I0118662

PROSPECTS FOR U.S.-RUSSIAN SECURITY COOPERATION

Stephen J. Blank
Editor

March 2009

*****

Published by Books Express Publishing
Books Express, 2011
ISBN 978-1-780395-51-7

Books Express publications are available from all good retail and online booksellers. For
publishing proposals and direct ordering please contact us at: info@books-express.com

CONTENTS

FOREWORD

Many might argue that this is a singularly inauspicious time to assess the prospects for U.S.-Russian security cooperation. Arguably, the prospects for bilateral cooperation lay buried under the wheels of Russia's invasion of Georgia in August 2008. As Vice-President Richard Cheney has said to Georgian President Mikhail Saakashvili, "Russian aggression must not go unanswered," and that "its continuation would have serious consequences for its relations with the United States."[1] Undoubtedly this invasion will have repercussions across the broad bilateral agenda, most of all insofar as regional security in the Caucasus is concerned. But ultimately, given their power, standing, and nuclear capability, dialogue and cooperation will be resumed at some point in the future. Therefore, an analysis of the prospects for and conditions favoring such cooperation is an urgent and important task that cries out for clarification precisely because current U.S.-Russian relations are so difficult. Russia, despite claims made for and against its importance, remains, by any objective standard, a key player in world affairs. It possesses this standing by virtue of its geographical location, Eurasia, its proximity to multiple centers of international tension and rivalry, its possession of a large conventional and nuclear force, its energy assets, and its seat on the UN Security Council. Beyond those attributes, it is an important barometer of trends in world politics, e.g., the course of democratization in the world. Furthermore, if Russia were so disposed, it could be the abettor and/or supporter of a host of negative trends in the world today. Indeed, some American elites might argue that it already is doing so. Even so, if U.S. policymakers and analysts see Russia more as a spoiler than as a constructive partner (whether rightly or wrongly), the fact remains that during the Cold War the Soviet Union was an active supporter of threats to world order such as international terrorism, and carried on a global arms race with the West. We negotiated productively with it on issues like arms control and proliferation.[2] Today, no matter how bad Russo-American or East-West relations may be, no such threats are present or immediately discernible on the horizon.

Therefore the chapters in this volume represent both a tribute to a vision of political order based upon such cooperation and a call to action to revitalize that cooperation. While the labor is arduous and unfulfilling and is unlikely to be completed on our watch; because of those stakes and scope we cannot abstain from carrying it out, for then everybody loses. George Kolt understood this truth deeply, and it was his combination of patriotism, wisdom, and concern for the larger issues that transcended personal interest that drove him to launch these conferences in the hope that they would facilitate the labor of bringing about this sorely needed cooperation.

We offer these chapters and the hope of subsequent similar conferences and publications in the same spirit that he did and look forward to the continuation of the dialogue.

DOUGLAS C. LOVELACE, JR.
Director
Strategic Studies Institute

ENDNOTES

1. George Jahn, "Oil Falls Despite Conflict," *Associated Press*, August 11, 2008.

2. Uri Ra'anan, Richard Schulz, Joshua Halperin, and Robert Pfaltzgraff, *Hydra of Carnage: Interational Linkages of Terrorism: The Witnesses Speak*, Boston, MA: Lexington Books, 1985.

CHAPTER 1

INTRODUCTION

Stephen J. Blank

Introduction.

Many might argue that this is a singularly inauspicious time to assess the prospects for U.S.-Russian security cooperation. Arguably, the prospects for bilateral cooperation lay buried under the wheels of Russia's invasion of Georgia in August 2008. As Vice-President Richard Cheney has said to Georgian president Mikhail Saakashvili, "Russian aggression must not go unanswered," and that "its continuation would have serious consequences for its relations with the United States."[1] Undoubtedly this invasion will have repercussions across the broad bilateral agenda, most of all insofar as regional security in the Caucasus is concerned. But ultimately, given their power, standing, and nuclear capability, dialogue and cooperation will be resumed at some point in the future. Therefore, an analysis of the prospects for and conditions favoring such cooperation is an urgent and important task that cries out for clarification precisely because current U.S.-Russian relations are so difficult. Russia, despite claims made for and against its importance, remains, by any objective standard, a key player in world affairs. It possesses this standing by virtue of its geographical location, Eurasia, its proximity to multiple centers of international tension and rivalry, its possession of a large conventional and nuclear force, its energy assets, and its seat in the United Nations (UN) Security Council. Beyond those attributes, it is an important barometer of trends in world politics, e.g., the course of democratization in the world. Furthermore, if Russia were so disposed, it could be the abettor and/or supporter of a host of negative trends in the world today. Indeed, some American elites might argue that it already is doing so. Even so, if U.S. policymakers and analysts see Russia more as a spoiler than as a constructive partner (whether rightly or wrongly), the fact remains that during the Cold War the Soviet Union was an active supporter of threats to world order such as international terrorism, and carried on a global arms race with the West. We negotiated productively with it on issues like arms control and proliferation.[2] Today, no matter how bad Russo-American or East-West relations may be, no such threats are present or immediately discernible on the horizon.

Therefore the chapters in this volume represent both a tribute to a vision of political order based upon such cooperation and a call to action to revitalize that cooperation. The vision is one that emerged out of the end of the Cold War and was based, as Jacob Kipp's chapter indicates, on the aspiration that a new era of Russo-American cooperation was dawning. In that new era, it was hoped that the two superpowers of the time would establish some kind of ill-defined, but no less real condominium in world politics based on their joint cooperation. In any event, this cooperation failed to take shape for multiple reasons and causes emanating out of both states' political choices. Nevertheless, some important elements of this vision have been salvaged and continue to this day. Presidents George Bush and Vladimir Putin recently signed a framework agreement outlining areas of cooperation, for example: counterterrorism, arms control, and proliferation. Both sides routinely declare (what they do may be quite different, however) that they are not enemies and see no reason for war between them. Arms control negotiations continue, and, despite much hostile rhetoric, observers have discerned the growth of practical East-West cooperation in the North Atlantic Treaty Organization (NATO).[3] Likewise, Russia continues to say publicly that it wants the dialogue to continue under the next administration, especially in regard to issues of the overall arms control agenda: a new strategic arms reduction treaty (START) and missile defenses, mainly in Europe, but probably also in Asia.[4] Similarly, at least some prominent Russian Parliamentarians like Retired General Viktor Zavarzin, who was Russia's Ambassador to NATO and now chairs the Duma's Committee on Defense, emphasize the ongoing need for continued cooperation against terrorism and the contribution of the NATO-Russia Council's plan of action in this field as important signs of the value of such cooperation and the need for extending it.[5] Finally, Russia's new Foreign Policy Concept of July 2008 emphasizes the great importance of Russo-American relations for global strategic stability and the overall international situation, not just the importance of large-scale bilateral and multidimensional economic, scientific, and other cooperation.[6]

Nonetheless, obviously the rise of Russia and its outspoken resistance to several U.S. policies have led to talk of a new Cold War, not least by Russian leaders. For example, in his press conference before the annual G-8 conference in Heiligendam, Germany, in June 2007, Putin told reporters that Russia and the West were returning to the Cold War and added that,

> Of course, we will return to those times. And it is clear that if part of the United States' nuclear capability is situated in Europe and that our military experts consider that they represent a potential threat then we will have to

take appropriate retaliatory steps. What steps? Of course we must have new targets in Europe. And determining precisely which means will be used to destroy the installations that our experts believe represent a potential threat for the Russian Federation is a matter of technology. Ballistic or cruise missiles or a completely new system. I repeat that it is a matter of technology.[7]

Or, as BBC correspondent Paul Reynolds wrote at that time in 2007 that based on such threats, "President Vladimir Putin's threat to target missiles at Europe indicates that the hostility between Russia and the West is more than a passing phase. It has become a permanent part of world diplomacy."[8] Similarly, despite its call for strategic dialogue and partnership on the basis of Russia's proverbial (and hence unrealizable) demand for equal security, the foreign policy concept breathes hostility to all kinds of U.S. policies.[9]

Thus the threats that we now hear about targeting the Czech Republic and possibly Poland for placing elements of a U.S. missile defense system in their countries, to cite only a few of Russia's bottomless well of threats to unsupportive European states, are already a matter of routine. Although Russian Foreign Minister Sergei Lavrov and Deputy Prime Minister Sergei Ivanov have both explicitly ruled out the Cold War as a label for Russo-American relations, their subordinates are not so soothing.[10] Thus Deputy Foreign Minister Aleksandr' Losyukov, speaking in Tehran, said that Washington was using Korea and Iran's proliferation as an issue to consolidate its global strategic position, i.e., invoking those two states to justify its missile defense program. If this issue cannot be resolved by diplomatic means, he warned, Russia will carry out a series of military acts to balance and establish security. And this could prompt an arms race.[11] This frosty warning, rather than the calculated and misleading efforts to invoke Russo-American partnership, more accurately characterizes the present state of Russo-American relations even if they are far from the Cold War. President Dmitry Medvedev's initial moves, challenging U.S. hegemony in international financial institution and vetoing a draft resolution on condemning Zimbabwe's President Robert Mugabe for his domestic brutality suggest as well a desire to strike at Washington and resist it rather than to find areas of practical cooperation. Certainly the Zimbabwe affair even before the Georgian war that only intensified concerns as to who really is in control had already caused observers to wonder if Medvedev really controls Russia, and if East-West cooperation is genuinely possible.[12]

Indeed, Russian leaders like Foreign Minister Lavrov have made clear their view that America is a power in moral decline that should no longer be entitled to the status of sole superpower, and Russia's new President Medvedev has already made that clear, along with his attack on America's economic, financial, and political leadership and a demand for an equal role for Russia.[13] It is hardly surprising, then, that Russian commentators now regularly say that "Russia's strategic worldview is fundamentally at odds with the American one and, perhaps, with American perspectives on international security."[14] Indeed, Lavrov stated that the United States was perhaps Moscow's "most difficult" partner and should learn from its mistakes in world politics.[15] Furthermore, U.S. influence is allegedly declining, and its hoped-for unipolar world cannot come into being. Instead, a multipolar world where Russia is a free standing independent actor is taking shape. In that context, Russia's independence is the primary achievement of Russian foreign and defense policy.[16] Lavrov also observed in 2005 that,

We can come to the conclusion that the whole complex
of our (foreign) relations, the weight of existing military
and strategic links between Russia and the (U.S.) . . .
will be constantly declining. We will never separate, but
drifting away from each other could have irreversible
consequences.[17]

Thus we are currently in a period of rising tension
that covers arms control, proliferation issues, and the
rivalry for regional influence in Europe, the former
Soviet Union, the Middle East, and even to some degree,
East Asia. The intensification of debate over the failure
of Russia to democratize and its regression instead
back to a system all too redolent of the Tsarist autocracy
with some Soviet admixtures has compounded these
issues and lent an ideological cast to the concurrent
geopolitical rivalry. Indeed, many observers, including
this author, would argue that it is the nature and logic
of this system that exercises a decisive influence upon
the goals, tactics, and operating principles of Russian
foreign policy.[18] Nonetheless, even an understanding
of Russian (and of U.S.) foreign policy that takes into
account domestic, structural, and ideological factors as
major drivers in the relationship need not and should not
exult over the downturn in Russo-American relations.
The experience of the Mikhail Gorbachev period 1985-
91 (encompassing both Presidents Ronald Reagan and
George H. W. Bush) strongly suggests that Russo-
American cooperation breeds further cooperation
between these two and possibly other states and has a
profound impact on outstanding international issues,
perhaps particularly arms control and proliferation.[19]
And, at the same time it has become abundantly clear
to all but the most prejudiced or intractable observers
that a diplomacy that places competing values above

shared interests as the goal of foreign policy is neither realistic nor successful in achieving either interests or values. When first principles become the daily stuff of diplomacy, states' most vital interests are immediately engaged and in a most hostile way. Thus diplomacy is "wrongfooted" from the start. The deterioration of the overall international security environment that we see today is testimony to that fact. Neither should we think that ideological grandiosity is a uniquely American failing or a distinctly American foreign policy tradition, or one that should be extolled and thus absolved of responsibility for our current predicaments or reviled for causing those predicaments.[20] Neither is this addiction to ideological universalism confined to the right wing of American politics. Rather it is a disease that is no less entrenched on the left, as several observers note.[21]

In fact, Russian foreign policy as currently conducted, suffers from a similar addiction to grand ideological perspectives which is no less rooted in earlier Russian history, both Tsarism which saw itself as the gendarme of Europe uniquely appointed to prevent revolution in the 19th century, and in the Soviet period which saw itself as the avatar of such revolution on a global scale. Although Russian spokesmen claim Russia no longer conducts foreign and defense policy based on ideology but purely on the grounds of pragmatic interest, they constantly feel impelled to lay out an ideological schema of trends in world politics just as their Soviet and Tsarist predecessors did.[22] In this respect, they are not merely emulating the Bush administration which might be the most self-consciously articulate exponent of an ideological, even millenarian view of the tasks of U.S. foreign policy which calls for the global triumph of democracy and involvement, if not intervention in other countries' affairs to encourage that trend. Rather, while they do emulate it, they are also responding to equally deeply rooted trends in Russian history and politics. Still, the particular brand of ideological universalism championed by the Bush administration openly proclaims our duty and right to intervene in the affairs of other states that were hitherto regarded as purely domestic matters and thus "sacrosanct," at least as external observers were concerned. As former Secretary of State Colin Powell wrote, in the current threat environment,

> This means we must do something statesmen have been reluctant to do since the birth of the modern state system. We have to understand and try to influence not just what states do *outside* their borders, but in some cases what goes on *inside* their borders. This marks a strategic rebalancing made necessary by circumstances.[23] (Italics in the original.)

Under the circumstances, we can hardly claim that today's deadlock was unforeseeable. Given Russia's determination not to answer or account to anyone for its behavior at home (or abroad for that matter) and its determined regression towards a neo-Tsarist autocracy with some Communist admixtures at home and in foreign policy, America's insistence on universal principles of democracy obviously represents a fundamentally antagonistic posture and a profound challenge to Russia. And, as other analysts point out, a diplomacy that places its priority emphasis on a ringing affirmation of universal values of democracy that license American intervention (or so it is seen) into the domestic affairs of other countries and which is prepared to use force to achieve that democratization, cannot but be seen as a threat to the most basic and vital institutions of those states.[24] Consequently, calls for restoring mutual confidence to East-West relations, e.g., German Prime Minister Angela Merkel's recent call for closer NATO-Russian ties, represent efforts to swim upstream or to limit the damage, not initiatives based on well-founded optimism.[25]

Yet despite the difficulties we now perceive in obtaining genuine security cooperation between Moscow and Washington, many elements of the previous vision have not been wholly lost. One of the key elements that continues and of which this monograph is a product is the idea of a regular strategic dialogue between Russian, American, and, if possible, European specialists on topical security issues of the day with a view towards outlining the grounds on which cooperation and understanding may be built. Such conferences among experts not only provide an atmosphere for developing both intimacy and candor, but also serve as a resource from which political leaders may ultimately elicit or extract useful ideas or suggested policy approaches to advance such cooperation. This is why these chapters represent a tribute to a vision of just such collaboration. A major reason why these dialogues have been able to continue was the efforts of the late George Kolt, the National Intelligence Officer (NIO) for Russia during the Clinton and both Bush administrations, to whom this book is dedicated. Having attained the rank of colonel in the Air Force, George subsequently became one of the most outstanding intelligence analysts of the Soviet Union and then the Russian Federation, rising to the post of the NIO for Russia during the first Bush presidency. Apart from his human qualities which this author was privileged to see, George believed passionately in the value of bringing experts from all sides into regular dialogue with each other, and into the policy debate on how the United States should relate to Russia. Through his leadership and sponsorship, we were able to hold such conferences annually from 1992-2003 at the Naval Postgraduate School, led by George and Professor Mikhail Tsypkin of the Naval Postgraduate School in Monterey.

These conferences were not only for the exchange of ideas, they also built and extended lasting personal ties among these experts, among whom this author was privileged to be one. They established a valuable channel by which experts in and out of governmental service were able to carry on a frank but professional dialogue on the issues of the moment and to build further insights as to what was happening either in Moscow or Washington. In the truest sense of the word, these conferences built international understanding and remain a valuable instrument for continuing to do so, and for giving our respective governments greater insight into what can and should be done and what might be achieved through dialogue and Russo-American cooperation. Though these conferences lapsed due to George's protracted final illness and the usual difficulties of obtaining sufficient funding, in March 2008 we were able to resurrect this program at the U.S. Army War College. On March 6-7 speakers from the United States, United Kingdom, and Russia met at Carlisle Barracks to present papers and conduct discussions on issues of Russo-American relations in light of the more or less concurrent presidential elections in both countries; arms control; nonproliferation; and regional security in both the Black Sea basin (comprising both Ukraine and the Caucasus), and Central Asia. The papers presented here are thus a tribute to the enduring vitality of the vision of dialogue that hopefully leads to better mutual understanding lasting relationships, and lasting practical cooperation between Russia and the West in general and with America in particular. It is our hope that we will once again be able to institutionalize these conferences and present their products to our audiences in service of this vision of civil, humane dialogue and practical efforts to enhance international security that George Kolt embodied in his life and service to his country.

A Call to Action.

At the same time, this volume, and hopefully succeeding ones in the years to come, also represent a call to action because of the grave need to avert further East-West hostility and the pressing need for international cooperation as new governments take center stage in Moscow and Washington. As we have noted, in the current environment, it is easy for both sides to attack each other not just because their foreign policy is driven by resentment, an over-inflated sense of Russia's importance to the world and to Washington, and even revanchist emotions as in Moscow's case, but also for reaffirmation of support from engaged domestic constituencies.[26] Among the most entrenched of such constituencies are clearly the Russian military and more broadly the Siloviki caste that Putin promoted into power. Numerous observers have cited the purely self-seeking use of this threat inflation in Russian politics. And besides the consolidation of a domestic bloc around the government, such rhetoric also reinforces the deep-rooted great power mystique of Russian elites concerning Russia's global role. As the Russian philosopher Sergei Gavrov writes,

11

The threats are utopian, the probability of their implementation is negligible, but their emergence is a sign. This sign — a message to "the city and the world" — surely lends itself to decoding and interpretation: we will defend from Western claims our ancient right to use our imperial (authoritarian and totalitarian) domestic socio-cultural traditions within which power does not exist to serve people but people exist to serve power.[27]

Vladimir Shlapentokh has written that an essential component of the Kremlin's ideological campaign to maintain the Putin regime in power and extend it (albeit under new leadership) past the elections of 2008 is anti-Americanism. As he wrote,

The core of the Kremlin's ideological strategy is to convince the public that any revolution in Russia will be sponsored by the United States. Putin is presented as a bulwark of Russian patriotism, as the single leader able to confront America's intervention in Russian domestic life and protect what is left of the imperial heritage. This propaganda is addressed mostly to the elites, particularly elites in the military and FSB [Russian federal security service] who sizzle with hatred and envy of America.[28]

Minxin Pei of the Carnegie Endowment similarly observes that besides serving domestic purposes of legitimating and reinforcing the domestic turn towards authoritarianism, a domestic turn towards autocracy has also driven the Russo-Chinese rapprochement.

The rapid improvement in ties and growing cooperation between China and Russia owes, to a great extent, not to any Chinese new initiative, but to Russia's changing relationship with the West under Putin's rule. As President Putin became increasingly authoritarian, he needed China as an ally in counterbalancing the West. The net strategic effect of Russia's reorientation of its policy toward the West has been tremendously positive for China.[29]

Indeed, already in the 1990s, the same convergence of opposition to democratization as well as to the supremacy of American power helped forge the Sino-Russian entente that began then.[30] Thus we cannot simply say that it is America's fault that Russia has taken a so-called wrong direction.[31] The domestic dynamics of Russian politics and Putin's, as well as his confederates', ingrained anti-Americanism cannot be simply excluded from the equation.[32]

Nevertheless American policy likewise has much to answer for. On the U.S. side, it is not just a question of ideological universalism run amok without due regard to the realities, let alone the interests of other players, it also is, as many have noted, the sheer refusal to take Russian interests into account that eroded the partnership that supposedly replaced mutual hostilities after September 11, 2001 (9/11). After that date, not only did the United States move into Central Asia, it abandoned the antiballistic missile (ABM) treaty, negotiated a strategic offensive reductions (SORT) treaty on arms control that decoupled the two nuclear superpowers from each other, expanded NATO, unilaterally invaded Iraq and disregarded Russian interests and equities there, leading to a quagmire that Moscow fears might lead to war with Iran or a kind of Huntingtonian clash of civilizations. Putin, in his speech of June 27, 2006, to the Foreign Ministry, emphasized the increasingly threatening nature of the international system, the unilateral American use of force and supposedly indiscriminate attacks on Islam, and the possibility of proliferation as major threats coming closer to Russia. Thus he said that,

> We need to be fully aware that, despite all our efforts, the potential for conflict in the world continues to grow.

13

After the collapse of the bipolar world order, there exists a lot of unpredictability in global development. Perhaps this is why we continue to hear talk of an unavoidable conflict of civilizations that could become a long-term confrontation on the lines of the Cold War. I am convinced that we have reached a point today where the entire global security architecture is indeed undergoing modernization, and you have probably noticed this for yourselves. If we let old views and approaches continue to hold sway, the world will be doomed to further futile confrontation. We need to reverse these dangerous trends and this requires new ideas and approaches. Russia does not want confrontation of any kind. And we will not take part in any kind of "holy alliance." . . . I must say, too, that the causes fuelling the desire of a number of countries to acquire weapons of mass destruction and carry out other military programs include not just national ambitions but also the overblown importance given to force in international relations that is being foisted on us all. In this respect, the stagnation we see today in the area of disarmament is of particular concern. Russia is not responsible for this situation. We support renewed dialogue on the main disarmament issues. Above all, we propose to our American partners that we launch negotiations to replace the START Treaty [Strategic Arms Reduction Treaty], which expires in 2009.[33]

From Moscow's point of view, Washington also mounted support for color revolutions, and finally it sought to supplant Russia in the Commonwealth of Independent States (CIS). From Russia's standpoint, then, it got little or nothing out of the alliance, while America, not Russia, became the rogue elephant of the epoch. Under the circumstances, a recovering Russia not only resisted U.S. policy, it pushed back and pushes back today with increasing anger and force. It is hardly surprising, then, that the most basic demand from Moscow to Washington is that it be listened to and treated as an equal. Moscow has similarly issued an endless stream of complaints that America does not take Russia sufficiently seriously, i.e., at Moscow's own self-serving and inflated valuation of itself. Putin's presidential envoy for relations with the European Union (EU), Sergei Yastrzhembskiy, stated that this was Russia's main objection to recent developments in world politics.[34] Similarly, Russia's Ambassador to America, Yuri Ushakov wrote that,

> What offends us is the view shared by some in Washington that Russia can be used when it is needed and discarded or even abused when it is not relevant to American objectives. . . . Russians do not need any special favors or assistance from the United States, but we do require respect in order to build a two-way relationship. And we expect that our political interests will be recognized.[35]

Following in this vein, in a televised address by Foreign Minister Lavrov, he again denounced U.S. unilateralism and demanded "total equality, including equality in the analysis of threats, in finding solutions, and making decisions." Therefore we should not be in any doubt that Russia sees itself once again as a sovereign, i.e., wholly independent, actor in world politics that should be regarded as a superpower equal to America and be able to constrain its policies while remaining free from such constraints on what matters most to it, i.e., the CIS. Indeed, Putin, in his now famous Munich Wehrkunde speech of 2007 (and even earlier as well), called for a new "architecture of global security," and his actions before and after that speech indicate that Russia is acting to bring such a structure—which it deems to be a multipolar one—into being.[36]

In light of the foregoing strategic environment, we have sought to address at least some of the most important and even possibly contentious issues in the bilateral relationship. Even if we do not agree with Moscow as to its role in world affairs, there can be no denying its intrinsic importance to international relations or the benefits of such cooperation and the costs of its absence. While the chapters cover a broad range of issues, they do not, and in the space of a single conference obviously cannot, address the entire bilateral agenda. This does not mean we are offering a comprehensive overview or set of presentations. For instance, we did not, at this conference, discuss energy issues or Russia's call for a new global architecture of international relations, or the international significance of its revived economy. Still, this volume offers an ample opportunity for interested audiences, whether they be specialists, policymakers, or merely interested laymen, to get a sense of unofficial perspectives from U.S., Russian, and in one case, British analysts. Such a perspective is necessary because, among other things, it is clear that one of the factors that most exacerbates the current tension is the lack of an accurate perspective on both sides of the other. American neglect of Russian interests, focus on millenarian values rather than concrete interests, and bureaucratic dissensions speak for themselves.[37] But on the Russian side, we also find that the leadership is quite badly informed. Medvedev's remarks that the United States is undergoing a depression betrays such ignorance and eagerness to exaggerate America's current problems. But it also fits in with a general and quite possibly sinister situation on the Russian side. As defense correspondent Pavel Felgengauer reports,

Russia has a Prussian-style all-powerful General Staff that controls all the different armed services and is more or less independent of outside political constraints. Russian military intelligence—GRU, as big in size as the former KGB and spread over all continents—is an integral part of the General Staff. Through GRU, the General Staff controls the supply of vital information to all other decisionmakers in all matters concerning defense procurement, threat assessment, and so on. High-ranking former GRU officers have told me that in Soviet times the General Staff used the GRU to grossly, deliberately, and constantly mislead the Kremlin about the magnitude and gravity of the military threat posed by the West in order to help inflate military expenditure. There are serious indications that at present the same foul practice is continuing.[38]

Similarly, Putin complained around the time of the 2007 Munich Wehrkunde conference that American politicians are invoking a nonexistent Russian threat to get more money for military campaigns in Iraq and Afghanistan. Putin's remarks represent a wholly fabricated analysis of Defense Secretary Robert Gates' testimony to Congress, but signify that he wants to believe the worst about American intentions as do the General Staff and like-minded Russian political leaders.[39]

Given such, dare we say, institutionalized misperception, it is important to let analysts and officials speak for themselves as is the case here. Indeed, these chapters should serve as an opening round in seeking to institutionalize a platform from which all the issues in that bilateral, or multilateral if we include Europe, agenda can be addressed. There is an immense need here, if not in Russia, for doing so because our present debate about Russia is limited to a narrow range of issues that distorts what is really happening in world politics and which badly serves our understanding of global trends and ability to deal with them constructively. A comparable myopia arguably affects Russian officialdom.

Chapter 2: U.S.-Russian Relations, 1991-the Present.

In Chapter 2, Jacob Kipp traces the trajectory of U.S.-Russian relations since 1991 through the present, highlighting the key issues like Kosovo, Iraq, and missile defenses that have led to current tensions. He also examines the differences in the campaigns for choosing successors to the previous presidents that were roughly concurrent as of the spring of 2008. While mindful of the difficulties and asymmetries of perspective on both sides, he clearly holds out the possibility of the resumption, if not of a real strategic partnership, of a meaningful strategic dialogue on key issues like Eurasian security and arms control. He concludes his assessment with the prospect of this revitalized dialogue on existing and new issues like the Arctic which has become an issue in 2007-08. This dialogue would permit the United States to sustain the Transatlantic community of democratic values while addressing key issues for Russia of arms control and disarmament.

A new look at U.S.-Russian relations should begin with a strategic vision encompassing multilateralism and regional interests, including those just emerging in the Arctic as a result of climate change. Russia and the United States may end up being more than neighbors across ice fields and have to share a new maritime highway and energy and resource potential. Being true to Western values, even as we compete in the emerging global economy, would permit us to sustain the Euro-Atlantic community and promote open societies, the rule of law, and human rights, while retaining the capacity for humanitarian intervention with international legitimacy. We would still share with Russia and the other nuclear powers the task of managing nuclear proliferation and disarmament well into the 21st century.

Chapters 3-6: Arms Control and Proliferations.

Historically, and even now, the arms control agenda represents the heart or foundation of the bilateral relationship, and even here we see contending perspectives. Whereas the Bush administration has stubbornly upheld the principle of unilateralism in force development, Russia, as stated in its Foreign Policy Concept, evaluates this dimension of the bilateral relationship not only for what it means to the two governments, but also for what it contributes to global strategic stability and peace, in particular regional balances and security in Europe and Asia.[40] Russia, like many American scholars but unlike the Bush administration, sees these issues of arms control and disarmament, and even proliferation of weapons of mass destruction (WMD) as being fundamentally a complex and interactive process involving all three of these issues. Moreover to the extent that one or both sides abandons that interactive perspective and tends to see weapons deployments and strategy, disarmament and proliferation as discrete, unconnected issues, the danger is that these force deployments on either side become not an instrument for strategic stability but rather they become instruments of increased destabilization and insecurity.[41]

These differing perspectives emerge in the chapters. Yet at the same time, they offer the possibility of bilateral agreement provided a serious negotiation occurs. Thus, Ambassador Linton Brooks holds open the possibility for agreement by both states on verification modalities for a Fissile Material Cutoff Treaty where he says both sides have similar interests, but which has stalled because the administration does not discern adequate measures of verification in existing draft treaties.[42] Brooks also notes that with regard to nonproliferation of WMD both sides cooperate much of the time. "The United States and Russia routinely work together to strengthen this regime, often working through the International Atomic Energy Agency [IAEA], which implements and monitors safeguards agreements with states operating nuclear facilities."[43] Other areas cited by Brooks include the cessation of nuclear testing since 1992, both sides' work in the Cooperative Threat Reduction Program (CTR), both sides' adherence to the Global Nuclear Energy Project (GNEP), and bilateral support for the Global Initiative to Combat Nuclear Terrorism.[44]

Nonetheless, there are substantial differences between the two states even though much nuclear cooperation will continue into the next administrations in both countries. Brooks lays out the two sides' differing approaches to the renegotiation of the START-1 Treaty that expires at the end of 2009 but emphasizes, as do other Bush administration spokesmen, that the U.S. position is not based on arms racing with Russia, quite the contrary.[45] Instead, Washington has been reducing both its nuclear arsenal and the role of nuclear weapons in American strategy. Similarly, Brooks reiterated that Washington does not see Russia as an adversary and even remarks that arms control is for adversaries, echoing Lavrov's point but disputing his assessment of the bilateral relationship. Therefore our planned missile defense in Poland and the Czech Republic are in no way intended to threaten Russia's nuclear forces or territory.[46]

From a Russian standpoint, Alexander Pikayev concurs with Brooks' assessment of the values of previous arms control negotiations and treaties between America and Russia. In this context, he openly relates the progress after 1970 on arms control to the conclusion of the Nonproliferation Treaty (NPT) of 1968, explicitly displaying the interactive aspect of the relationship between arms control and disarmament on the one hand and nonproliferation on the other. Since the collapse of the Soviet Union, however, though armed confrontation has disappeared, noncooperative competition and partnership have emerged as the dominant aspects of the bilateral strategic relationship. Subsequent discords over NATO enlargement, missile defenses, Kosovo, etc., thus led to a situation where force postures, though vastly reduced, remained in a deterrent, i.e., adversarial, mode targeted against each other. Russia's sense of vulnerability grew immensely, and, given the huge imbalance of power between America and Russia, Russia had to rely ever more on nuclear weapons in its strategy even as its ability to maintain them shrank at an alarming rate until 2000.

Paradoxically, after 2000 Western power fragmented, Russia recovered and successfully tested new systems with which to replace its aging deterrent, and as a result has become more able to think about resuming arms control which had been discredited due to developments in the 1990s. Of particular interest is renegotiating the START-I treaty and possibly globalizing the Intermediate-range Nuclear Forces (INF) treaty of 1987. In other words, while it may not be as urgent as was the case a generation ago to negotiate such treaties, arms control opportunities are again coming into focus for both sides.[47] At the same time, there exists a critical relationship between arms control and issues of nonproliferation. At the diplomatic level, it will be impossible to sustain the NPT regime at the next Review conference of 2010 if there is not progress on major power disarmament. That has already been proven at the 2000 and 2005 conferences. While such failure is not decisive in and of itself in persuading a country's leaders to go nuclear; it removes some important political obstacles to their doing so. Second, in view of the centrality of the arms control agenda to the bilateral U.S.-Russian relationship, failure here to move beyond the Cold War relationship impedes the Russo-American unity that is needed to persuade would be proliferators to desist from doing so, as was the case in the "golden decade" of 1987-96 when such unity was effective in retarding or blocking many countries' aspirations for nuclear weapons.[48] Indeed, given the heightened U.S.-Russian tension, it is not surprising to find that recently "Yuri Yekhanurov, Ukraine's defense minister, has intimated regret over his country's 'foolish' decision to give up all its nuclear weapons after independence."[49] As it is clear that a nuclear armed Ukraine represents the greatest possible and conceivable threat to Russia, the centrality of agreements such as the 1994 Tripartite Treaty among Kyiv, Washington, and Moscow stands out as an ideal to be striven for in subsequent cases. North Korea already is a nuclear weapons state, even if we lack precise estimates of its weapons capability. And Iranian proliferation would uproot the nonproliferation regime especially in the two most troubled regions of the world the Middle East and South Asia. Thus there is a link between our chapters on the arms control agenda and the chapters by Alexei Arbatov and Stephen Blank on proliferation issues and the prospects for bilateral cooperation on that agenda.

- Arbatov and Blank both concur that there are positive opportunities for cooperation between Moscow and Washington on these issues, but the fundamental asymmetry of Russian and American views on why and how such cooperation should take place is quite visible in their chapters. Arbatov, for example, reviews the sources and reasons for Russia having a very different idea of the degree to which proliferation threatens it than does the United States, and concludes that based on that perspective we can expect the following policy orientations from Moscow. Specifically, he writes that Russia has an interest in enhancing the nonproliferation regimes, but this is not the main priority in its foreign policy or security strategy.
- Russia views with a lot of skepticism the global strategy of nonproliferation and counterproliferation declared by the United States, seeing in it a policy based in the practice of double standards and an attempt to veil other political, military, and commercial interests, including nuclear exports, with the goal of nonproliferation.
- Russia is not inclined to sacrifice its own economic and political interests in peaceful nuclear cooperation with other countries for the sake of the abstract nonproliferation ideal (especially in the unilateral interpretation of the United States). It will not initiate any further tightening of the regime (especially one

associated with economic losses), while at the same time observing the letter of the provisions of the NPT, IAEA safeguards, and agreed-upon norms for nuclear exports.

- Relations with the United States are of considerable significance for Russia (including CTR and GNEP programs), and it is prepared within certain limits to take U.S. demands into account.

- At the same time Moscow will resist Washington's pressure to abandon its dealings with other countries that are legal from the standpoint of the NPT, even if these countries at this point in history are not to the liking of the current U.S. administration and even if there is suspicion about the military nuclear proclivities of Russia's foreign partners. In this sense, the continuation of the Bushehr project and its possible expansion have gained not only practical significance for Moscow ($5 billion in income), but a sense of principle and political significance as well.

- Russia will object, as will the majority of U.S. allies, to using force to resolve nonproliferation problems (although for political considerations, it has supported the Proliferation Security Initiative [PSI]), and will give preference to diplomatic and economic instruments in reinforcing the NPT. Russia has supported recent United Nations Security Council (UNSC) resolutions on Iran and People's Democratic Republic of Korea (PDRK) but will resist "hard sanctions" (i.e., oil embargo, cutting communications, etc.) and will veto the use of force.

- Russia's nonproliferation policy (just as defense and arms control postures) will probably stay passive and mostly reactive, except when promising direct economic benefits (as with the multilateral uranium enrichment plant in the Siberian city of Angarsk). Without initiatives from outside, Russia would hardly initiate or readily endorse more strict export controls, embargoes on sales of nuclear fuel cycle components or more intrusive IAEA guarantees. However, it may use nuclear and missile proliferation as a pretext for withdrawing from some treaties, foremost the Intermediate Range Nuclear Forces-Strategic Rocket Forces (INF-SRF) Treaty of 1987, apparently motivated by other military and political reasons.[50]

Stephen Blank, on the other hand, underscores the many and diverse ways in which the proliferation of not just nuclear weapons but also of missiles represents serious threats to both American and Russian interests and therefore the urgency of joint action undertaken on behalf of both sides. He cites over 10 reasons why such cooperation is necessary in the Middle East, South Asia, and Northeast Asia, clearly articulating the American sense of the urgency of the issue that, according to Arbatov, is not felt so strongly in the Kremlin. Nonetheless, both authors concur that for nonproliferation cooperation to take place and to be successful, the next administration will have to depart from the Bush team's perspectives. Both authors agree that we can expect continuity, rather than change, from the Medvedev administration on this issue. Therefore the change that will have to take place will have to come from the White House. Specifically, according to Blank, future efforts at nonproliferation and at inducing both bilateral and multilateral cooperation to achieve it, must renounce using nonproliferation policy as an attempt to impel or coerce regime change from without. Arguably the more recent U.S. policy towards North Korea, and possibly Iran, suggests this is already happening. Blank offers an analysis derived from contemporary political science thinking as to why reaching agreements with potential or actual proliferators actually may set in motion a process leading over time to substantive alteration in the makeup of those governments. But this does not mean we will get democracies in proliferating states, although hopefully better government and more pro-Western policies from those governments will develop over time.[51] The important points of agreement here are that first, unilateral answers will not work and impose greater costs than benefits across the international system; second, regime change cannot be the stated or even implicit goal of such exercises; third, coercive military means will, unless absolutely necessary, fail and can only succeed if they enjoy multilateral backing and legitimacy. These conclusions are based on hard practical experience and will not, in and of themselves, necessarily lead to a convergence of Russo-American perspectives on why proliferation is a threat, to what degree, and what should be done about it. But from those starting points arrived at in those conclusions, we can get to a point where the practical policies of both Washington and Moscow overlap sufficiently so that they can devise coordinated and cooperative responses to the threat posed by proliferation.

Chapters 7-8: Issues of Regional Security in Eurasia.

Regional security is one of the most contentious issues in Eurasia as the current crises over Georgia's and Ukraine's desire to enter NATO illustrate. And thanks to the war over South Ossetia, it will be even more contentious. Although Moscow's line here is that Georgia was an aggressor that committed war crimes and therefore does not deserve to rule over South Ossetia and Abkhazia, the story is more complicated. Close analysis of the Russian and world press reveals the following scenario. After a long series of provocations and Russian attempts to isolate Georgia and overthrow its government, Moscow reacted forcefully to the NATO-EU decision to recognize Kosovo's independence and to consider Georgian application for a membership action plan (MAP) from NATO. Russia reacted by unilaterally dispatching Russian forces to Abkhazia and offering Abkhazia and South Ossetia consular and legal status. Thus, Russia has initiated a typical example of coercive diplomacy. Russia clearly sought to coerce Georgia into renouncing NATO membership and any hope of regaining those two territories under its sovereignty. It also sought to force Georgia to negotiate these provinces' destiny exclusively with them and Moscow, thereby conferring upon it a dominant status in the Caucasus and excluding NATO and/or the EU from that negotiation which the EU clearly seeks to influence.[52] Otherwise, as it had done since the 1990s, it steadfastly blocked any effort by Georgia to negotiate with these provinces directly without Russian interference. By pursuing that exclusive status, Moscow also shows just how little concern it has for Abkhazia's or South Ossetia's self-determination. The principle of their self-determination is merely camouflage for eroding Georgia's sovereignty, integrity, and independence, and for augmenting Russia's power in the Caucasus and elsewhere in the CIS. In this respect Russia follows Soviet precedents of using self-determination to destroy competing governments and to reunify their peoples around the Russian state.[53]

As part of its diplomatic campaign at the recent St. Petersburg CIS conference in June 2008, Russia once again admonished Georgia and Ukraine not to join NATO, called such membership a breach of the Russo-Ukrainian treaty of 1997, threatened to double Ukrainian gas prices, and piously stated that, while it is up to Georgia to improve bilateral relations, there was no problem between them that could not be solved if they met bilaterally and did not involve others in their dispute.[54] While demanding that Georgia meet with Abkhazia and South Ossetia and renounce the use of force, Moscow, of course, threatened both sides in these projected talks with violence and demanded its full participation and the exclusion of all other actors from those talks.[55] Thus Russia sought to isolate Georgia from its Western supporters by defaming Georgian policy abroad, separating it from European support, and then intimidating it by bringing the full weight of its power to bear on an isolated regime. Then that intimidated regime would have had no choice but to yield to Russian pressure and accept a Russian-dictated truncation of its sovereignty, integrity, and independence.

However, the situation became progressively more complex by July 2008. Here we must consider the nature of the Russian government and of its satrapies in South Ossetia and Georgia. In both of these provinces, the local regime was essentially an FSB regime controlled by ethnic Russians and/or officials of the FSB, a hallmark of Putin's regime. Moscow reportedly has also placed FSB officers throughout Abkhaz President Bagpash's entourage and even threatened his life if he negotiated with Georgia.[56] Moscow reportedly tries to exercise similar kinds of pressure upon South Ossetia.[57]

The primary interests of these "South Ossetian" officials lay in holding power, profiting from the widespread racketeering that they lead, and in blocking any rapprochement with Georgia. Resumption of direct talks or ties to Georgia was, in their eyes, a sign that Moscow was selling them out. Thus they were willing collaborators with Moscow and the Siloviki who commanded the power structures and were themselves getting rich off the proceeds of this pervasive criminality. Moscow provided them with weapons, and gave passports to their citizens so it could claim with no justification that they were Russian citizens whom Moscow was obliged to defend. Thus the Russian peacekeeping forces in these provinces were anything but peacekeepers. Rather, they were conscious instruments of a policy intended to prevent conflict resolution and eventually move these provinces into formal reincorporation into Russia. It is natural that Georgia bitterly resented this and believed that Russia was behind every effort to block it from regaining its sovereignty, apart from the visible emotionalism and inflated rhetoric of the Georgian regime and political culture. Not surprisingly, there had been a pattern of escalating Russian provocations going back years, including assassination attempts against Saakashvili's predecessor, Edvard Shevarnadze, boycotts, bombings, subversion efforts to overthrow the Georgian government, missile launches, and more recently military buildups and the moves of March-

April to establish direct ties between the government in Moscow and these provinces. However, perhaps due to the pressure generated by Russian provocations and Georgian counterprovocations, the Russian government announced its support for direct South Ossetian-Georgian negotiations in July.

But at this point, the nature of the Russian government became a factor in this equation and a decisive one at that. There have been multiplying signs of a developing rivalry, if not struggle, between President Medvedev and Prime Minister Putin. Although the issues joined were domestic political issues, it is clear that Putin was also trying to control Russian foreign policy and relying upon the Siloviki, the same people who supervised the officials in South Ossetia and Abkhazia. A close reading of the military press, for example, would suggest that the military (and presumably the intelligence services) were itching for a chance to destroy Saakashvili's power, and show him and NATO who's boss in the Caucasus. These officials' pecuniary motives, always uppermost in their minds, also stood to lose if there were direct negotiations between Tbilisi and the South Ossetians in Tskhinvali, the provincial capital. Indeed, Russian officials contributed to the buildup of tensions by publicly dismissing a peace plan offered by German Foreign Minister Frank-Walter Steinmeyer after privately praising it, and having the commander of Russian airborne forces raise the possibility of their descent into the area in support of South Ossetia.

Thus it appears that the South Ossetian leaders decided, with support from their friends, to ratchet up the already high level of armed provocations to deliberately incite a forceful Georgian response that could then be used to justify Moscow's retaliation.

The size, swiftness, and scope of the operation, plus its widening objectives cited above, all lend credence to this assessment.[58] Although Saakashvili had offered Russia a role of a guarantor of South Ossetian autonomy within Georgia and a cease-fire, for reasons not yet clear, within 3 hours Georgian forces invaded Tskhinvali.[59] Allegedly, this humiliation by force of Russia and its new president could not be accepted. But it is clear that Russia was ready and waiting for this. At least one Russian commentator has hinted at the likelihood that Moscow, or more specifically the Siloviki, had planned a grand provocation here. Writing on August 8, the newspaper *Gazeta* observed that,

> The relative passivity of official Russia has already made a decisive impact on the events of recent days. The Foreign Ministry's wrathful tone and theatrical curses from parliament deputies do not count. As long as the military fist is not engaged, this is all just a noisy background for the advancement of Georgian troops. The Russian forces in the region, including the nominal peacekeepers deployed there, have failed and may even never tried to put an end to tribal feuds in South Ossetia. Yet, it would not have been a problem for them only several days ago to stop the Georgian Army at the beginning. Contrary to the usual cast of roles. It was never done. What is the reason? Artful foreign-policy maneuvers by Saakashvili? Putin's Olympic absence? Medvedev's tour of the Volga region? Or a decision, made in advance and being implemented in cold blood, to let events run their own course? If so that would be the greatest turn in Russia's Transcaucasian policy in the past 15 years. If not and if a forcible intervention is eventually to take place, its cost—both political and the one paid with blood of all the conflict participants—will prove much higher than it could have been only just recently. If it is not a turn of the course but just a delay in the intervention, the reasons for the delay may be very banal. Apart from the usual mess, there is also no full clarity as to whose order

31

the Siloviks (Power Officials) should receive. Although the conventional wisdom is that they are commanded by the premier, it is still the new president with all his constitutional powers who is the official commander in chief. And Dmitry Medvedev is the one who will bear most of the political responsibility for whatever decision will be made and whoever will make it. It is possible that he needs time to answer himself a question of whether he is ready to take it on his shoulders.[60]

These remarks underscore not just the possibility of a conspiracy or provocation launched by Siloviki in Moscow to get Medvedev, possibly against his better judgment, to support a war in Georgia, but they also point to the enduring crisis potential that resides in Russia's failure to institute democratic controls over the power structures.

Consequently, this operation also confirms what this author has said before in other forums.[61] A regime such a Putin's represents a permanent standing invitation to military adventurism. The absence of democratic controls over all the instruments of force—regular military, paramilitary, internal troops, and intelligence forces—renders Russia permanently vulnerable to domestic and external coups as in 1994, 1999, and now in 2008. Just as the Chechen war of 1999 was in many respects a provocation and coup d'etat against more democratic elections and accountability, so, too, today's operation partakes of elements of the Siloviki's unremitting desire to seize and hold power even at the risk of foreign war.

Admittedly, throughout the entire period Georgia has displayed a lamentable penchant for stormy rhetoric and its own brand of provocative action compelling Western leaders to restrain Georgia repeatedly. It even contemplated a military action against South Ossetia and Abkhazia in 2006. But contemplation is not action, and its provocations were far surpassed by the consistent and escalating nature of Russian provocations dating back several years. In this confrontation, Georgia was the bull in the ring responding to the Russian matador's red cape. Russia was by no means the offended party as its leadership wants to make out.

Neither is it likely this war will end with whatever denouement plays itself out in Georgia. We can expect heightened Russian pressure against pro-Western states in the CIS like Azerbaijan and Ukraine. Indeed, Ukraine is already being threatened by Moscow. At the NATO-Russia Council in Bucharest in April 2008, President Putin told President Bush, "But, George, don't you understand that Ukraine is not a state?" Putin further claimed that most of its territory was a Russian gift in the 1950s. Moreover, while Western Ukraine belonged to Eastern Europe, Eastern Ukraine was "ours." Furthermore, if Ukraine did enter NATO, Russia would then detach Eastern Ukraine (and the Crimea) and graft it onto Russia. Thus Ukraine would cease to exist as a state.[62] Putin also said that Russia regards NATO enlargement as a threat, so if Georgia received membership, Moscow would "take adequate measures" and recognize Abkhazia and South Ossetia to create a buffer between NATO and Russia.[63]

So nothing that has occurred since then should have surprised us. Russian politicians are using every resource at their disposal to meddle in Ukraine's politics and extend the Black Sea Fleet's presence there beyond 2017; and they are now attacking Ukraine for its alleged arming of Georgia to the teeth and support for genocide. Ukraine, for its part, has said it may bar Black Sea Fleet ships that participated in this conflict from returning to their base, opening the way to further recriminations with Moscow.[64]

Thus even if one believes, as does Andrei Tsygankov in Chapter 8, that possibilities for such cooperation exist, it still must be admitted, as he does, that the obstacles to it are formidable.[65] Indeed, given Ukraine's pro-Georgian role in this war, those obstacles are likely to grow. Although these lines are being written during the war in Georgia, it is entirely conceivable that a Russian move on Tbilisi could lead to a new insurgency in the Caucasus which can little afford it. Alternatively, even if a new government replaces the Saakashvili regime, it is quite likely that it will be an irredentist government in outlook even if it is incapable of regaining its territories. Russia may well find that, despite a victory that makes it preen as if it was the boss of the CIS, again it has stepped on a rake. Tsygankov largely attributes these obstacles to psychological and cognitive factors in both countries' policymaking processes that prevent them from seeing each other clearly. Nevertheless, he argues that Washington and Moscow could contribute together to jointly assuring the integrity and stability of states menaced by threats to those attributes, e.g., Georgia, Ukraine, and Azerbaijan. Joint cooperation on economic development and reduction of poverty might also be possible. He also raises the point of whether it might be possible to find a way to avoid crises over Georgian and Ukrainian membership in NATO which is a red line for Moscow precipitating what its leaders consider to be a threat to Russia's vital interests.

For instance, in response to Russia's concerns, President Victor Yushchenko has recently suggested that he has no plans of stationing any foreign military troops on Ukrainian territory.[66] If NATO is indeed a political organization and not merely a military alliance as many in the West claim, then such solutions should not seem unfeasible. Enforcement of the Article 5 in such cases should be a subject of a separate negotiation. Other joint security arrangements, with or without NATO participation, must also be considered.[67] Much of this analysis, however, may turn out to have been superseded by events.

Tsyagankov also contends that both sides could collaborate on assuring the integrity of the threatened states — Georgia, Azerbaijan, and Ukraine — and work together to bring about poverty reduction and economic development, helping to demilitarize the Caucasus which is awash in conflicts and armed forces. But first, of course, the two sides, and particularly America, will have to overcome the cognitive and psychological blinders that impede cooperation.[68]

James Sherr, on the other hand, though he agrees that Russian policy is rooted in the psychological and cognitive dispositions of its elites, argues that this psychology combines resentment with an excessive self-confidence that masks the fact that Russia's regime feels threatened by developments like the Orange Revolution in Ukraine or Georgia's Rose Revolution because those events engender repercussions within the Russian Federation itself. And those repercussions, especially towards democratization, are anathema to the ruling elite. Meanwhile, these states' own internal weaknesses have long since drawn both East and West into their internal affairs as rivals. Thus the bilateral antagonism that we now see in regional security issues, as well as elsewhere in the bilateral agenda, is rooted in a clash pertaining to the nature of the state in the East and West or to what he calls the culture of power. Thus this conflict is rooted in the intrinsic nature of the rival polities, making it all the more difficult to overcome and resolve. But not only does this condition lead to conflict over regional security, energy, and

35

defense issues, given the nature of the Russian state and its permanent ongoing intrigues and rivalries, foreign policy issues are implicated in the very fabric of those domestic rivalries, e.g., the recent succession to Putin.[69]

Thus it is as much for domestic reasons as foreign policy and defense considerations that Russian elites from Putin on down do not consider Ukraine (or any other CIS state for that matter) to be a genuinely independent, self-standing, and sovereign state.

Under the circumstances, and as we see in real life, restoring cooperation on the regional security points of the agenda or on any of the other outstanding issues touched upon here will clearly be difficult both for the Bush administration and for its successor. Nevertheless, given the stakes and scope of the issues that encompass this agenda, there is no alternative. While the labor is arduous and unfulfilling and is unlikely to be completed on our watch; because of those stakes and scope we cannot abstain from carrying it out, for then everybody loses. George Kolt understood this truth deeply, and it was his combination of patriotism, wisdom, and concern for the larger issues that transcended personal interest that drove him to launch these conferences in the hope that they would facilitate the labor of bringing about this sorely needed cooperation. We offer these chapters and the hope of subsequent similar conferences and publications in the same spirit that he did and look forward to the continuation of the dialogue.

ENDNOTES - CHAPTER 1

1. George Jahn, "Oil Falls Despite Conflict," *Associated Press*, August 11, 2008.

2. Uri Ra'anan, Richard Schulz, Joshua Halperin, and Robert Pfaltzgraff, *Hydra of Carnage: Interational Linkages of Terrorism: The Witnesses Speak*, Boston, MA: Lexington Books, 1985.

3. Patrick Keller and Thomas Kunze, *In the Light of the NATO Summit: Chances and Limits of Eastward Enlargement*, Konrad Adenauer Stiftung, Anlaysen & Argumente, No. 51, May 2008, p. 5.

4. Moscow, *Interfax in English, July 7, 2008,* Foreign Broadcast Information Service, Central Eurasia (henceforth *FBIS SOV*), July 7, 2008; Moscow: *ITAR-TASS*, in English, July 7, 2008, *FBIS SOV*, July 7, 2008.

5. Moscow, *Agentstvo Voyennykh Novostey Internet Version*, in Russian, May 26, 2008, *FBIS SOV*, May 26, 2008.

6. Ministry of Foreign Affairs of the Russian Federation, *Kontseptsiya Vneshnei Politiki Rossiiskoi Federatsii*, Moscow, July 15, 2008, *www.mid.ru*, p. 20.

7. "Putin Interviewed by Journalists From G8 Countries–Text," *www.kremlin.ru*, June 4, 2007, Retrieved from Nexis-Lexis.

8. Paul Reynolds, "New Era of Discord for Russia and the West," *BBC News*, June 8, 2007, *news.bbc.co.uk/2/hi/europe671927.stm*.

9. *Kontseptsiya Vneshnei Politiki.*

10. Moscow, *Agentstvo Voyennykh Novstey internet version*, in English, May 16, 2007, *Open source Committee, FBIS SOV*, May 16, 2007; Moscow, Ministry of Foreign Affairs *Internet Version, Press Conference of Foreign Minister Sergei Lavrov with Secretary of State Condoleezza Rice*, May 16, 2007, *www.mid.ru*.

11. Tehran, *Mehr News Agency Internet Version*, in English, May 14, 2007, *FBIS SOV*, May 14, 2007.

12. "Russia's Zimbabwe Sanctions Veto Angers West, Raises Questions About Medvedev," *Associated Press*, July 15, 2008.

13. Thomas Gomart, *EU-Russia Relations: Toward a Way Out of Depression*, Paris, France; IFRI (IFRI), 2008, *www.ifri.org*.

14. Vladimir Olegovich Rukavishnikov, "Values, Interests and Threats in U.S. and Russian Grand Strategies and Politics," Review of International Affairs (Belgrade), No. 1118, April-June 2005, p. 60.

15. Steve Gutterman, "Russian Calls U.S. 'Difficult'," *Associated Press*, February 4, 2007.

16. "U.S. Influence in World Affairs Weakening-Russian FM," *RIA Novosti*, March 17, 2007.

17. "Russian Foreign Minister Acknowledges Growing Divergence with US," *Mosnews*, December 5, 2005, cited in Andrew Monaghan, "'Calmly Critical': Evolving Russian Views of U.S. Hegemony," *Journal of Strategic Studies*, Vol. XXIX, No. 6, December, 2006, p. 988.

18. Stephen Blank, *Towards a New Russia Policy*, Carlisle Barracks, PA: Strategic Studies Institute, U.S. Army War College, 2008.

19. Christopher Jones, "The Axis of Nonproliferation," *Problems of Post-Communism*, Vol. LIII, No. 21, March-April 2006, pp. 3-16.

20. See the following Debate, Robert Kagan, "Neocon Nation: Neoconservatism, c. 1776," *World Affairs*, Spring 2008, *www.worldaffairs/journal.org*; and David Rieff, George Parker, Ronald Steel, and Robert Kagan, "An Exchange: Neocon Nation?" *World Affairs*, Summer 2008, *www.worldaffairs.org*.

21. Rieff.; Hans-Joachim Spanger, *Between Ground Zero and Square One: How George W. Bush Failed on Russia,* Peace Research Institute, Frankfurt, Germany, Report PRIF Reports No. 82, 2008.

22. "Summary of Remarks by Russian Minister of Foreign Affairs Sergey Lavrov at the International Symposium 'Russia in the 21st Century'," Moscow, June 20, 2008, *www.mid.ru/*.

23. Colin L. Powell, "Understanding and Strategy," *SAIS Review*, Vol. XXV, No. 1, Winter-Spring 2005, p. 170.

24. Spanger.

25. Judy Dempsey, "Merkel Calls for Closer-NATO-Russia Ties," *International Herald Tribune*, May 27, 2008, *www.iht.com*.

26. Spanger, passim; Gomart, passim.

27. Sergei Gavrov, "Is the Transition to Authoritarianism Irreversible?" *Russian Social Science Review*, Vol. XLVIII, No. 3, May-June 2007, pp. 22-23.

28. Vladimr Shlapentokh, "Are Today's Authoritarian Leaders Doomed to Be Indicted When They Leave Office? The Russian and Other Post-Soviet Cases," *Communist and Post-Communist Studies*, Vol. XXXIX, No. 2, Autumn 2006, pp. 462-463.

29. Minxin Pei, *Assertive Pragmatism: China's Economic Rise and Its Impact on Chinese Foreign Policy,* IFRI Proliferation Papers, No. 15, Paris, France, IFRI, 2006, p. 17, *www.ifri.org*.

30. Constantine C. Menges, *China: The Gathering Threat*, Nashville, TN: Nelson Current Publishers, 2005; Stephen Blank, "Towards Alliance?: The Strategic Implications of Russo-Chinese Relations," *National Security Studies Quarterly*, Vol. VII, No. 3, Summer 2001, pp. 1-30.

31. Council on Foreign Relations, *Russia's Wrong Direction: What the United States Can and Should Do*, New York, *www.cfr.org*, 2006.

32. Richard Pipes, "What Is to Be Done?" *Commentary*, May 2008, *www.commentarymagazine.com/viewarticle.cfm/what-is-to-be-done-11358*.

33. Vladimir Putin, Speech at Meeting with the Ambassadors and Permanent Representatives of the Russian Federation, Ministry of Foreign Affairs, Moscow, June 27, 2006, *www.president.ru*.

34. Moscow, *Ekho Moskvy*, in Russian , February 17, 2007, *Open Source Committee, FBIS SOV*, February 17, 2007.

35. Yuri Ushakov, "From Russia With Like," *Los Angeles Times*, February 1, 2007, *www.latimes.com*.

36. "Speech and the Following Discussion at the Munich Conference on Security, February 10, 2007," *www.kremlin.ru/eng/speeches/2007/02/10/0138*.

37. Spanger.

38. Pavel Felgenhauer, "Russia's Imperial General Staff," *Perspective*, Vol. XVI, No. 1, October-November 2005, *www.bu.ed./iscip/vol16/felgenhauer*.

39. Moscow, *Agentstvo Voyennykh Novostey, Internet Version*, in English, February 14, 2007, *FBIS SOV*, February 14, 2007.

40. Kontseptsiya Vneshnei Politiki, p. 20.

41. Stephen J. Cimbala, *The New Nuclear Disorder*, Unpublished manuscript, pp. 1-3, cited with consent of the author.

42. Ambassador Linton Brooks, *Arms Control and U.S.-Russian Relations*, Paper Prepared for the Conference on "U.S. and Russia: Post-Elections Security Challenges," U.S. Army War College, Carlisle Barracks, PA, March 6-7, 2008.

43. *Ibid.*

44. *Ibid.*

45. Kerry M. Kartcher, "U.S. Nuclear Weapons and Nonproliferation: Dispelling the Myths," Presentation to the Carnegie Moscow Center, February 2, 2007, available at *www.carnegie.ru/en/pubs/media/101192007.02.02.Presentation.ppt*.

46. Brooks.

47. Alexander A. Pikayev, *Arms Control and U.S.-Russian Relations*, Paper Prepared for the Conference on "U.S. and Russia: Post-Elections Security Challenges," U.S. Army War College, Carlisle Barracks, PA, March 6-7, 2008.

48. Christopher Jones, "The Axis of Nonproliferation," *Problems of Post-Communism*, Vol. LIII, No. 21, March-April 2006, pp. 3-16.

49. Alex Vatanka, "Editor's Notes, *Jane's Intelligence Digest*, July 24, 2008, *www4.janes.com/subscribe/jid/doc_view.jsp?K2DocKey=/ content1/janesdata/mags/jid/history/jid2008/jid70416.htm@ current&Prod_Name=JID&QueryText=*.

50. Alexei Arbatov, "Terms of Engagement; WMD Proliferation and U.S.-Russian Interests," Paper Prepared for the U.S. Army War College Conference, "U.S. and Russian: Post-Elections Security Challenges," Carlisle Barracks, PA, March 6-7, 2008.

51. Stephen Blank, "Promoting Russo-American Cooperation in Halting Nuclear Proliferation," Paper Prepared for the U.S. Army War College Conference on Russo-American Cooperation, Carlisle Barracks, PA, March 6-7, 2008.

52. Moscow, *Agentstvo Voyennykh Novostey Internet Version*, in English, June 6, 2008, *FBIS SOV*, June 6, 2008.

53. Richard Pipes, *The Formation of the Soviet Union: Communism and Nationalism, 1917-1923*, Revised Ed., Cambridge, MA: Harvard University Press, 1997.

54. Sophia Kishkovsky, "Georgia is Warned By Russia Against Plans to Join NATO," *New York Times*, June 7, 2008, p. 8; Moscow, *ITAR-TASS*, in English, June 6, 2008; Moscow, *Interfax*, in English, June 6, 2008, *FBIS SOV*, June 6, 2008; Moscow, *Agentstvo Voyennykh Novostey* internet version, *in English*, June 6, 2008, FBIS *SOV*, June 6, 2008.

55. Moscow, *ITAR-TASS*, in English, June 6, 2008, *FBIS SOV*, June 6, 2008; Moscow, *Interfax*, in English, June 6, 2008, *FBIS SOV*, June 6, 2008.

56. Conversations with Georgian officials, Washington, DC, May, 2008.

57. Tbilisi, *Rezonansi*, in Georgian, June 6, 2008, *FBIS SOV*, June 6, 2008.

58. Dov Lynch, *Engaging Eurasia's Separatist States: Unresolved Conflicts and De Facto States*, Washington, DC: United States Institute of Peace Press, 2004, p. 57; James Traub, "Taunting the Bear," *New York Times*, August 11, 2008, *www.nytimes.com*; Vladimir Frolov, "Russia Profile Weekly Experts Panel: Russia Going To War With Georgia," *ww.russiaprofile.com*; "Georgia: A Fresh Outbreak of Violence During Negotiations," *www.stratfor.com*, August 7, 2008; "Geopolitical Diary, Decision Time in South Ossetia," *www.stratfor.com*, August 8, 2008; Vladimir Socor, "Berlin Consultations on Abkhazia Derailed," *Eurasia Daily Monitor*, August 1, 2008; Vladimir Socor, "Ossetian Separatists Are Provoking A Major Russian Intervention," *Eurasia Daily Monitor*, August 7, 2008; Boris Dolgin, "Military Continuation: What Is Happening Around South Ossetia," Moscow, *Polit.ru Internet Version*, August 8, 2008, *FBIS SOV*, August 8, 2008; Vadim Dubnov, "Who Fired the First Shot," Moscow, *Gazeta*, in Russian, August 6, 2008, *FBIS* SOV, August 6, 2008; Moscow, *Interfax*, in Russia, August 6, 2008, *FBIS SOV*, August 6, 2008; Yevgeny Shestakov, "From South to North Evacuation of Children From South Ossetia Continues," Moscow, *Rossiyskaya Gazeta*, in Russian, August 5, 2008, *FBIS SOV* August 5, 2008; "Talking Through Gritted Teeth," *BBC Monitoring*, August 6, 2008; Yuliya Latynina, "South Ossetia Crisis Could Be Russia's Chance To Defeat Siloviki," *Radio Free Europe Radio Liberty*, August 8, 2008; Georgi Lomsadze, "Georgia Tensions Flare Over Breakaway South Ossetia, *Eurasia Insight*, August 4, 2008; "Who's To Blame In South Ossetia," *Radio Free Ruope Radio Liberty*, August 8, 2008.

59. Moscow, *Interfax*, in English, August 7, 2008, *FBIS SOV*, August 7, 2008.

60. Lomsadze; Moscow, *Gazeta.ru Internet Version*, in Russian, *FBIS SOV*, August 8, 2008.

61. Stephen Blank, "Is Russia a Democracy and Does It Matter?" *World Affairs*, Vol. MCLVII, No. 3, Winter, 2005, pp. 125-136.

62. Socor; "Ugroza Kremlya," www.kommersant.com, April 7, 2008, *Radio Free Europe Radio Liberty Newsline*, April 8, 2008; "Putin Hints At Splitting Up Ukraine, "*Moscow Times*, April 8, 2008; "Putin Threatens Unity of Ukraine, Georgia," *Unian*, April 7, 2008, *www.unian.net.*

63. "Ugroza Kremlya."

64. "Georgian Breakaway City in Ruins," Tbilisi's Blog, *tbilisiwebinfo/woodpress.com/2208/08/10georgia-breakaway-city-in-ruin;* "Russian War Ships Sail For Georgia," *Russia Today*, August 10, 2008, *www.russiatoday.ru/news/news/28759.*

65. Andrei P. Tsyagankov, "Obstacles to U.S.-Russian Cooperation in the Caucasus and Ukraine," Paper Prepared for the Conference on "U.S. and Russia: Post-Elections Security Challenges," U.S. Army War College, Carlisle Barracks, PA, March 6-7, 2008.

66. Victor Yuschenko, "Ukraine's Membership in NATO Will Pose No New Threats to Russia," *Vremya Novostei*, No. 29, February 22, 2008.

67. Tsyagankov.

68. *Ibid.*

69. James Sherr, "Russian & American Strategic Rivalry in Ukraine & Georgia," Paper Presented to the U.S. Army War College Conference on Russo-American Cooperation, Carlisle Barracks, PA, March 6-7, 2008.

CHAPTER 2

PRESIDENTIAL ELECTIONS AND THE FUTURE OF U.S.-RUSSIAN RELATIONS: A TIME FOR REFLECTION

Jacob W. Kipp

Introduction.

Professor Stephen Blank, an old and dear friend, had asked me to undertake this topic from the perspective of my analysis of the Russian side of this equation. Owing to events beyond our control, that task has evolved into an assessment of the two sides of the equation. Now those of you who know me are well aware that I have made a career of not commenting on U.S. affairs. The logic of this has been quite apparent to me. I have been trained and worked as a scholar of Russia and the Soviet Union and have accepted the challenge of making the Russian state, society, and history comprehensible to American, and to a lesser extent, European audiences. I will now violate the rule to enhance discourse upon this topic or create intellectual confusion. Wish me well. My first task is to provide you with an appropriate intellectual/ speculative frame for the discourse.

Framing the Question.

As an historian, I have am quite comfortable with the *Annales* paradigm for historical discourse on the problem of change over time with its distinct differentiations. The Annales drew attention to long-term continuities based on structural patterns of human interactions within cultural communities, the *longue duree* which gives birth to collective mentalities — much like the very depths of the ocean. These historians focused specific attention on processes of socio-economic change on a generational basis — much like ocean currents with their continuous, directed movement that affect life at sea and ashore. In this context, specific events, such as immediate political events — the stuff of classical history, the Annales saw as transitory — much like the crash of waves, powerful, awesome, but random and unpredictable, their deeper meaning concealed unless understood against the larger temporal context. Presidential elections appear in this context to be of immediate interest, but one must look deeper to appreciate longer term continuities and more substantial generational shifts. As a historian of Russia, I am more likely to agree with the basic narrative of Count Aleksei Konstantinovich Tolstoy's poem, "*Istoriya gosudarastva Rossiiskogo ot gostomysla do Timasheva.*" This witty review of a thousand years of Russian History is based on a persistent refrain about a land of untold riches and a perpetual search for order (*Zemlya u nas bogata, Poryadok v nei lish' net*).[1] The state has been the focus for such a search for order, even as it assumed direction over a social order that has been collectivist (*sobornost'*) in its mentality. This play on interaction between Russia and the outside, between the distant sea and the vast land, has always been a part of Russian exceptionalism, making for a unique sense of culture and history. Since 1991 Russia has had its national identity reshaped out of the Communist model and back towards one that emphasizes that Russian exceptionalism, in the absence of an ideology claiming a universal mission, to impose its order on others as manifestation of historical progress.

I can claim no such inspired reflection on the American experiment. But for purposes of comparison, I have drawn upon Alexis de Tocqueville's *de la Démocratie en Amérique*, in which the author observed both the threats to democracy and the threats from democracy in the republic.[2] I find particular relevance in his insights into the American national character. It is the attention to social bonding based upon pragmatic criteria, a search for personal advantage and profit and an inclination to the forging of secondary associations to further such goals that give life to the society and reduce the central importance of the state. In its post-modern democratic manifestation, this view embraces American exceptionalism and democratic universalism. Unipolarity has made it possible to speak of an American supplied security, which makes possible the universal triumph of democracy as both an inevitable and positive culmination of history.[3] While both nations conquered continents and built great states, they differed in certain fundamental principles of social organization and political discourse. At this time with the end of the post-Cold War order and the waning of the naïve assumption that globalization, the end of Soviet Communism, and common Western values meant an end of history, it seems appropriate to put the current electoral coincidence into a larger historical and societal context—not an inevitable clash of civilizations as much as a need to recognize that differences exist and must impact the character of the relations between these two great experiments. If this sounds like a critique of Samuel Huntington's *Clash of Civilizations*, let me assure you that while I share a bias towards the Western values and institutions, I do not see a clash between Russia and the West as inevitable. Indeed, I have argued that a bridge across this cultural divide would serve the interests of both. Those supporting such a clash can argue their case as certainly a persistent theme. Certainly, they can refer to the Marquis de Custine's scathing criticism of the pretense that was Nicholas I's Russia and even invoke his vision of a future clash between Russia as oppressor and threat to the West.[4] When George Kennan offered containment as a strategy to deal with the Soviet Union after World War II, it was assumed that a post-Soviet Russia would revert to some elements of its historical experience in building a new order. Those who are disappointed in Russia's neo-authoritarian turn in Russian statehood would do well to reflect on Alexis de Tocqueville's other great work, *L'Ancien Regime et la Revolution*, with its emphasis upon continuity between Bourbon and post-Revolutionary France.[5] In the current Russian case, it is precisely the absence of pretense to a universal transformational mission at this time in Russia's ideology that suggests the possibility of a bridge between the Euro-Atlantic world and Eurasia, for if such cannot be built on this axis, then the 21st century will see another long and bitter struggle. As James Billington has suggested, Russia's search for its identity is not resolved. While the naïve Westernism of the early 1990s has given way to a deeper search for national identity across the political spectrum and drawing upon historical experiences, there remains the tension between a more critical Western path toward an "inventive economy, and open society, and a more accountable government for a multiethnic continent-wide nation" and an authoritarian illusion of the well-regulated police state under the banner of Eurasianism.[6] That question has not yet been resolved, and a prudent Western policy that sought common interests in conjunction with shared values would aid the positive resolution of the question. The unstated question in this context is whether that prudent Western policy will be a matter of *diktat* imposed by the superpower hegemon or renewed dialogue among the Atlantic-European community—now encompassing Central and Eastern Europe—about the best approach to a recovered Russia seeking to play new role as a great power in a multipolar world.

Political Calendars, Candidates, and Policies.

The political calendars of the United States and the Russian Federation have created a political coincidence of some import. Both states are in the midst of an electoral process leading to the selection of a new head of state after long tenures by the current incumbents of those offices. As of the time of this meeting, Russia had elected Dmitry Medvedev, Putin's designated successor, to be its next president by an overwhelming majority. In May Medvedev assumed the office of President, and one of his first acts was to appoint Vladimir Putin as Prime Minister, further assuring continuity in administrations, even as the appointment raised issues regarding the de facto power-sharing arrangement between sponsor and successor. The American electoral process is still ongoing with Senator McCain and Senator Barak Obama as the candidates. Nevertheless, we shall have two new presidents in both nations by January 2009.

There is, of course, a very great difference in our ability to forecast the political courses of the American and Russian future presidents. One can clearly see a fundamental asymmetry on the questions of future policies and key personnel appointments. Not only has Medvedev already been elected, but one of his first official acts was to appoint his predecessor Prime Minister and to confirm many of his appointees to serve in a Medvedev administration. Indeed, the emerging capital issue seems to be whether Russia's constitution of 1993 with its strong presidency will give way to a more parliamentary government, given Putin's role as both Prime Minister and Party leader. While Medvedev has made numerous comments about a more liberal economic order, it seems that Putin's policies, especially his emphasis on energy policy, will remain a guiding principle. Most observers expect a general continuity in domestic and international policies between the Putin and Medvedev presidencies since Medvedev is one of the group of lawyers and security personnel from St. Petersburg who joined Putin's team in the new administration. His association with *Gazprom*, the semi-public energy giant, and his advocacy of open markets have led most observers to expect a continuation of a "controlled liberalism" in state policy.[7] The more interesting discussions have concerned the duration and direction of the Medvedev presidency. Mark Smith has speculated about a short interval for Medvedev to reign while Putin would rule as prime minister, followed by a resignation and another Putin election to the presidency, which would be within the Constitution. Smith also looked at a short-term tenure by Putin as prime minister, providing a transition to full-blown Medvedev presidency in law and deed. Such a transition could strengthen the Duma and the emerging executive-dominated party system. Smith, however, saw as more likely a sorting out of arrangements with the Russian ruling elite around the two pillars, with the power ministers (*Siloviki*) and the energy elite driving the struggle. This would be more a struggle within the *rentier* elite over access to wealth than deep policy disputes. Smith did not see this outcome as bringing any fundamental break in Russian foreign policy.[8] We can certainly expect the Council on Foreign and Defense Policy under Sergei Karaganov to continue to be one of the leading public institutions influencing foreign policy.[9]

Of the American candidates for President, John McCain would seem to be the candidate offering the greatest chance of policy continuity towards Russia. The Republican nominee, he inherits Bush's foreign policy whole cloth. And in some areas, i.e., Iraq and the Global War on Terrorism (GWOT), McCain has made clear his commitment to President Bush's goals. In other areas, including Russia, McCain seems closer to more conservative elements in his party, who are opposed to the authoritarian direction of Russian policy and support a policy to challenge Russia's sphere of interest politics in the near abroad. A year ago, McCain challenged Bush's assessment of Putin as a man with whom the United States could do business, and called for a harsh response to Russia's anti-democratic policies.[10] McCain supports the Bush policy of expanding the North Atlantic Treaty Organization (NATO) to include Ukraine and Georgia, but has been much more outspoken about following a policy of confrontation with Russia in case of conflict over the near abroad. He has also supported Gary Kasparov and The Other Russia in the latest elections.[11] The candidate's chief advisor on Russia, Stephen Biegun, combines time as both a former staffer on the Senate Foreign Relations Committee and as an appointed official in the Department of Defense (DoD) under the First Bush administration. He has the reputation for being a solid professional without academic credentials.[12] To what extent McCain will draw upon the leading Russianist in the current Bush administration is an unknown.

Secretary of State Condoleezza Rice combines Russian expertise with more general foreign policy credentials and her own political influence, making her into a major Republican operative and even a potential vice presidential candidate, which would balance McCain's ticket by bringing strength in a number of areas. As the architect of Bush's opening to Putin in the early years of the current administration, she would to have find a way of adjusting her position to that of a strong-willed McCain. In a recent issue of *Foreign Affairs*, the Secretary of State called a continuation of Bush administration policies under the banner of a "unique American realism," which emphasizes values in place of interests in shaping America's approach to a new international order. In this policy, democratization on a global scale becomes the foundation of such an order. On U.S.-Russian relations, Rice spoke of a "strategic framework" between Washington and Moscow, but lamented Moscow's anti-U.S. rhetoric, and its tendency to treat its post-Soviet neighbors as in its sphere of influence. She held out the hope that international economic conditions would lead Russia towards values more in keeping with her global democratic order.[13]

The Democratic challenger, Barack Obama, has attracted both the young and the old. Michael McFaul, one of the brightest of the younger generation of Kremlinologists, joined the campaign after writing in *Foreign Affairs* about the myth of Putin's political-economic successes.[14] Zbigniew Brzezinski, a leading Obama supporter, if not advisor, has a reputation as a scholar of deep geo-strategic insights. His work, *The Grand Chess Board*,[15] is well known to the Russian foreign policy elite and contributed to the Russian debate of the 1990s on geopolitics. His first extensive critique of the Bush administration's foreign and security policies appeared in 2005, emphasizing a clear strategic choice between imposing a global domination or restoring American leadership of like-minded states.[16] Brzezinski has been a vocal critic of superpower over-reach, which he warned was creating geopolitical conditions for a Beijing-Moscow axis in Eurasia that would oppose American interests.[17] Having served as National Security Advisor to President Jimmy Carter, Brzezinski is associated with that part of the Democratic Party with a distinctly *Mitteleuropaicsher* perspective on post-cold war geopolitics. In this view, the linkage of Eastern and Central Europe to Western Europe serves to balance Russian influence as does a strong and independent "near abroad" in Eastern Europe and the Caucasus. An independent and vital Ukraine serves as the bridge to Russia that acts like another state. This is a view heard more often in Warsaw today than Berlin.

Candidate Obama's own pronouncements in favor of more diplomacy with those whom the Bush administration has labeled as rogue states, a rapid withdrawal from Iraq, and his domestic focus seem to suggest an initial period when Moscow would not loom large in U.S. foreign relations, and those relations would not become fraught with potential conflict. One area where Obama has asserted interest in close U.S.-Russian cooperation is nuclear policy. Unlike the Bush administration that sought to enlist Russia in a case-by-case counterproliferation program, Obama has reasserted a nuclear arms control agenda as capital in U.S.-Russian relations and in supporting the Non-Proliferation Treaty (NPT). He has spoken of a move towards "a nuclear free world." His foreign policy position paper calls for radical measures involving close cooperation with Russia:

He will stop the development of new nuclear weapons; work with Russia to take U.S. and Russian ballistic missiles off hair trigger alert; seek dramatic reductions in U.S. and Russian stockpiles of nuclear weapons and material; and set a goal to expand the U.S.-Russian ban on intermediate-range missiles so that the agreement is global.[18]

Given the Russian attitude on nuclear issues and their perpetual importance to the strategic relationship between Washington and Moscow, one must assume that bilateral relations in other areas will be subject to the prism of nuclear cooperation in the spirit of Nunn-Lugar from the 1990s.

Some Russian experts have speculated that Obama, with his youth and reform ambitions, would be more likely to find a partner in Medvedev. It is unlikely that Obama would be dealing with Medvedev in the context of a free hand. Putin and his legacy will shape strategic choices until there are fundamental shifts in the international environment, and Obama's inexperience would more likely engender some hard testing from Putin over issues related to the near abroad and NATO expansion.

The Post-Cold War Era.

That this electoral coincidence has served to bring about this current meeting between U.S. and Russian specialists interested in the relations between these two states and upon the general impact of these elections on the international system should be expected. The history of these meetings, which began in the immediate aftermath of Soviet withdrawal from Afghanistan in 1989 and continued through the tumultuous events of the end of the Cold War, the disintegration of the

Soviet Union, and the emergence of the Russian Federation as the chief successor to the Soviet Union, has been much conditioned by the political processes involved in selecting new national leaders. The very dynamic of the early years, when a bipolar international system based on a militarized ideological competition collapsed, underscored the importance of the political processes in both states for the emerging post-Cold War international order.

When these conversations began, no one in Washington or Moscow doubted the centrality of U.S.-Russian relations in determining the prospects for post-Cold War stability and order. The common assumption was that cooperation was the most effective means "to win the peace" and to ensure stability and order in the post-Cold War geo-strategic space. The first Bush administration even seemed to doubt the wisdom of the rapid and disordered disintegration of the Soviet Union. That process, however, quickly got beyond the control of either Washington or Moscow after the August 1991 Putsch. The logic of the Bush administration from the perspective of what statesmen in Moscow and Washington saw as the core problem of the former strategic confrontation was unassailable. Critics of this course spoke of President Bush's "Chicken Kiev" speech in August 1991 as a slap in the face to Ukrainian national aspirations for independence; what he had actually warned against was a suicidal nationalism that could have fired ethnic tensions between Ukrainians and Russians in the context of a dispute over strategic nuclear weapons. He had not ruled out a political process leading to a plebiscite on national self-determination for Ukraine.

Nuclear weapons, which had been at the very heart of the militarized confrontation, were seen as matters of grave strategic concern, with the disposition of the remaining Soviet arsenal a mutual concern of Moscow and Washington. Nuclear weapons and their delivery systems seemed to ensure that Russia and the United States would be involved both in managing the reduction of such arsenals and in cooperation to ensure positive and active control of the remaining weapons systems. The two nations shared an interest in managing nuclear proliferation, even as they set about the reduction of their own nuclear arsenals. The United States backed Russia's "gathering in" of the Soviet arsenal under Moscow's control and quickly enacted measures to assist Russia in ensuring the management of that arsenal to reduce the risks of proliferation of weapons, technology, and expertise. This cooperation gave the U.S.-Russia relationship the flavor of a strategic partnership of global significance. After the election of the Clinton administration in 1992, much initial rhetoric spoke of a broader strategic partnership involving cooperation on a wide range of security issues. The Yeltsin administration expected to gain serious political capital for dismantling the Soviet system within Russia and for promoting the disintegration of the Soviet Union, the recognition of the successor states, and for endorsing the concessions made by Mikhail Gorbachev towards the removal of Soviet hegemony in Eastern Europe, including the arrangements necessary to bring about German unification. Making the reduction of its own nuclear arsenal under the terms of the Strategic Arms Reduction Treaty (START) was expected to be a long-term political chit that Washington and Europe would value and respect.

Yet Washington's rhetoric about the United States as the "sole surviving super power" and its mission to create a "new world order" raised concerns in Moscow and brought into play subtle and not-so subtle efforts to create mechanisms that would limit the freedom of action of the United States on issues vital to Russia and forge an axis of cooperation with Beijing and New Delhi, as Foreign Minister Primakov described it. These efforts, which included ambitious programs of arms sales, proved more successful with Beijing than New Delhi.

The leaderships in Moscow and Washington also shared a common perspective on the end of the Soviet Union, the emergence of Russian democracy, and the initiation of the capitalist transformation of Russia. Both leaderships expected Russia to join the West as a full partner in an emerging global order, based on open societies and market economics. However, the road to economic recovery in Russia proved long delayed and the social costs of the transition period cost much of the Russian population dearly. Those who benefited from the dismantling profited to a degree that assured their politico-economic leadership under the telling phrase, the oligarchs. The emergence of an obvious redistribution of wealth that enriched the few and impoverished the many led to popular speculation about corruption and collusion between those in government and those who became the giants of Russian business.

Some observers became alarmed because these economic troubles began to call into question the survival of Russian democracy, especially after the open conflict between the executive and legislative branches led to the storming of the Russian "White House" in November 1993. In the aftermath of those events Russia adopted a new constitution stressing presidential power in December, and the elections for the Duma resulted in the largest party bloc there being that of Vladimir Zhirinovsky's Liberal Democratic

Party, which combined national chauvinism and authoritarianism with political farce. Boris Yeltsin's re-election in 1996 after a stunning political recovery in the wake of the disastrous first year of the War in Chechnya represented more of a vote against Russia's Communists than a popular endorsement of Boris Yeltsin's government or policies. Some foreign observers noted flaws in the electoral process that ensured Yeltsin's reelection. Knowledgeable observers of the Russian military spoke of a failed program for reform of the armed forces in the context of a "time of troubles" (Smuta).[19] Others feared the rise of authoritarian nationalism bent upon revanche in a "Weimar Russia."[20] Renewed fighting in Chechnya in the summer of 1996 and the political alliance that Yeltsin was forced to make with Alexander Lebed to ensure victory over the Communists quickly brought about a negotiated end of hostilities between Lebed and President Maskhadov at Khasvayurt, Dagestan.[21] Neither side was satisfied with this temporary settlement, but both were too weak to renew the fighting. The bloom was off Russian democracy in Washington and Moscow. Washington saw Russia as a declining power, whose recovery seemed to be either long postponed or unlikely. Corruption in both the state apparatus and in the economy raised serious questions concerning Russia's integration into the global economic order. The role of Russian organized crime in international finance became a salient feature of discussions of transnational criminal activities.[22]

As noted above, the spring of strategic partnership between Washington and Moscow proved premature and ill-founded. While there was much talk of Russia's integration into a Western economic model, the actual deconstruction of the Soviet economy rapidly turned into a general collapse of production, spiraling inflation, and bandit privatization executed at the expense of much of the Russian population. Not until 1997, after Yeltsin's remarkable re-election in the face of monumental public disapproval of his administration's management of the economy, public disorder, the war in Chechnya, and Russia's decline as a great power, did the economy briefly look like there would be some economic recovery and growth of the gross domestic product (GDP) back towards pre-1989 levels. But that interval was short-lived and ended with the financial, fiscal, and monetary meltdown of August 1998. Russia appeared to be a marginal power. Its nuclear weapons, the state's last claim to superpower status, were irrelevant to the most pressing issues before European security.

The political efforts to integrate Russia into a post-Cold War security regime in Europe followed a line based upon managing the integration of Central Europe into a NATO-dominated structure. NATO's evolution from its Cold War role as a defensive security system designed to keep "the Soviets out, the Americans in, and the Germans down" depended upon finding a new role. In the early and mid-1990s, the emphasis was upon transforming NATO into a collective security system that could manage European security problems via Russia's active engagement. Efforts to transform the Organization for Security and Cooperation in Europe (OSCE) into the Commission on Security and Cooperation in Europe (CSCE) and make the latter a major security nexus quickly collapsed. The emerging security challenge of ethno-national conflicts in Europe and among the former states of the Soviet Union posed a new challenge to U.S.-Russian relations. The "near abroad" became a complex set of regional problems, which Russia sought to deal with through its own bilateral measures, collective actions of the successor states through the Commonwealth of Independent States (CIS), and via existing international mechanisms, i.e., the United Nations (UN) and the newly extant European institutions such as the transformed OSCE and the Council of Europe. The tension between Russia's claims in the "near abroad" and its involvement in a series of ethno-national conflicts across this vast region brought further complications with the successor states from Moldova, through the Caucasus and into Central Asia. Russian concern about such conflicts increased when the same tensions threatened the territorial integrity of the Federation itself. The Yeltsin government's badly executed military intervention in Chechnya underscored the weakness of Russian military power and the ineffectiveness of its national leadership. These issues still complicate Russia's relations with Moldova over Pridnestrovia and with Georgia over Abkhazia and South Ossetia. The one success story for Russian military intervention came in Tajikistan, but the political settlement between Tajik factions in that civil war owed much to the victory of the Taliban in Afghanistan and the threat that radical Islam posed to both Tajik factions.

The emergence of Balkan instability with the disintegration of the Yugoslav Federation in 1991 proved to be one of the most challenging and complex issues confronting Russian foreign policy. Russia joined in the UN effort to establish a security regime in Croatia under the UN Protection Force (UNPROFOR) and took part in its extended operations into Bosnia-Herzegovina. NATO proved to be the most difficult institution for the Russian Federation to reach an accommodation with over the next decade. This problem became more complex when NATO set upon the path of expansion into Central Europe. Russia signed on for Partnership for Peace but became disillusioned with that institution when it became apparent that NATO intended to expand beyond its admission of the three Central European states—Poland, the Czech Republic, and Hungary. NATO-Russian relations became more strained as the Clinton administration called for the alliance to take on increasing responsibility for a successor security regime in Bosnia-Herzegovina, as UNPROFOR proved less and less effective in managing the conflict. The mass murder of Bosnian Muslims at Srebrenica, a UN-mandated "safe haven" under UNPROFOR protection, changed the dynamics of the conflict from one of ethnic cleansing to genocide and moved the United States and NATO to take direct military action against the forces of the Republic of Serbia.[23] The Yeltsin government's immediate response to NATO's use of force over Bosnia brought a temporary crisis of relations between NATO and Russia that only improved after the negotiation of the Dayton Accords and the bilateral arrangement for Russian participation in the NATO Implementation Force (IFOR) as part of Multi-National Division (North) (MND[N]) under a U.S. division headquarters. The Russian deployment assumed a long-standing character when IFOR gave way to the NATO Stabilization Force (SFOR).[24] This situation set the stage for the NATO-Russia Charter of 1997, which established the Permanent Joint Council and provided for on-going dialogue between Russia and NATO over political and security issues confronting the continent.

For Washington, managing the reduction and security of Russia's nuclear arsenal required continued bilateral engagement, but European security issues were now left to the newly developed NATO-Russia structures. These were never designed to be the basis of a strategic partnership but rather to assure Russian support or at least acquiesce to a redefined and radically expanded NATO, which went well beyond the initial three new members of 1999 (Czech Republic, Poland, and Hungary) and laid out a Membership Action Plan (MAP) to expedite the admission of other states to the alliance. This change in strategic direction towards Russia coincided with the economic and fiscal crisis of 1998, which seemed to confirm Russia's marginal status on the periphery of Europe. Seeking to engage Russia in a solution over an emerging insurgency in Kosovo and the repressive counterinsurgency measures mounted by Belgrade, the United States and NATO turned its attention to direct political pressure upon the Yugoslav Federation, demanding political concessions and the end of repressive measures. Memories of the rapid shift from ethnic cleansing to genocide in Bosnia underscored the need for rapid and decisive action to NATO. Russia parted company with the United States and NATO over the direct use of force to compel Yugoslav compliance with the Rambouillet II conditions. What followed was the initiation of Operation ALLIED FORCE against Yugoslavia and a distinct cooling of NATO-Russia relations. The air campaign, which was supposed to achieve rapid political concessions and military withdrawal from Kosovo, turned into a protracted campaign and mass population expulsion of Kosovars by Yugoslav forces, and brought mounting tensions between Moscow and Washington. Astute observers of Moscow recognized a sea change in Russian elite attitudes towards international security and relations with the United States and the West.

In the post-Cold War international security environment, Russian military and civilian analysts have shared some basic assumptions. First, general nuclear war is not likely. The risk of general conventional war is not imminent. However, the probability of local conflicts turning into regional wars and inviting foreign intervention on Russia's periphery is high in some regions and carries with it the risk of the escalation of such conflicts into regional and even general war. The risk of a local conflict becoming a regional war with foreign intervention grew substantially in the aftermath of NATO's intervention in Kosovo in the spring of 1999. As Aleksei Arbatov, a member of the State Duma's Defense Committee, stated: "The bombing of Yugoslavia revived the worst instincts of the Cold War" among the Russian civil and military leadership. More exactly, Russia's isolation and NATO's willful disregard of its interests confirmed the threat assumptions that only a few years before had been confined to the extreme nationalist and communist circles.

The events of the spring of 1999 marked the end of the post-Cold War era in U.S.-Russian relations. NATO bombing of Yugoslavia brought large scale protests in Moscow. NATO's admission of the first set of new members in April and the articulation of the MAP for even more members from Eastern Europe and the former Soviet Union confirmed that Moscow had no effective check on the creation of an all-European security system, even in the face of Russian concerns and objections. The Russian government itself was in a deep crisis, with the Duma threatening to impeach the President before his second term ended in 2000. While the negotiation of the Ahtisaari-Chernomyrdin duo with President Milosevic brought an end to fighting in Yugoslavia and the occupation of Kosovo by a UN-mandated NATO force, Russian reactions pointed to a much deeper rift with the United States and NATO. An alliance among the military and the security services initiated a sharp symbolic turn away from the cooperation. In June Russian paratroopers assigned to SFOR in Bosnia were ordered to march from Uglivic to Pristina via Serbia. The small detachment represented no serious military challenge to NATO but did highlight a Russian intention to carve its own zone of occupation within Kosovo. That deployment, which created tensions within the NATO high command, was greeted in Moscow as a sign of Russian will to protect its interests and those of the Serbian minority within Kosovo. On June 21 the Russian government, through the head of the Security Council, Vladimir Putin, announced the first large-scale strategic exercises of the Russian armed forces since the end of the Cold War, ZAPAD 99, the scenario of which involved Russian forces defending Belarus from an attack from the West and ended with what the General Staff described as nuclear first-use to stop the aggression and "de-escalate" the conflict. While the exercise focused on the Baltic, Russia's political and military elite had much graver concerns in the south, where increasing tensions in and around Chechnya held out the prospect of renewed fighting.[25]

It was in this context that Putin moved to prominence in the Russian government. When fighting erupted in Dagestan, the initial response seemed to be one to contain the conflict without escalation into a full-scale war in Chechnya. In mid-August, President Yeltsin sacked his Prime Minister, the loyal Sergei Stepashin, and named Putin Prime Minister, identifying him as his chosen successor as President. Putin emerged as the champion of decisive action in conjunction with a series of bombings against Russian military and civilian targets, including an apartment complex in Moscow. Putin marshaled the means of the Russian state to impose a military solution upon Chechnya and end the threat of seccession and external intervention.[26] However well Russian troops functioned in the fight for Chechnya, Putin made certain that the Russian state would win the information war at home and that the conflict would be Chechenized as far as possible to undercut the notion that this was a Russian colonial war and not a struggle against "Islamic terrorism."

The Presidencies of Vladimir Putin and George W. Bush.

Boris Yeltsin resigned from the Presidency and Putin became acting President on December 31, 1999. His presidency began with broad plans to restore the national economy, strengthen the central state apparatus, and prosecute the Chechen War to a victorious conclusion. His so-called millennium speech laid out a gradual program of reforms and economic development that would restore the national economy and the living standards of the Russian population.[27] In these early days, the primary question for Russian and foreign observers was "Who is this Vladimir Putin?" The answers have varied, depending upon the viewer's perspective and timing and have included: a son of Leningrad and protégée of the late Anatoly Sobchak; the appointed heir to Boris Yeltsin; the Russian President who restored prosperity and order; a former KGB *Apparatchik* who side-tracked Russian democracy; the sworn enemy of Chechen rebels, terrorists, and Islamic extremists; a Russian imperialist bent on subjugating the Near Abroad; a supporter of U.S. War on Terrorism; Chairman of the G-8 for 2006; a German in the Kremlin; a great centralizing tsar reuniting the Russian land; an Orthodox Christian and champion of his faith; a sportsman and judo enthusiast; and/or a democrat into whose soul George Bush looked.[28]

From its first days, the new administration displayed a strong desire to control the national media and ensure that the government's message on the causes, course, and costs of the Chechen War was the only one to be heard. Putin offered Russia's oligarchs a straightforward deal: Concentrate on making money, recognize the state's special place in the national economy, and stay out of opposition politics. In February, Russian forces began their general offensive in Chechnya with the objective of occupying the Chechen capital and, by taking it, rob the Aslan Maskhadov government of any de facto claim to legitimacy and so undercut any basis for foreign intervention. Russia was engaged in a war with terrorists/extremists, and it would be a fight to the end. The government, however, made a point of enlisting and using Chechen fighters under Akhmad Kadyrov, the Chief Mufti of Chechnya in the 1990s. Putin also put his own stamp upon Russian foreign policy by abandoning the failed search for strategic partnership with the West and proclaimed Russia a Eurasian power. Ilan Berman noted what he called "slouching towards Eurasia."[29] Putin, however, never adopted the ideological posture of the Russian Eurasianists who claimed for Russia both an exceptionalist and a universalist role as rival to a U.S.-dominated West for global hegemony.[30] In 2001, Russia and China joined three Central Asian states to transform the Shanghai Five, which had been created in 1996, into the Shanghai Cooperation Organization (SCO) with the goal of countering the terrorist threat and opposing the hegemony of the United States.

As the Putin administration was putting Russia's house in order, the Bush administration announced a new orientation towards Russia. The Bush administration proclaimed that Cold War issues were relics of the past and a new bilateral relationship was in order based on current international realities. Washington's attention seemed initially to be focused on Pacific security issues and mounting tensions with the People's Republic of China (PRC) over the growing threat of Chinese military power to Taiwan. In late 2001 the United States gave warning that it was withdrawing from the AntiBallistic Missile (ABM) Treaty of 1972 to go forward with its own plans for a missile defense system against rogue states seeking to acquire nuclear weapons. The Putin government questioned the wisdom of this course of action and assured the Russian public and the world that Russia possessed strategic offensive means to counter any such rudimentary missile defense system. By this time, however, Washington and Moscow had entered into a close relationship as a result of the events of September 11, 2001 (9/11), and the obvious evidence that the Taliban and al-Qaeda had used Afghanistan as a base of operations for the terrorist attacks. Russia not only joined NATO in invoking chapter V of the collective defense provisions of the alliance, but also entered into intelligence sharing with Washington. Russia accepted the need for U.S. basing in Central Asia as a temporary requirement to support military operations in Afghanistan and did not object to the use of Northern Alliance forces against the Taliban. Moscow's clear expectation was that the United States would conduct a limited operation against the Taliban and al-Qaeda and then disengage from the region. Putin wasted no time in declaring his support for the struggle against terrorism and his support for operations against the Taliban and al-Qaeda.[31] Putin expected Washington to be understanding about his own operations against "Islamic terrorism" in Chechnya. Given its own experience with operations in Afghanistan, Moscow may have assumed prudence would direct Washington's policy.[32] That proved incorrect with adverse consequences for more than U.S.-Russian relations.

In the spirit of the new global security environment, in May 2002 Washington and Moscow had concluded the Strategic Offensive Reductions Treaty (SORT), which provided for major cuts in both state's nuclear arsenals.[33] However, further progress in improving U.S.-Russian relations collapsed as a result of another fundamental shift in the international system. The Bush administration saw no future in "detailed technical arms control agreements" and was reluctant to extend existing operational arms control agreements, which did not reflect the new realities of American power. For a decade, administrations in Washington had spoken of the United States as the sole surviving super power. Moscow had spent much of the same decade warning of the risks of a unipolar world order. Now the Bush administration decided that it would employ the implied power in that statement to a new security challenge. There would no ambiguity about the debt that a new world order would owe to American military power. This course of action precisely represented Moscow's worst fear for its own position in the international order.

For the Bush administration, the events of 9/11 had ushered in a new global challenge, which demanded decisive U.S. actions against terrorism, states supporting terrorism, and rogue states engaged in weapons of mass destruction (WMD) proliferation. The strategy for this new challenge, which the Bush administration labeled the Global War on Terrorism (GWOT), demanded that the U.S. "act preemptively" in using military power against such threats.[34] In his State of the Union address of January 2003, Bush specifically labeled Iraq, Iran, and North Korea as an "axis of evil" against which the United States would apply the full measure of its power, beginning with Iraq.[35]

The U.S. intervention in Iraq was supposed to be a rapid and decisive action that would eliminate the supposed WMD threat from Iraq, remove the Baathist regime from Baghdad, and create the strategic context for the democratic transformation of the Middle East. Washington chose to organize a coalition of the willing and to act without a direct UN mandate and against the objections of major European allies, particularly France and Germany. While U.S.-Russian relations deteriorated in the approach to the invasion of Iraq, they did not occupy a prominent place in Washington's calculus. The wrath of the administration was directed primarily against "old Europe," as Secretary of Defense Donald Rumsfeld referred to Germany and France, as opposed to the "new Europe" of Eastern Europe where governments were eager to join the coalition band wagon in Iraq. President Putin had publicly remarked in February that he did not want to see the United States suffer defeat in Iraq but also pledged that Russia would avoid involvement in the conflict.[36] When the invasion began, Putin put his objections not in terms moral principles but strategic miscalculation, calling the invasion "a great political error."[37]

The actual operations to remove Saddam Hussein and his government proved to be the lightning success envisioned by Secretary Rumsfeld and his military advisors, much to the chagrin of Russian military observers, who had expected a much more difficult fight. General Makhmut Gareyev, President of the Russian Academy of Military Science, spoke of an internal collapse of the Iraqi military as the chief cause of the U.S.-led coalition's easy success.[38] The fall of Baghdad came after less than 3 weeks of war. In May, President Bush declared combat operations ended from the deck of the USS *Lincoln* with a huge banner on the carrier's island declaring "mission accomplished."[39]

What was supposed to have been a *fait accompli* turned into a protracted struggle combining chaos, insurgency, and civil war. Russian commentators spoke of a partisan war being fought against the United States and its allies in terms that sounded strikingly similar to Western discussions of the Soviet quagmire in Afghanistan decades before.[40] Washington proved particularly reluctant to acknowledge the rapid deterioration of the situation on the ground or the long-term consequences for the U.S. geo-strategic situation. What was to have given Washington room to maneuver in the region became a dead weight upon its foreign policy and a security burden that drained national resources for the indefinite future. By fall 2003, the sole super power faced an insurgency in Iraq and the recovery of the Taliban in Afghanistan. A modest step towards internationalization of the Afghan conflict came in August 2003 when the UN Security Council mandated NATO's International Security Assistance Force (ISAF) to take over responsibility for the stability of Kabul and in October 2003 took responsibility for the regions of Afghanistan not then affected by the Taliban insurgency.[41] Russia endorsed this action as contributing to the peace and stability of Afghanistan.[42]

Iraq remained the albatross around the Bush administration's neck. Plans for a speedy withdrawal of forces and rapid transfer of authority to an Iraqi government had to be shelved. The White House made efforts to entice Russia to join a *post facto* coalition, but Putin had no reason to join what had become by the late summer of 2003 a disaster in the making. Russia joined the rest of the UN Security Council to condemn the terrorist attack on the UN mission in Iraq in August 2003.[43] Following that attack, Putin stated that Russia would not oppose an international force deployed in Iraq if it were under a UN Security Council mandate. He declined, however, to offer Russian forces for such a mission.[44] Regarding other rogue states that Bush had identified as threatening international order and aiding terrorism, Iran and North Korea, the U.S. administration initially dismissed negotiations and again gave particular weight to military options. However, as that course of action failed to move either Tehran or Pyongyang toward concessions on their nuclear programs, the United States shifted towards a position of multilateralism. In 2003 when North Korea announced its withdrawal from the Non-Proliferation Treaty, Washington embraced the six-party talks with North Korea. On Iran, the United States joined the other five permanent members of the Security Council and Germany to present Iran with carrots and sticks to end uranium enrichment and to make its entire nuclear program transparent. In the face of Iranian refusals, the United States embraced the UN Security Council and International Atomic Energy Commission (IAEC) as instruments to pressure Iran to comply with uranium enrichment controls or face increasingly rigorous sanction regimes. Russia played a role in both multilateral efforts. In the North Korean case, it was both

71

a neighboring state and a nuclear power. In the Iranian case, Russia was deeply involved in the development of Iranian nuclear power through the construction of the Bushehr Nuclear Power Facility. Moreover, it engaged in the sale of sophisticated weapons to Iran, including advanced air defense systems, leading at least one observer in 2005 to conclude that Russia had acquiesced to Iran's nuclear program.[45] In 2006, however, Russia and China joined the United States and the other European members of the six-power talks to support UN sanctions but negotiated for a gradual approach to the escalation of such sanctions. Putin has been consistent in warning of the risks of preemptive military action by any power against Iran. At a meeting of the Caspian states in Tehran in 2007, Putin stated: "We should not even think of making use of force in this region." The remarks came at a time when the Bush administration had pointedly stated it would not exclude military action to halt what Washington considered a convert nuclear weapons program in Iran.[46] In short, in the North Korean and Iranian cases, Washington found Russia to be a necessary, if difficult, partner in its multilateral attempts at solution, reflecting a retreat from its initial unilateralism in favor of protracted diplomacy.

Putin's geopolitical realism in such issues and his prudence toward the use of force went hand-in-hand with a deliberate commitment to *Machtpolitik*, if vital Russian interests were at stake. His hand in the prosecution of the Second Chechen War left no doubt that he would use all instruments of state power to pacify a secessionist region, including state control and manipulation of the media to guarantee success in information operations. His refusal to negotiate with those who had taken up arms even as he used Chechens loyal to Moscow to "Chechenize" the conflict and keep it under control if not resolved underscored his own vision of statecraft in the Russian sphere of influence, which he extended across the Caucasus.[47] Putin's tenure has been marked by an explicit geo-strategic reorientation, the beginnings of which can be found in Russian-NATO relations over Kosovo, and represented an explicit shift from a European-oriented policy of the Yeltsin administration to a Eurasian policy under Putin. As Arbatov stated, "The bombing of Yugoslavia revived the worst instincts of the Cold War" among the Russian civil and military leadership. More exactly, Russia's isolation and NATO's willful disregard of its interests confirmed the threat assumptions that only a few years before had been confined to the extreme nationalist and communist circles.[48]

With the growing expansion of NATO into post-Soviet space, Moscow concluded that a Eurasian balance was the only effective countermeasure. Given the expanding economic power and influence of the PRC, the Putin administration had compelling reasons to see China as a potential economic partner in the development of the Russian Far East and a strategic countermeasure to U.S. initiatives in Central Asia. Both the PRC and Russia saw Islamic radicalism as a threat to the stability of Central Asia and their own Muslim regions. The founding of the SCO in June 2001 by its five initial members made explicit the Eurasian orientation of Russian policy.[49] This event preceded the 9/11 attacks and reflected the attention that its member states were already paying to the role of the Taliban in spreading Islamic extremism into Central Asia.

From the "Rose Revolution" in Georgia, which brought to power a democratically elected President bent on de facto independence from Russian influence and the reassertion of the territorial integrity of the state, Eurasianism has included a distinct hostility towards the emergence of democratic regimes seeking Western support against Russian influence. The "Colored Revolutions" in Georgia (Rose), Ukraine (Orange), Kyrgyzstan (Tulip), and the riots in Uzbekistan were all seen by Moscow as manifestations of external interventions intended to reduce Russian influence. Where Western observers and the indigenous activists spoke of a victory for civil society and nongovernmental actors to restore democratic institutions, Putin and Russian commentators have spoken of political subversion by pro-U.S. elements as the core of each revolution based on a zero-sum game over Russia's influence. In this context, Russian theorists invoked the concept of "information warfare" as the locus of the struggle in peace and war, called for an active and intense information counterstruggle to counter the "information-financial-terrorist war" unleashed against Russia after 1991, and spoke of the need to extend Eurasia into a "continental bow" (*kontinental'naia duga*), which would embrace Paris-Berlin-Moscow-Beijing-New Delhi-Tehran.[50]

At the same time, Putin has to oversee a fundamental recasting of Russia's geostrategic position within a world becoming increasingly multipolar. Working against the stereotype of Russia as a great power only through its military strength, Putin has hedged his bets on military expansion and accepted a downsized military on a slightly reformed model to play for influence on the periphery without becoming a major military challenge.[51] Stagnation and corruption had become the mark of the transformed military. What the Putin administration did do was take advantage of the expanding demand in global energy markets to grow the Russian national economy on the basis of that international demand and to transform Russia's position in the global economy into a major energy player as a "petro state" of a very distinct character and vigorous energy diplomacy. The secret to the new model was not just spiral prices for oil but also Russia as an emerging player in the production and distribution of natural gas through Gazprom.[52] According to Marshall Goldman, even before coming to power Putin understood the political-economic influence to be found in Russia's vast reserves of natural gas, the largest in the world, and in its pipeline system which dominated Eurasia.[53]

The heavy-handed use of state power and the courts to bring about the break-up of the YUKOS oil company and the arrest and imprisonment of its chief and reputedly the richest man in Russia, Mikhail Khodorkovsky, seems to have been aimed at the firm and the man for their roles in domestic politics and the international oil regime. The signal from the Kremlin in 2003 was that oligarchs could make money but not engage in political challenges to Putin and his team.[54] Whereas the Yeltsin years had seen Russian capitalism as a poor hand maiden of the developed West and facing persistent structural problems and crises as it sought to make the transition to a market economy,[55] Putin's Russia practiced a national system of political economy that Frederick List and Sergei Witte would have understood and applauded. This global energy role based upon oil exports and its dominant position in Eurasian natural gas resources and infrastructure have translated into "energy diplomacy" of a subtle and not so subtle character, depending on character relations with other states.[56] In this new situation, Putin's Russia had the capacity to exercise a new form of indirect influence that went beyond its ability to disrupt energy supplies. As Fiona Hill observed, "Russia has a new 'soft power' role that extends far beyond its energy resources."[57]

American commentators are quick to point to Putin's anti-U.S. rhetoric at the 43rd Munich conference on Security Policy, where Putin took on the Bush administration's unilateral actions. "One state and, of course, first and foremost the United States, has overstepped its national borders in every way. This is visible in the economic, political, cultural and educational policies it imposes on other nations."[58] Some conservative commentators labeled these remarks "the Putin Doctrine" and the foundation for another U.S.-Russian military confrontation.[59] Russian commentators saw Putin's remarks as part of what they called a "love-hate relationship" between Washington and Moscow and not a sharp break.[60] While he rhetorically asked who liked such unilateralism, his central point was to declare the end of any claim to a unipolar world revolving around an American axis. Putin depicted a dynamic international landscape in which an array of regional powers was emerging, with the economic powers to be major players in their own rights. He noted the growing size of the GDP's of India and China in comparison with the United States, and cited the emerging economic power of Brazil, Russia, India, and China (BRIC) as a new force in the global economy which other players would have to consider.[61] Putin was, in effect, announcing the end of deference to the claims of the "one sole superpower" as the indispensible keystone of the international system. This new situation will depend upon the creation of new partnership relations among the major players in the emerging multilateral system. As experts have noted, building such partnerships with the BRIC states will require distinct efforts reflecting the bilateral dynamics between the European Union (EU) and the BRIC partners.[62] In discussing the EU-Russia partnership, Sabine Fischer describes it as contested in the sense that it has evolved from the paternalism of EU assistance to a prostrate Russia to one of conflict as Russia has reasserted its role as a global player. While there is every evidence of mutual economic interaction and interdependence, there is less room to speak of a "strategic partnership" based on shared values. [63] Dmitri Trenin from the Moscow office of the Carnegie Endowment for International Peace (CEIP) took a different tact on an EU-Russian partnership and spoke of a process of redefining the strategic partnership in terms of the situation 2 decades hence and to look towards cooperation in a world increasingly dominated by Asia.[64] Trenin seems to have been privy to the resource-economic vision shared by the elite around Putin with its stress on energy diplomacy and Russia's trump cards of natural gas reserves and pipelines crossing Eurasia.

Speaking in February 2008, as his presidency was coming to its end, Putin addressed the accomplishments of his tenure in office and his expectations for Russia in 2020. The accomplishments included economic growth, higher per capita income, domestic stability, a strong central state, large dollar reserves, and a renewed position in the world as a great power. At the same time he laid out a set of strategic directions to shape Russian policy well into the next decade. This was a vision shaped by Russian values but in the context of global pressures for Russia to adapt and meet new challenges.[65] The emphasis was upon a state-directed, capitalist economy that would be regionally and globally integrated.

At present, there is no domestic discussion of a reappraisal of a U.S.-Russian strategic partnership. That really cannot come about until there is a restoration of a global vision beyond that of super power hegemony as a national objective. Applying military power to remake the world into its democratic image will neither change this perception nor undercut the emerging multipower international order. The new situation demands prudence and agility in the current situation with greater attention to political economy and less to *Machtpolitik*. Many commentators have sought to articulate a strategy for the United States that would play to American strengths to ensure global stability and U.S. interests in such an emerging order. As Fareed Zakaria has observed, the United States has many unique advantages associated with American ideas and ideals which will permit it to "shape and master the changing global landscape." He warns, however, that it must first recognize "that the post-American world is a reality" and embrace that reality.[66]

A new look at U.S.-Russian relations should begin with a strategic vision encompassing multilateralism and regional interests, including those just emerging in the Arctic as a result of climate change. Russia and the United States may end up being more than neighbors across ice fields and have to share a new maritime highway and energy and resource potential.[67] Being true to Western values, even as we compete in the emerging global economy, would permit us to sustain the Euro-Atlantic community, promote open societies, the rule of law, and human rights, and retain the capacity for humanitarian intervention with international legitimacy. We would still share with Russia and the other nuclear powers the task of managing nuclear proliferation and disarmament well into the 21st century, a task that will involve arms control, deterrence, and preemption.[68]

Epilogue.

This chapter was completed in the early summer of 2008 when the Russian elections had already been decided and the "dual power" of Putin as Prime Minister and Medvedev as President had emerged. On the U.S. side, the process had narrowed to McCain as the Republican nominee designate and Obama as the leader on the Democratic side. The description of the policy choices open to each elite in pursuing U.S.-Russian relations were well-defined, given the existing international context. Speculations about the probable winner—Obama at this writing—and the likely cabinets of both contenders have shed even more light on the probable figures that will shape U.S.-Russian relations in Washington. Obama's team appears to be more bipartisan and technocratic in this area, including the continued service of sitting Secretary of Defense Robert Gates.[69] While some Russians have speculated about the advantages of an Obama administration for U.S.-Russian relations, Western analysts have warned of more similarity than differences.[70] In the same article, Steve Blank warned his Russian colleague to be aware of Obama's greater concern for the domestic political situation in Russia, especially the retreat from democratic values and toward Putin's authoritarian state at the expense of the rule of law and towards bureaucratic arbitrariness and corruption.

In the meantime, while those trends were confirmed—Obama and McCain became their party nominees — a set of seismic shocks recast the context of U.S.-Russian relations. The first event was the war between Georgia and Russia over South Ossetia. That conflict turned into full-scale warfare when the Saakashvili government, responding to provocations from the South Ossetian side, decided to seize the region's capital, Tsikhinvali, by coup de main. The Russian response was a yeoman-like application of conventional combined arms, cyber attacks, and irregular warfare that speedily defeated the Georgian military, drove it from South Ossetia, and set up a temporary zone of Russian occupation in other parts of Georgia. Moscow followed this military success with a political failure. It recognized the independence of both South Ossetia and Abkhazia but found few other states which would follow suit. In the aftermath of the fighting, the Russian occupation set the environment for the ethnic cleansing of Georgian settlements in South Ossetia and Abkhazia by pro-Moscow irregular forces, including the notorious Chechen Vostok battalion.[71]

Russia reaped a military victory but at significant diplomatic costs. Russia had used military power for the first time since the collapse of the Soviet Union to impose its will upon a successor state and change existing boundaries. Both U.S. presidential candidates recognized the importance of the event for the international environment and defended the territorial integrity of Georgia. McCain spoke of grave consequences for Euro-Atlantic stability and security and sided directly with Georgia as a victim of Russian aggression.[72] Obama also recognized the challenge to international stability but couched his response in terms of calling for restraint by both parties and international crisis management.[73]

As the crisis unfolded, McCain, whose senior foreign policy advisor, Randy Scheunemann, has been a lobbyist for Georgia, became more strident in his anti-Russian and pro-Georgian rhetoric. The Russian military action was part of a broader campaign to intimidate any state in Russia's near abroad from seeking close ties with the West. McCain embraced the Georgian cause as one worthy of an American strategic commitment. In a phone conversation with President Mikhail Saakashvili, whom he referred to as "Misha," McCain reported that "I know I speak for every American when I say to him today, we are all Georgians." Obama called on Russia to execute the cease-fire negotiated by President of France Nicolas Sarkozy on behalf of the EU, of which he was then serving as President. Obama put more emphasis on building a common Euro-Atlantic position than on rushing ahead into a U.S.-Russian showdown over Georgia. Russian arms had already created the de facto conditions for Russian supremacy in the disputed provinces, even as Moscow championed the region's independence.

In resorting to arms as the final arbitrator of this ethno-national dispute, Russia turned a question of interests, subject to negotiation and compromise, into a conflict over values, which would separate Russia and the West and leave little room for negotiations. The team of Putin and Medvedev had managed to recast Russia's place in the international system from one of great power among a community of nations into a unilateral actor willing to move outside that community's values. Russia's economic recovery and Putin's political swagger seemed to have recast post-Cold War European security. The Russian administration announced major plans for increased defense spending, and mounted a series of foreign deployments of air and naval assets that placed Russian military presence in regions noteworthy for their anti-American cast and potential instability, i.e., Venezuela and Syria.[74] Finally, in early September, the Russian Ministry of Defense began a large-scale military exercise with global dimensions, including strategic nuclear forces. Russian commentators were quite sure that the exercise, "Stabil'nost' 2008," was aimed at the United States and NATO as the probable opponents.[75] The exercise, as Pavel Felgengauer pointed out, represented "a direct preparation of the special services, state staff, and army for a full-scale nuclear war against the United States and NATO."[76]

If the seismic shifts had remained confined to that of *Machtpolitik*, the impact of change would have been clearly one directional and favorable to candidate McCain as the man of iron will and decisive action. That, however, was not to be the case. International economics, beginning with a meltdown in U.S. housing securities and extending into global banking and finance, announced not just the end of the post-Cold War economic order but a more fundamental challenge to the very institutional foundations of international finance, which had emerged after World War II. Globalization in the form of global capital markets now brought lightning declines to market values around the world.[77] Predator practices undermined the trust of people around the world in the transparency of markets. Floundering responses undermined public faith in the capacity of governments to regulate those same markets and to protect the well-being of their citizens from economic collapse. As James Galbraith asserted with regard to the challenge to the preeminent role of the United States in the global economic order,

"We spoke instead of community, of freedom, of common purposes and common values. And the world took us seriously because we had paid our dues. What's happened to those values?"[78] The New York Stock Exchange witnessed the steepest decline in share values in 60 years, bringing with it talk of a deep and prolonged recession or even, God forbid, a depression. Some economic observers, like Nouriel Roubini of New York University, have noted the impact of the global financial crisis upon the global economy and warned of "a self-fulfilling animal spirit recession that is more severe than otherwise" because of the collapse of credit markets and weak consumer and corporate spending.[79]

In short, the international economic order recast the place of all actors and made self-evident the profound interdependence upon which the system depends. Short-sighted players in both Moscow and Washington could point to the mounting crisis that the other faced. Secretary of State Condoleezza Rice warned on September 18 that the "dark turn" of Russian foreign policy towards unilateral use of force could undermine Russia's prosperity and doom it to authoritarianism and international isolation. She cited capital flight as a major factor in supporting her analysis.[80] Less than a month later, Prime Minister Putin was declaring to the world that the U.S. financial crisis had irreparably damaged the positions of both Washington and Wall Street. "Trust in the United States as the leader of the free world and the free economy, and confidence in Wall Street as the center of that trust, has been damaged, I believe, forever. There will be no return to the previous situation."[81] In both cases, political analysis overcame political-economic perspective. Neither Washington nor Moscow has the capacity to provide sole leadership for a global recovery. Given the extractive energy bias of the Russian economy and its modest share of the global GDP, this should come as no surprise. Russia, which had been riding high on world energy prices, saw world price for oil decline from $140/barrel to under $70/barrel. Putin's neo-Listian dream of a national system of political economy based on energy domination suffered a series of blows. The Russian stock market fell, foreign capital fled, and Ural crude oil fell below $60/barrel. Russian energy entrepreneurs were gripped by fear: "There's a persistent and growing fear of a total collapse."[82] Russia's once majestic energy giants have been forced to go hat-in-hand in search of foreign loans for oil. The most immediate case has been a deal under negotiation between the Chinese government and Russian firms for long-term oil deliveries in exchange for immediate loans of $20-30 billion.[83] But Washington and New York have had to recognize that global leadership will not be retained if other nations see the United States seeking temporary political advantage in a global crisis that is sweeping away peoples' hopes and spreading fears. In this context, Washington and Moscow, like other capitals, will learn to work together or they will face a much deeper, more protracted, and finally more traumatic crisis of the global economy. Only those who will provide effective international leadership will retain any claim to special status in creating a new political-economic order. The alternative to such a course is what came with the Great Depression, a turn to economic nationalism, the rise of authoritarianism from the streets, and a global political-economic climate that will make war among major blocs of powers more likely. Neither the new administration in Washington or in Moscow can afford such a course.

ENDNOTES - CHAPTER 2

1. Aleksei Konstantinovich Tolstoy, "Istoriya gosudarstva Rossiiskogo ot gostomysla do Timasheva," in A. K. Tolstoy, *Sobranie sochinenii v chetyrekh tomakh*, Moscow: Izdatel'stvo Khudozhestvennoi literatury, 1963, Vol. I, pp. 384-400. Tolstoy, an intellectual of the 1850s and 1860s, combined service at the court of Nicholas I and Alexander II with a career devoted to literature, drama, and poetry. He composed the *Istoriya* in 1868 when the bloom had gone off the great reforms and did not extend his satiric history to the last two tsars, "because it is slippery to walk over some stones, so it is better to keep our mouths shut about things that are too close," turning his attention to their ministers and ending with praising the Lord for granting the Russian nation Minister Timashev as the "light of dawn" to once again create "order."

2. Alexis de Tocqueville, *De la Démocratie en Amérique*, 12th Ed., Paris, France: Pagnerre, Editeur, 1848, 4 volumes. See also Peter Rutland, "Why Is Russia Still an Authoritarian State? (Or What Would De Tocqueville Say?)," Washington, DC: American Political Science Association, September 2-4, 2005, *www.allacademic.com//meta/p_mla_apa_research_citation/0/4/1/8/4/pages41841/p41841-1.php*, accessed May 15, 2008.

3. Edward A. Kolodziej, "American Power and Global Order," in Edward A. Kolodziej and Roger E. Kanet, eds., *From Superpower to Besieged Global Power: Restoring World Order after the Failure of the Bush Doctrine*, Athens: The University of Georgia Press, 2008, pp. 3-30. On the ideological underpinning of this interpretation of the end of the Cold War and the triumph of liberal democratic values, see Francis Fukuyama, *The End of History and the last Man Standing*, New York: The Free Press, 1992. The victory was not just of the United States but also the common values of what was assumed to be a West united by common values.

4. Phyllis Penn Kolher, *Journey for Our Time: The Journals of the Marquis de Custine*, New York: Pellegrini & Gudahy, 1951.

5. Alexis de Tocqueville, *L'Ancien Régime et la Révolution*, 7th Ed., Paris, France: Michel Lévy Frères, 1866.

6. James H. Billington, *Russia in Search of Itself*, Baltimore, MD: Johns Hopkins University Press, 2004, p. 165. On Eurasianism, see Jacob W. Kipp, "Aleksandr Dugin and the Ideology of National Revival: Geopolitics, Eurasianism, and the Conservative Revolution," *European Security*, Vol. XI, No. 3, Fall 2002, pp. 91-125.

7. "Dmitri Medvedev" in *Russian Profile, Org: Unwrap the Mystery inside the Enigma*, *www.russiaprofile.org/resources/whoiswho/alphabet/m/medvedev.wbp#7*, accessed May 15, 2008.

8. Mark A. Smith, "The Russian Presidential Succession," Advanced Research and Analysis Group, UK Defence Academy, Russian Series, No. 1, 2008.

9. On the role of the Council on Foreign and Defense Policy in the Putin years, see *Sovet po vneshnei i oboronnoi politike (SVOP)*, Strategiya dlya Rossiya: 10 let SVOP, Moscow: Vagrius, 2002, pp. 1-7.

10. "McCain: Russia Deserves 'Harsh Treatment'," MSNBC, April 2, 2006, *www.msnbc.msn.com/id/12121191/*, accessed February 8, 2008.

11. Vladimir Frolov, "Russia Profile Weekly Experts Panel: 'Should Moscow Root for Obama?'" *Johnson's Russia List*, No. 41, March 21, 2008, *www.cdi.org/russia/johnson/2008-61-41.cfm*, accessed March 25, 2008.

12. *Ibid*.

13. Condoleezza Rice, "Rethinking the National Interest: American Realism in a New World," *Foreign Affairs*, July-August 2008, pp. 2-26.

14. Michael McFaul and Kathryn Stoner-Weiss, "The Myth of Putin's Success," *Foreign Affairs*, January-February 2008, pp. 68-84.

15. Zbigniew Brzezinski, *The Grand Chess Board: American Primacy and Its Geostrategic Imperatives*, Cambridge, MA: Basic

Books, 1997. Of particular interest in Moscow was the map of the "potential scope of a Chinese sphere of influence and coalition points," which included all of Southeast Asia and more importantly for Russia, Central Asia and the Russian Far East. On the Russian response, see V. V. Karpov, *Geopolitika: Konspekt lektsii,* In *Seriya "Vysshee profesional'noe obrazovanie",* St. Petersburg: Izdatel'stvo Mikhailova V. A., 2000, pp. 25-33.

16. Zbigniew Brzezinski, *The Choice: Global Domination or Global Leadership,* Cambridge, MA: Basic Books, 2004.

17. Zbigniew Brzezinski, *Second Chance: Three Presidents and the Crisis of American Superpower,* Cambridge, MA: Basic Books, 2007.

18. Barack Obama, "Towards a Nuclear Free World," *www.barackobama.com/issues/foreignpolicy/#nuclear,* accessed May 15, 2008.

19. Pavel Baev, *The Russian Army in a Time of Trouble,* London, UK: SAGE, 1996.

20. Alexander Yanov, *Weimar Russia and What Can We Do About It,* New York: Slovo/WoTd, 1995.

21. Anatol Lieven, *Chechnya: Tombstone of a Super Power,* New Haven, CT; and London, UK: Yale University Press, 1998.

22. Phil Williams, *Russian Organized Crime,* London, UK: Frank Cass, 1997; William Webster *et al., Russian Organized Crime and Corruption: Putin's Challenge,* Washington, DC: Center for Strategic and International Studies, 2000; and Sovet po vneshnei i oboronnoi politike, "Korruptsiya v sisteme gosudarstvennogo upravleniya Rossii: Znachenie, prichiny, I mekhamizmy iskoreneniya," in *Strategiya dlya Rossii 10 let SVOP,* pp. 562-581.

23. Richard Holbrooke, *To End a War,* New York: Random House, 1998.

24. Jacob W. Kipp, ed., *Lessons and Conclusions on the Execution of IFOR Operations and Prospects for a Future Combined Security System: The Peace and Stability of Europe after IFOR,* Ft. Leavenworth, KS:

Foreign Military Studies Office and Center for Military-Strategic Studies of the Russian General Staff, 1999.

25. Jacob W. Kipp. "Russian Non-Strategic Nuclear Weapons," *Military Review*, Vol. 81, No. 3, May-June 2001, pp. 27-38.

26. Jacob W. Kipp, "Putin and Russia's War in Chechnya" in Dale Herspring, ed., *Putin's Russia: Past Imperfect, Future Uncertain*, Lanham, MD: Rowman & Littlefield Publishers, 2002.

27. On the continuity and discontinuity between Yeltsin and Putin administrations, especially the role of bureaucratic capitalism, see Lilia Shevtsova, *Russia – Lost in Transition: The Yeltsin and Putin Legacies*, Washington, DC: Carnegie Endowment for International Peace, 2007.

28. Alexander Rahr, *Wladimir Putin Der "Deutsche" im Kreml*, Munich, Germany: Universitas, 2000; Shevtsova, *Russia – Lost in Transition*; Liliya Shevtsova, *Putin's Russia*, Washington, DC: Carnegie Endowment for International Peace, 2003; Dale Herspring *et al.*, Putin's *Russia: Past Imperfect, Future Uncertain*, 2nd Expanded Ed., Lanham, MD: Rowman & Littlefield Publishers, Inc., 2003; Andrew Jack, *Inside Putin's Russia*, Oxford, UK: Oxford University Press, 2004; Janusz Bugajski, *Cold Peace: Russia's New Imperialism*, Washington, DC: CSIS Praeger, 2004; Anna Politkovskaya, *Putin's Russia*, New York: Henry Holt & Company, 2004; and James Billington, *Russia in Search of Itself*, Baltimore, MD: Johns Hopkins University Press 2004.

29. Ilan Berman, "Slouching towards Eurasia," Institute for the Study of Conflict, Ideology and Policy, *Perspectives*, Vol. XII, No. 1, September-October 2001, *www.bu.edu/iscip/vol12/berman.html*, accessed February 10, 2008. Berman correctly noted both the ideological and geopolitical elements in this focus and correctly identified the sources of the ideology as nationalist and authoritarian. The basic text for post-modern Eurasianism is Aleksandr Dugin, *Osnovy geopolitiki: Geopoliticheskoe budushchee Rossii*, Moscow: Arktogeia, 1997. For a further discussion of geopolitics and Eurasianism, see Jacob W. Kipp, "Aleksandr Dugin and the Ideology of National Revival: Geopolitics, Eurasianism, and the Conservative Revolution," *European Security*, Vol. XI, No. 3, Fall 2002, pp. 91-125.

30. For a complete exposition of Dugin's claims in this regard, see Alexander Dugin, *The Paradigm of the End*, *www. gnosticliberationfront.com/The%20Paradigm%20of%20The%20 End.htm*. Dugin draws heavily upon the *Grossraum* theory of Karl Schmitt and his concept of conflict between the maritime and continental powers. See Karl Schmitt, *Land und Meer: Eine weltgeschichtliche Betrachtung*, Leipzig, Germany, 1942.

31. Jacob W. Kipp, "Tectonic Shifts and Putin's Russia in the New Security Environment," *Military Review*, March-April 2002, pp. 58-71.

32. Maksim Iusin, "Five Lessons of Afghanistan: The Experience of the Russian 'Limited Contingent' Can Serve the Americans," *Izvestiya*, September 19, 2001, p. 3.

33. Richard Weitz, "Russian-American Security Cooperation after St. Petersburg: Challenges and Opportunities," Carlisle, PA: Strategic Studies Institute, U.S. Army War College, 2007, p. 3.

34. *The National Security Strategy of the United States*, the White House, September 17, 2002, p. 2, *slomanson.tjsl.edu/NSS.pdf*.

35. "President Delivers State of the Union Address," The White House, January 29, 2003, *www.whitehouse.gov/news/ releases/2002/01/20020129-11.html*, accessed February 21, 2008.

36. "Putin on Iraq, Meetings with U.S. Officials and 'War Opponents'," Norsk Utenrikspolitisk Institutt (NUPI), Centre for Russian Studies, April 4, 2003, *www.nupi.no/cgi-win/Russland/ krono.exe?6179*, accessed January 15, 2008.

37. "Russians See Iraq War As 'Crime'," *Angus Reid Global Monitor*, March 24, 2004, *www.angus-reid.com/polls/view/russians_ see_iraq_war_as_crime/*.

38. Makhmut Gareyev, Tainye pruzhiny Irakskoi voiny," *Krasnaia zvezda*, July 18, 2003, p. 2.

39. "Commander-in-Chief Lands on USS *Lincoln*," CNN, May 2, 2003, *www.cnn.com/2003/ALLPOLITICS/05/01/bush.carrier. landing/*.

40. "Berdanki protiv vertoletov. Knigi," *Nezavisimoe Voyennoye Obozreniye*, December 16, 2005, p. 8.

41. North Atlantic Treaty Organization, "NATO in Afghanistan: International Security Assistance," March 31, 2008, *www.nato.int/issues/isaf/index.html*.

42. "New UN Resolution on Afghanistan Aids National Unity-Russian Foreign Ministry," BBC Monitoring International Reports, October 14, 2003, *www.accessmylibrary.com/coms2/ summary_0286-24692021_ITM*.

43. United Nations Security Council, "Security Council Condemns Terrorist Attack against Baghdad Headquarters, States UN Iraq Mission 'Will Not Be Intimidated'," August 20, 2003, *www.un.org/News/Press/docs/2003/sc7850.doc.htm*, accessed March 24, 2008.

44. Steven Eke, "Putin Changes Tack on Iraq Force," BBC News, August 30, 2003, *news.bbc.co.uk/2/hi/middle_east/3194525. stm*, accessed March 24, 2008.

45. Robert O. Freeman, "Russia, Iran and the Nuclear Question: The Putin Record," Carlisle, PA: Strategic Studies Institute, U.S. Army War College, 2006, p. 44.

46. Nazila Fathi and C. J. Chivers, "In Iran, Putin Warns Against Military Action," *New York Times*, October 17, 2007, *www. nytimes.com/2007/10/17/world/17iran.html?_r=1&hp&oref=slogin*.

47. Jacob W. Kipp, "Putin and Russia's War in Chechnya" in Dale Herspring, ed., *Putin's Russia: Past Imperfect, Future Uncertain*, Lanham, MD: Rowman & Littlefield Publishers, 2002; and "Changing Threat Perceptions and Russian Military Reform—The War Scare over Pankisi Gorge: Threat Perceptions in the Age of the War on Terrorism," in A. Aldis and Roger McDermott, eds., *Russian Military Reform, 1992-2002*, London, UK: Frank Cass, 2003.

48. Alexei Arbatov, *The Transformation of Russian Military Doctrine: Lessons Learned from Kosovo and Chechnya, The Marshall Center Papers*, No. 2, Garmisch-Partenkirchen: The George C. Marshall Center, 2000, p. 9.

49. John Daly, "'Shanghai Five' Expands to Combat Islamic Radicals," *Jane's Terrorism & Security Monitor*, July 19, 2001, *www.janes.com/security/international_security/news/jtsm/jtsm010719_1_n.shtml*.

50. Igor Panarin, *Informatsionnaya voina i geopolitika*, Moscow: Pokolenie, 2006, pp. 5-7.

51. A. Gol'ts, *Armiia Rossii: odinnadtsat' poteriannykh let*, Moscow: Zakharov, 2004.

52. Marshall I. Goldman, *Petrostate: Putin, Power and the New Russia*, Oxford, UK: Oxford University Press, 2008; and Michael T. Klare, *Rising Powers, Shrinking Planet: The New Geopolitics of Energy*, New York: Henry Holt and Company, 2008. On Gazprom and Russia's place in the global political-economy of natural gas, see Julian Darley, *High Noon for Natural Gas: The New Energy Crisis*, London, UK: Chelsea Green Publishing, 2004; U.S. Energy Information Administration, "Country Analysis Brief: Russia, Natural Gas," *www.eia.doe.gov/cabs/Russia/NaturalGas.html*, accessed June 20, 2008; and Gazprom, "Gazprom Today," *www.gazprom.com/eng/articles/article8511.shtml*, accessed June 20, 2008.

53. *Ibid.*, pp. 136-144.

54. Elena Chinyaeva and Peter Rutland, "The YUKOS Affair: Politics Trumps Money," *The Jamestown Foundation*, Vol 2, Issue 15, July 22, 2003, *www.jamestown.org/publications_details.php?volume_id=16&&issue_id=627*, accessed July 30, 2003.

55. Jeffrey Surovell, *Capitalist Russia and the West*, Aldershot, UK: Ashgate, 2000.

56. Fiona Hill, "Energy Empire: Oil, Gas and Russia's Revival," The Foreign Policy Centre, September 2004, reprinted by Brookings, *www.brookings.edu/articles/2004/09russia_hill.aspx*.

57. Fiona Hill, "Russia's Newly Found 'Soft Power'," *The Globalist*, August 26, 2004, reprinted by Brookings, *www.brookings.edu/articles/2004/0826russia_hill.aspx*.

58. "Putin's Prepared Remarks at 43rd Munich Conference on Security Policy," *Washington Post*, February 10, 2007, *www.washingtonpost.com/wp-dyn/content/article/2007/02/12/AR2007021200555.html*, accessed May 15, 2008.

59. Charles Krauthammer, "The Putin Doctrine," *Washington Post*, February 16, 2007, *www.washingtonpost.com/wp-dyn/content/article/2007/02/15/AR2007021501282.html*, accessed May 15, 2008.

60. V. A. Nikonov, "Rossiya I SShA — Love-Hate Relationship," *Materialy XIII Ezhegodnogo Rossiisko-Amerikanskogo seminara*, St. Petersburg: Izdatel'stvo S-Peterburg. Un-ta, 2004, pp. 21-26.

61. "Putin's Prepared Remarks at 43rd Munich Conference on Security Policy."

62. Giovanni Grevi and Alvaro de Vasconcelos, eds., "Partnerships for Effective Multilateralism: EU Relations with Brazil, China, India and Russia," in *Chaillot Paper No. 109*, May 2008.

63. Sabine Fischer. "The EU and Russia: a Contested Partnership" in *ibid.*, pp. 115-132.

64. Dmitri Trenin, "Russia and the European Union: Redefining Strategic Partnership," in Grevi and Vasconcelos, pp. 116-143.

65. "Putin's Speech on Russia's Development Strategy through 2020," February 8, 2008, Ministry of Foreign Affairs, *www.mid.ru*, accessed February 20, 2008.

66. Fareed Zakaria, "Is America in Decline?" *Foreign Affairs*, May-June 2008, pp. 21-43.

67. Scott G. Borgerson. "Arctic Meltdown: The Economic and Security Implications of Global Warming," *Foreign Affairs*, March/April 2008, *www.foreignaffairs.org/20080301faessay87206/scott-g-borgerson/arctic-meltdown.html*, accessed March 3, 2008.

On Russia's political-economic aspirations in the region and the state and business interests supporting Rosshelf, see Evgeny P. Velikhov and Vyasheslav P. Kuznetsov, *Russia's Marine Oil and Gas Industry Approaches the Arctic Shelf: A History of Rosshelf,* Oslo: Europa-programmet, 1997.

68. Thom Shanker, "Gates Gives Rationale for Expanded Deterrence," *New York Times,* October 28, 2008, *www.nytimes. com/2008/10/29/washington/29gates.html?scp=2&sq=robert%20 gates&st=cse#,* accessed October 28, 2008.

69. Peter Baker and Jackie Calmes, "Building a White House Team before the Election Is Decided," *New York Times,* October 25, 2008, *www.nytimes.com/2008/10/25/us/politics/25transition. html,* accessed October 26, 2008; "Russians Prefer the More 'Approachable' Obama," *Deutsche Welle,* October 27, 2008, in *Johnson's Russia List,* October 27, 2008, No. 195, *davidjohnson@ starpower.net;* and Stephen Blank *et al.,* "Russia Profile Weekly Experts Panel: Waiting for Obama," *Johnson's Russia List,* October 27 2008, No. 196, *davidjohnson@starpower.net.*

70. Baker and Calmes.

71. Stephen Blank, "Georgia: The War Russia Lost," *Military Review,* November-December 2008, pp. 39-46; and Brian Whitmore, "Did Russia Plan Its War in Georgia?" *Radio Free Europe Radio Liberty,* August 15, 2008, *www.globalsecurity.org/military/library/ news/2008/08/mil-080815-rferl07.htm,* accessed October 28, 2008. On the Vostok battalion, see Ralph Peters, "Devil Sent Down to Georgia: Russia Unleashes Chechen Thugs," *New York Post,* August 18, 2008, *www.nypost.com/seven/08182008/news/columnists/ devil_sent_down_to_georgia_124993.htm,* accessed August 19, 2008.

72. Michael Cooper, "War Puts Focus on McCain's Hard Line on Russia," *New York Times,* August 11, 2008, *www.nytimes. com/2008/08/12/us/politics/12mccain.html?ref=europe,* accessed August 12, 2008.

73. Michael Falcone, "Obama Emerges to Talk about Georgia," *New York Times,* August 11, 2008, *thecaucus. blogs.nytimes.com/2008/08/11/obama-emerges-to-talk-about-*

georgia/?scp=1&sq=obama%20georgia%20august&st=cse, accessed August 12, 2008.

74. Ian James and Vladimir Isachenkov, "Russian Defense Spending Increased by 25 Percent," *Pravda.ru*, September 19, 2008, P. A 11, *english.pravda.ru/news/russia/19-09-2008/106406-russia_defense_budget-0;* "Russian Bombers Land in Venezuela for Drills," *Washington Post*, September 11, 2008, p. A11, *www.washingtonpost.com/wp-dyn/content/article/2008/09/10/AR2008091003524.html*, accessed September 20, 2008; and "From Syrian Fishing Port to Naval Power Base: Russia Moves Into the Mediterranean," *The Guardian*, October 8 2008, *www.guardian.co.uk/world/2008/oct/08/syria.russia*, accessed October 15, 2008.

75. Victor Litovkin and Vladimir Mukhin, "Big-Time Maneuvers," *Defense & Security*, No. 106, September 24, 2008.

76. Pavel Felgengauer, "Stable Armament," *Novaya Gazeta*, No. 72, September 29, 2008, p. 5.

77. James K. Galbraith, *The Predator State: How Conservatives Abandoned the Free Market and Liberals Should Too*, New York: The Free Press, 2008.

78. "Interview with James K. Galbraith," *Bill Moyer's Journal*, October 24, 2008, *www.pbs.org/moyers/journal/10242008/transcript2.html*, accessed October 26, 2008.

79. John Brinsley, "US Should Enact $400 Billion Stimulus, Roubini Says," *Bloomberg*, October 27, 2008, *www.bloomberg.com/apps/news?pid=20601087&sid=aJ4TTEocITV0&refer=home*.

80. Nicholas Kralev, "Rice: Russia's 'Dark Turn' Could Hurt the Economy," *Washington Times*, September 18, 2008, *www.washingtontimes.com/news/2008/sep/18/rice-russias-dark-turn-could-hurt-economy/*, accessed September 20, 2008.

81. "Putin: US Image Damaged Forever over Economic Woes," *Associated Press*, October 9, 2008, *ap.google.com/article/ALeqM5hAow61U7kW5ktEJ4qIzEUoLSeI4AD93N6OBG1*, accessed October 25, 2008.

82. Ira Iosebashvili, "Market Plummets Despite Oil Cuts," *The Moscow Times*, October 27, 2008, p. 2.

83. Andrew E. Kramer, "Russia Seeks to Trade Oil for Loans from China," *New York Times*, October 29, 2008, *www.nytimes.com/2008/10/29/world/europe/29russia.html?_r=1&ref=todayspaper&oref=slogin*, accessed October 29, 2008.

CHAPTER 3

ARMS CONTROL AND U.S.-RUSSIAN RELATIONS

Linton F. Brooks

Chapter 3 discusses the prospects for nuclear arms control between the United States and the Russian Federation after the impending change of administration in both countries.[1] The two countries are bound together by a complex set of nuclear arrangements that include, but go far beyond, traditional east-west arms control as practiced during the Cold War. Their nuclear relations include:

- Involvement in the international nonproliferation regime, including leading roles in strengthening both the Nuclear Nonproliferation Treaty (NPT) and the International Atomic Energy Agency (IAEA) and in augmenting their efforts by embracing "coalitions of the willing" such as the Proliferation Security Initiative.
- Parallel efforts to ensure that the anticipated global increase in the use of nuclear energy does not lead to proliferation of nuclear weapons, primarily by attempts to limit the spread of technology to enrich uranium or reprocess spent nuclear fuel to obtain plutonium.
- Extensive joint efforts under the Cooperative Threat Reduction Program (CTRP) to assist Russia in eliminating excess strategic weapons left over from the Cold War and in improving the security of nuclear weapons and nuclear materials.
- Cooperation, primarily through their co-leadership of the Global Initiative to Combat

Nuclear Terrorism, in efforts to prevent terrorists from inflicting mass casualties for political purposes through obtaining or using nuclear weapons or improvised nuclear devices.

- Bilateral nuclear relations including formal arms control, reciprocal unilateral initiatives, and a general practice of taking account of each other's forces in internal military planning, although Russia is not now regarded by the United States as posing a significant threat.

Prior to discussing the prospects for formal arms control, it is useful to review these other areas of cooperation and to assess the prospects for change following the U.S. and Russian elections.[2]

Nonproliferation.

The heart of the international nonproliferation legal regime is the 1972 Treaty on the Nonproliferation of Nuclear Weapons, currently adhered to by every state in the world except India, Pakistan, Israel, and North Korea (which was a signatory but has withdrawn). The United States and Russia routinely work together to strengthen this regime, often working through the IAEA, which implements and monitors safeguards agreements with states operating nuclear facilities.

Two treaties, the Comprehensive Test Ban Treaty (CTBT), banning all nuclear weapons tests, and a Fissile Material Cutoff Treaty, banning the production of plutonium or highly enriched uranium (HEU) for weapons purposes are regarded by much of the international community and some (but not all) U.S. experts as important steps to strengthen the international nonproliferation regime. Many argue that moving forward on these two treaties is essential for the nuclear weapons states to demonstrate the seriousness with which they take their obligations under Article VI of the Nuclear Nonproliferation Treaty.[3]

Both Russia and the United States have signed the CTBT, although the Bush administration has made it clear that it will not seek ratification.[4] Neither state has tested since 1992. The United States has no plans to resume nuclear testing, although it maintains the Nevada Test Site capable of resuming underground testing on approximately 24 months notice. There is no indication that the Russians have plans to resume testing, although many observers assume they would do so if the United States did. A future Democratic administration will almost certainly seek U.S. ratification of the CTBT; it is unclear whether the votes will be present in the Senate.[5] In any event, it is difficult to see any unique U.S.–Russian implications of CTBT ratification.

In 2006, the United States tabled a draft Fissile Material Cutoff Treaty in the Conference on Disarmament, a United Nations forum in Geneva. The United States concluded that no effective verification regime was possible, a position that has been criticized both domestically and internationally. If negotiations actually commence, it will be important for the United States and Russia to work together, since they have similar interests. This will be especially true if the new administration chooses to add verification provisions. For now, however, actual negotiations appear unlikely; in recent years, the requirement for consensus in the Conference on Disarmament has prevented the beginning of negotiations on any subject.

Nuclear Energy.

It is widely believed that the world (with or without U.S. participation) is moving toward a dramatic increase in the use of nuclear power, driven in part by the combination of growing global energy demand and growing concern for the effect on global climate from burning fossil fuels. Russia in particular envisions being a major player on the international nuclear power scene. Such an expansion carries proliferation risks if states elect to establish their own facilities for enriching uranium or for reprocessing of spent nuclear fuel to obtain plutonium. Commercial reactor fuel typically is enriched to contain around 5 percent of the isotope U^{235}. The necessary technology can easily be adapted to allow further enrichment to levels useful for nuclear weapons, perhaps as high as 90 percent U^{235}. (Concern with enrichment is a major current issue with respect to Iran.)

An alternate approach to commercial reactor operation is to reprocess spent fuel to obtain plutonium that can then be made into fuel for further operations. But plutonium can also be used for nuclear weapons; North Korean reprocessed spent fuel from their Yongbyon reactor to obtain the plutonium used in its October 2006 nuclear weapon test.

To counter the threat posed by proliferation of enrichment and reprocessing capabilities, President George Bush proposed in 2004 that nations interested in peaceful uses of nuclear energy and willing to foreswear enrichment and reprocessing be guaranteed an assured reactor fuel supply by the international community. Some uranium declared excess to U.S. weapons use has been set aside as the U.S. contribution to such a supply. Russia's President Vladimir Putin made a similar proposal, built around an international fuel center at Angarsk, Russia, from which nations could obtain fuel, but without gaining access to the underlying technology. Neither proposal has yet gained international consensus.

In 2006, the United States launched the Global Nuclear Energy Partnership, with a goal of developing technologies that will reprocess spent nuclear fuel without creating the separated plutonium that could be used in nuclear weapons. In July 2007, the United States and Russia agreed to a joint Nuclear Energy and Non-Proliferation Initiative to help states which want peaceful nuclear energy to field more proliferation-resistant nuclear power reactors. The two states have not yet signed the necessary implementing Agreement for Cooperation in Peaceful Use of Nuclear Energy required by Section 123 of the Atomic Energy Act; at their April 2008 summit Presidents Bush and Putin pledged to sign the document "in the near future."[6] While it is virtually certain that both the United States and Russia will continue to encourage expansion of nuclear energy while limiting proliferation risks, the degree to which they will cooperate in this area is uncertain.

Cooperative Threat Reduction.

When the Cold War ended and the Soviet Union collapsed, the Russian Federation was left with significant weaknesses in the security of nuclear weapons and nuclear materials. Facing major economic problems, Russia was unable to improve security unaided. As a result, the United States established the CTRP, which, among other things, worked with Russia to dramatically improve security.[7] The improvements, which are implemented by the Departments of Defense and Energy, will be largely complete in 2008. For several years thereafter, there will be a transition program to help the Russians maintain the improvements that have been made. U.S. funding for this purpose will end in 2013.

Despite Russian security concerns over allowing U.S. access to some sensitive weapons sites, the program is well regarded in both countries. It should continue unchanged following the changes of administration in the two countries. Related work by the Department of Energy to assist in shutting down plutonium production reactors (due to complete in 2010) and to improve Russia's ability to interdict nuclear smuggling at its borders (called the Second Line of Defense program) should also continue without interruption. While some individuals in both countries advocate the United States and Russia working together in a global version of Cooperative Threat Reduction, there appears little actual interest in such an idea on the part of the two governments.

Nuclear Terrorism.

Presidents Bush and Putin have consistently stated that international nuclear terrorism is one of the greatest threats facing each of their countries and the international community generally. Much of the motivation for improving security of Russian nuclear weapons and nuclear material under the CTRP has been to ensure that these materials do not fall into terrorist hands. Cooperation with Russia (and others) against nuclear terrorism is extensive. In a recent speech, National Security Advisor Stephen Hadley outlined some of the international efforts:

The President has also created strong international partnerships to address the threat of nuclear terrorism. In 2003, he launched the Proliferation Security Initiative to stem the flow of illicit materials used for weapons of mass destruction programs. More than 85 nations are now partners in this effort to coordinate their individual national capabilities to detect and interdict illicit materials — whether moving by land, sea, or air.[8]

In 2004, the United States cosponsored and helped secure the approval of U.N. Security Council Resolution 1540. This resolution requires states to enact and enforce effective export controls for dangerous weapons and materials, and to prosecute those who transfer weapons of mass destruction (WMD) or sensitive technologies to terrorists.

In 2006, the United States and Russia launched the Global Initiative to Combat Nuclear Terrorism, which is helping to build international capacity to prevent, defend against, and respond to nuclear terrorism. Through this initiative, more than 60 nations have joined the United States and Russia to exchange information, share best practices, and develop new solutions to the challenge of nuclear terrorism.

Russia is an active participant in all of these efforts, especially the Global Initiative to Combat Nuclear Terrorism. There is every reason to assume that this cooperation will continue in the coming years.

Bilateral Relations and Arms Control.

As this brief survey notes, there will continue to be substantial cooperation in nuclear areas regardless of what happens to the bilateral arms control relationship. The future of Cold War-style formal arms control is less certain, and some would argue that arms control treaties of the past are no longer relevant in the modern era. The bilateral nuclear relationship between Russia and the United States has four components:

1. The 1987 Intermediate Range Nuclear Forces (INF) Treaty requires the elimination of ground-launched cruise and ballistic missiles with ranges between 500 and 5,500 kilometers. All reductions under this treaty are complete. The Russians have suggested that the Treaty no longer serves their interest unless it is expanded to include other states. They contend that the treaty unfairly precludes Russia from having weapons that its neighbors, such as China, are developing. The United States and Russia issued an October 25, 2007, statement at the United Nations (UN) General Assembly reaffirming support for the treaty and calling on all other states to join in renouncing the missiles banned by the treaty.[9]

2. The 1991 Strategic Arms Reduction Treaty (START)[10] limits strategic delivery vehicles, warheads (both overall and on ballistic missiles),[11] and ballistic missile throw-weight, and contains a number of subsidiary limits to preclude circumvention and to aid verification. START, which is exceptionally complex (primarily to ensure effective verification), will expire in December 2009 unless extended (this point is discussed below).

3. A series of 1991-92 reciprocal, unilateral steps referred to in the United States as the Presidential Nuclear Initiative removes nuclear weapons from Navy ships and submarines, eliminates nuclear artillery and short range missiles, and withdraws many so-called tactical, or nonstrategic nuclear weapons to central storage.[12]

4. The 2002 Treaty of Moscow will reduce operationally deployed strategic warheads to between

1,700 and 2,200 by 2012. Because the Treaty of Moscow lacks verification provisions and allows an immediate increase in deployed forces after 2012, it is widely regarded as little more than a joint declaration of intent expressed in treaty form.

The immediate question facing the United States and the Russian Federation is what, if anything, should replace the START Treaty when it expires in December 2009. Neither the United States nor Russia wishes to extend the Treaty in its present form.[13] Both see advantages to a replacement regime that would preserve the benefits of START while reducing burdensome and expensive requirements. Russia seeks a formal follow-on treaty that would include legal limits on forces. The Bush U.S. administration, convinced that the era of large-scale East-West arms control has ended and that it must retain flexibility to adjust future force structures, initially preferred an informal agreement on transparency and confidence-building. In their U.S.-Russia Strategic Framework Declaration of April 6, 2008, however, Presidents Bush and Putin stated that the two sides "will continue development of a legally binding post-START arrangement."[14]

The difference between what the United States and Russia believe should replace START reflects a broader disagreement over the role of arms control in the post-Cold War world. One perspective, generally adopted by the Clinton administration, was to see the breakup of the Soviet Union as allowing much more progress in arms control—deeper reductions, more intrusive verification, and solutions to the problems posed by nondeployed nuclear warheads and their dangerous fissile material, among other things. The Bush administration view has been the exact opposite. It saw the lengthy and cumbersome negotiation process as *delaying* the continued reductions that both sides sought. It saw complex verification procedures as reflecting (and perhaps contributing to) an atmosphere of confrontation and suspicion inappropriate for the new partnership relationship that both countries desired.[15] As a result, the Bush administration has discounted the need for and the value of formal arms control, preferring reciprocal unilateral steps.

The reluctance to embrace formal arms control does not imply any U.S. interest in an arms race. Shortly after taking office, the administration conducted a review of America's nuclear posture. One outcome was a decision to reduce operationally deployed strategic weapons to between 1,700 and 2,200 by the year 2012, thus continuing a trend of reductions prevalent throughout the 1990s. This level was subsequently codified in the Treaty of Moscow. Many observers believe that the actual deployed levels in 2012 will be considerably lower.

In addition to reducing deployed warheads, the United States has also reduced total warhead levels. In May 2004, the President approved a plan to dramatically lower the number of nondeployed weapons retained as a hedge against unforeseen geopolitical or technical problems and thus to significantly reduce the total stockpile. Although the reductions were initially planned for completion in 2012, in December 2007 the White House announced that they had been attained 5 years ahead of schedule. As a result, the U.S. nuclear stockpile is now the smallest it has been since the Eisenhower administration. The weapons removed from the stockpile are being eliminated. Russia is also reducing overall stockpile levels, although it is deploying replacement systems for intercontinental ballistic missiles (ICBMs) and constructing (slowly) a new class of ballistic missile submarines. Its plans for future reductions are unclear.

The lack of current U.S. interest in formal bilateral arms control arises from doubts as to its relevance. Virtually all analysts and administrations of both parties accept the principle that arms control is not an end in itself but a means to ensure national security and international stability. It is thus useful to consider traditional benefits of U.S.-Soviet or U.S.-Russian arms control to see if they are still relevant.

While each analyst and policymaker will have a slightly different list, the following are commonly considered benefits of formal bilateral arms control:

- *Provide predictability and avoid an action-reaction cycle where each side builds new systems in anticipation of similar moves by the other.* Called arms race stability, this was a major motivator during the Cold War. Today, however, with no new strategic systems in development in the United States and with Russian modernization proceeding at a very slow rate, it is irrelevant.

- *Reduce incentives to preempt in time of crisis (provide crisis stability).* Much of the Cold War arms control effort was aimed at encouraging a shift away from ICBMs with multiple warheads that were seen as "use or lose" systems during a crisis. While this concern is still theoretically valid, economic conditions in Russia preclude massive restructuring no matter what arms control agreements say. Further, it is difficult to envision a scenario leading to a crisis severe enough to involve consideration of a nuclear strike. Finally, in such a hypothetical future crisis, the dangers from the antiquated Russian warning system outweigh any pressures caused by force structure.

- *Save money by capping expenditures on new systems.* This advantage has vanished due to the very slow rate of strategic spending on both sides.
- *Reduce suspicion and avoid misunderstanding through increased transparency and predictability.* This benefit remains important and argues for retention of data exchanges and other transparency measures regardless of whether or not there are any numerical limits on force structure.
- *Improve the overall political relationship between the two sides.* This is probably the strongest argument for extending or replacing the START Treaty and was a major reason for concluding the Treaty of Moscow. It has been given increased urgency by the deterioration in political relations between Russia and the United States incident to Russia's turn away from democracy and transformation into a security state.

Despite legitimate philosophic doubts about the relevance of arms control in the post-Cold War world, the need for halting the deterioration of relations between Russia and the United States will almost certainly result in some formal agreement to replace START. It is possible that such an agreement will be completed in 2008; if not, it will be an immediate task facing the new U.S. President.

Strategic Defenses.

The bilateral nuclear relationship, and indeed the overall U.S.-Russian political relationship, has been complicated by the U.S. decision to deploy elements of a ballistic missile defense system in Europe, with interceptors in Poland and radar in the Czech Republic. It is important to realize that the ballistic missile defense program of today is very different, both technically and strategically, from strategic defenses of the past. During the 1980s, worried about instability and uncertain of the value and dependability of arms control, many looked to defenses as a better solution. In 1983, President Ronald Reagan launched the Strategic Defense Initiative (SDI), an extremely ambitious plan to deploy non-nuclear land, sea, air, and space-based ballistic missile defenses. Some outside government claimed this would make the United States invulnerable, but its internal goal was to so disrupt any nuclear strike that the Soviets would not be able to accomplish any meaningful military mission and thus would be less likely to attack. Whatever the merits of this argument, the end of the Cold War saw the end of SDI.

When it took office, the Bush administration concluded that the proliferation of ballistic missiles by rogue states, especially Iran and North Korea, represented a significant threat. It also concluded that defenses are necessary because the operation of deterrence is less certain against such regimes. That does not mean that such states cannot be deterred. But we understand relatively little about how they process information and what drives the value system of the top decisionmakers and, especially in Iran, the relative influence of the various centers of power.[16]

The United States has no interest in deploying defenses against Russian forces and believes that the Russians should recognize that U.S. deployments pose no threat to Russia's security. A combination of political factors, a tendency toward worst-case analysis, and a claimed fear that the initial deployment will lead to much greater deployments has caused Russia to react forcefully to U.S. plans. If, as is likely, the next administration continues with current plans, some accommodation of Russian concerns may be appropriate. The most common suggestion is integrating some elements of Russia's ballistic missile attack warning system with the U.S. system, thus ensuring that the two sides would have a common understanding of the strategic situation. Indeed, two of the most respected analysts in Russia have suggested that integrating warning and defenses could be the basis for a transformed strategic relationship between the two states, although their proposals are almost certainly too sweeping to be negotiable in the present political circumstances.[17]

Formal Arms Control Other Than START.

In addition to a follow-on to START, arms control advocates sometimes call for a treaty codifying the Presidential Nuclear Initiatives or constraining (or even eliminating) nonstrategic nuclear weapons. In addition, there are periodic calls for transforming START into a multilateral treaty by expanding it to include China, France, and the United Kingdom. Neither of these options appears likely.

Negotiations on nonstrategic nuclear weapons are unlikely for three reasons: verification, inequality, and the North Atlantic Treaty Organization (NATO). There simply are no good ways to verify limits on numbers of warheads, yet without verification, treaties are simply unilateral declarations under another name. An equally daunting problem is the disparity between the nonstrategic arsenals of the United States and Russia, with the Russian arsenal substantially larger, although authoritative public numbers are lacking on both sides. Finally, in any such negotiation the Russians would certainly seek the removal of the remaining U.S. nuclear weapons (all bombs) from Europe. While the numbers of U.S. weapons deployed in Europe is less than one-tenth of Cold War levels, they remain politically important to the defense ministries of some of our allies. Although it is possible that a future administration would seek negotiations, it is difficult to see how these problems can be overcome.

Multilateral strategic arms control is even less likely. France and the United Kingdom both have minimal deterrents. China is modernizing its very small nuclear force, but at a relatively slow pace. In the past, all three have been uninterested in participating in strategic arms control. There appears little likelihood of this position changing in the future. Despite significant reductions, both U.S. and Russian stockpiles are an order of magnitude larger that those of the other three NPT states. China, in particular, is unlikely to be interested in formally codifying such an inequality. (China also historically has been suspicious of the concept of transparency, which many Chinese see as a weapon the strong use to maintain their power over weaker states.)

Conclusion.

There is a rich web of nuclear interactions between Russia and the United States. Those interactions will continue in some form regardless of who the new leaders of the two states are. Formal arms control of the sort practiced during the Cold War will, however, play a relatively minor role. Some replacement for

START is almost certain, perhaps before the new U.S. administration takes office. Beyond that, the situation is less clear. It is possible, though not likely, that there will be an attempt to reach a formal agreement on strategic defenses. Other areas are unlikely to be attempted and even less likely to come to fruition.

Arms control advocates tend to decry the lack of prospects for formal U.S.-Russian agreements. They are right to be concerned, but wrong to focus that concern on arms control. Arms control is for adversaries. Russia, despite the increasing strains in the relationship, is not a military adversary, and it is in our interest to keep it that way. While formal treaties can help improve relations between states, they cannot substitute for political action. Our intellectual effort should not go to devising ever more complex — and impractical — ideas for elaborate formal treaties. Instead, we should do the hard diplomatic work of building better political relations with Russia. This is likely to be difficult, especially over the next few years, but it is essential. Better political relations will make formal arms control both easier to obtain and, perhaps paradoxically, far less important.

ENDNOTES - CHAPTER 3

1. Although the Russian Federation elected Dmitry Medvedev as President on March 2, 2008, most analysts assume that current President Vladimir Putin will continue to dominate Russian political life. Thus, substantial continuity can be expected in Russian approaches to nuclear issues, including arms control. In contrast, while none of the Presidential candidates have, as of this writing, expressed significant views on nuclear issues, it is virtually certain that the approaches of the two U.S. parties would be significantly different. Thus for the purposes of this analysis, the U.S. election is the more important of the two.

2. For an optimistic survey of ideas for expanding cooperation in nuclear security, see "Leadership Through Partnership: A Vision for the 2015 Nuclear Security Relationship Between the United States of America and the Russian Federation," presented by Ambassador Linton F. Brooks, at *The Future of the Nuclear Security Environment in 2015*, An International Workshop Sponsored by the U.S. National Academies and the Russian Academy of Sciences, Vienna, Austria, November 12-13, 2007. The article is reprinted in *Comparative Strategy*, Volume 27, Issue 2, March 2008, pp. 211-219.

3. Article VI states: "Each of the Parties to the Treaty undertakes to pursue negotiations in good faith on effective measures relating to cessation of the nuclear arms race at an early date and to nuclear disarmament, and on a Treaty on general and complete disarmament under strict and effective international control."

4. During the Clinton administration any attempt to gain Senate advice and consent to ratification failed by a significant margin.

5. Whatever the symbolic and policy benefits of U.S. ratification, a CTBT is unlikely to actually come into effect in the foreseeable future. Under the terms of the Treaty, 44 specific states must ratify it for it to take effect, including such unlikely candidates as North Korea, India, and Pakistan.

6. The White House, Office of the Press Secretary, "U.S.-Russia Strategic Framework Declaration," April 6, 2008.

7. The CTR effort was far broader than security and included assistance in dismantling strategic weapons and eliminating chemical weapons. Much of the effort was aided by international contributions from other members of the G-8.

8. Remarks by National Security Advisor Stephen Hadley to the Center for International Security and Cooperation, Stanford University, Palo Alto, CA, February 8, 2008.

9. Arms Control Association Fact Sheet, "The Intermediate-Range Nuclear Forces Treaty at a Glance," February 2008, accessed at *www.armscontrol.org/factsheets/INFtreaty.asp*.

10. The treaty is sometimes called START I to distinguish it from a January 1993 START II Treaty that was signed but never entered into force and is no longer relevant.

11. More precisely, the Treaty limits the ability to carry warheads.

12. Non-strategic nuclear weapons (also called tactical or battle field weapons) were extensively deployed in the Cold War where they served as a counterweight to Soviet conventional superiority and a means to link the defense of Europe to the U.S. nuclear arsenal. The term "nonstrategic" is a misnomer; in political terms, all nuclear weapons are strategic.

13. Ukraine, Belarus, and Kazakhstan are also parties to START but play no meaningful role in decisions on its future.

14. The White House, Office of the Press Secretary, "U.S.-Russia Strategic Framework Declaration," April 6, 2008.

15. I owe this insight, although in a significantly different form, to Dr. Edward Ifft's presentation on "The Future of START" at a June 2007 Arms Control Association press roundtable.

16. For amplification of this point, see Keith Payne, *Deterrence in the Second Nuclear Age*, Lexington: University Press of Kentucky, October 1996.

17. See Alexei Arbatov and Vladimir Dvorkin, *Beyond Nuclear Deterrence: Transforming the U.S.-Russian Equation*, Washington DC: Carnegie Endowment for International Peace, 2006, pp. 141-162.

CHAPTER 4

ARMS CONTROL AND U.S.-RUSSIAN RELATIONS

Alexander A. Pikayev[1]

The United States and Russia are engaged in various arms control regimes—bilateral, multilateral, and global. Bilateral political relations affect their attitudes towards the regimes and cooperating inside them. But the opposite is also true: The regimes might also shape the bilateral relations. The format of this volume does not permit us to analyze a link between the bilateral relationship and arms control. Instead, strategic nuclear arms control was chosen as a case study. The role of this segment of bilateral arms control has faced dramatic change during the last 40 years. Recently, due to the expiration of the Strategic Arms Reduction Treaty (START I) in 2009, we might witness the last chapter of this formerly central bilateral and, sometimes, global issue.

For 40 years, strategic nuclear arms control has played an important role in U.S.-Russian relations. Some of the bilateral arms control agreements, including their approaches and provisions, have demonstrated their viability. They survived the rise and fall of the détente policy, the war in Afghanistan, President Ronald Reagan's Star Wars, the collapse of the Soviet Union, the end of the Cold War, and the North Atlantic Treaty Organization (NATO) enlargement. In the late 1960s, U.S. President Lyndon Johnson and Soviet Prime Minister Alexei Kosygin started the process. The foundations of the regime created to regulate the bilateral strategic balance still continue to determine some domestic and international policies in the United States and Russia.

At the same time, radical transformation since the late 1980s affected the role and implementation of the bilateral arms control regime. The regime was primarily based on Cold War imperatives and under approximate parity in sizes of the strategic nuclear forces of both countries. The regime's erosion, which became evident in the early 2000s, emerged not because of tactical considerations and occasional events, but because of fundamental changes both at the global level and in the realm of bilateral U.S.-Russian relations.

ROLE OF ARMS CONTROL DURING THE COLD WAR

During the Cold war, strategic arms control played several important roles. First, arms control negotiations were held regularly, except for a relatively short interruption in the mid-1980s, which followed deployment of U.S. intermediate range missiles in Western Europe. The negotiations created a unique channel of the regular U.S.-Soviet dialogue and helped to maintain critically important bilateral interaction between two leading and mutually confrontational states. The dialogue facilitated confrontation and regulated the bilateral relationship. Given the role of these bilateral relations in the global system of that time, this also contributed to a certain stability on the global level.

Second, the process also was a unique military tool permitting the both sides to influence each other's strategic nuclear activities through cooperative measures. Despite the will of both Moscow and Washington to subordinate negotiated ceilings to their unilateral strategic nuclear forces' modernization plans, the arms control talks, nevertheless, forced both sides' national defense programs, to an extent, to adopt to these cooperative efforts. Thus, under the 1979 Strategic Arms Limitation Treaty (SALT) II, which legally has never entered into force, the Soviet Union had to refrain from using Tu-22 *Backfire* bombers for implementing strategic intercontinental missions by agreeing not to equip them with air refueling capabilities. As a result, they were unable to hit targets on U.S. soil.

Third, arms control provided both sides with predictability of their future developments. Due to data exchanges and verification, they were able to obtain more reliable knowledge on composition and structure of the other side's forces as compared with information gathered by unilateral intelligence. This helped avoid exaggerated estimates of the capabilities of the other side, and, consequently, saved funds on unnecessary military buildups.

A famous episode from the 1950s illustrates the importance of the relative transparency offered by arms control. During one of the parades in Red Square in Moscow, then Soviet leader Nikita Khrushchev ordered a small number of strategic nuclear bombers to make several rounds over the parade. He wanted to demonstrate to the gathered foreign diplomats that the Soviet Union possessed a stronger capability than was actually the case. As a result, the United States debated about its window of vulnerability. The debates led to a decision for a considerable buildup of the U.S. bomber force. Both sides suffered. The United States has spent considerable funds, while the Soviet Union faced even larger U.S. predominance.

Strategic arms control fixed a principle of approximate numerical parity of the U.S. and Soviet forces. On paper it was codified in equal ceilings and subceilings for deployed delivery vehicles and the warheads associated with them. This alleviated their mutual concerns that the other side could suddenly obtain a decisive superiority by a breakthrough. Also, the military planning of both sides was facilitated as well. Due to the arms control, they could both quite confidently forecast the dynamics and structure of the force of the other side for a relatively long period of time.

In the late 1960s, U.S. agreement on the principle of strategic nuclear parity became a pleasant surprise and a considerable military and political achievement for the Soviet Union. In practice, by terms of the agreement, Washington abandoned the policy of maintaining superiority over the Soviet Union in one of the important sectors of bilateral balance of forces. The Soviet Union was accepted as an equal partner. It became an important political and propagandistic message for both Soviet allies and adversaries, and provided the Soviet leadership with the argument on overcoming a qualitative barrier in the competition of two systems. It should also be mentioned that the U.S. agreement on strategic numerical parity was a sudden victory for the Soviet leadership. According to knowledgeable sources, in instructions to the Soviet delegation for the SALT I negotiations the *Politburo* permitted it to accept an overall limit on strategic nuclear forces in a proportion of 5 to 4 in favor of the United States.

The mutual recognition of strategic nuclear parity was based on a fundamental assumption that deterrence is determined by unavoidable retaliation. In other words, under all conditions both sides' strategic nuclear forces should be capable of inflicting unacceptable damage to the adversary in a second strike. Everything that limits the retaliatory capability undermines deterrence and is destabilizing. According to the logic, vulnerability to a retaliatory attack stabilizes the strategic nuclear balance, and invulnerability destabilizes it. Therefore, defense systems capable of intercepting strategic nuclear delivery vehicles would undermine a retaliatory strike and, thus, are destabilizing and should not be deployed.

It is the principle of inevitability of retaliation, which explains why limitation of strategic nuclear forces was linked with imposing restrictions on missile defense systems. It is interesting to remember that in the 1960s the Soviet Union supposed that missile defenses were stabilizing since they limit the destructive power of nuclear weapons. During the meeting between U.S. President Johnson and Soviet Prime Minister Alexei Kosygin in Glassboro in 1968 when they agreed to start talks on SALT I and anti-ballistic missiles (ABM), Johnson had to read a lecture to his Soviet counterpart as to why the ABM destabilizes strategic nuclear relations between the superpowers. Later, the Soviet Union accepted the U.S. point of view. But until the early 1980s, it was the United States, not the Union of Soviet Socialist Republics (USSR), which insisted on imposing tougher restrictions on deploying the ABM strategic systems.

Probably, the U.S. position could be explained by much less philosophical considerations. Failed development and testing of the U.S. missile interceptors in 1950s and 1960s did not allow the United States to develop them in large scale due to their inefficiencies. At the same time, the Soviets decided to deploy missile defenses. Under parity, an unlimited quantity of Soviet missile interceptors could lead to an undetermined increase in numbers of first-rate targets for the U.S. strategic forces. The U.S. military would have to maintain a considerable part of its strategic nuclear delivery vehicles targeted at the ABM capabilities of the other side, but not at its strategic nuclear forces. This could create a imbalance in favor of the Soviet Union. The imbalance could be avoided by imposing clear and tough restrictions on ABM deployments.

Bilateral U.S.-Soviet strategic nuclear arms control became possible due to the relative unimportance of the nuclear capabilities of third nuclear powers— the United Kingdom, France, and China. Due to the massive Soviet nuclear buildup in the 1960s, the U.S. ally, the United Kingdom (UK), appeared quite behind the Soviet arsenals and could be discarded from strategic nuclear consideration. Also, due to the distance to the Soviet Union, the UK represented a target for intermediate range nuclear forces, but not for the strategic ones. The other two powers, France and China, during the late 1960s remained at an early stage of the nuclear buildup, and their arsenals remained small. Also, it is believed that the Chinese did not have capabilities to hit the targets on the U.S. soil until the early 1980s.

Beginning the U.S.-Soviet SALT negotiations was possible only after concluding the Nuclear Nonproliferation Treaty (NPT). It was signed in 1968 and strictly limited the number of recognized nuclear powers. It also legally confirmed a non-nuclear status for the vast majority of the countries, including those which possessed the technological capability to acquire nuclear weapons. Therefore, another necessary condition for bilateral arms control had been created and nuclear bipolarity had received a legal basis. After completion of the NPT, both the United States and the

Soviet Union faced a reduced risk of an uncontrollable increase in the number of targets for their strategic forces due to nuclear proliferation and expansion of the number of nuclear states in the world.

On the other hand, after concluding the NPT, both superpowers appeared under pressure from non-nuclear states, which required commencing talks on nuclear disarmament. In exchange for agreement from a vast majority of countries to refrain from obtaining nuclear weapons, nuclear powers had to accept an obligation to conduct nuclear disarmament negotiations in good faith. Article VI of the NPT required this obligation. The U.S.-Soviet SALT talks were the most immediate case of implementing the NPT Article VI obligations by the United States and the Soviet Union.

THE POST-COLD WAR GEOPOLITICAL ENVIRONMENT

Collapse of the 1990s.

The collapse of the Soviet Union and the end of the Cold War led to three major radical changes. First, confrontation was removed from the relations between the United States and the Russian Federation—the prime successor state of the Soviet Union—which inherited all its nuclear capability and a permanent seat in the United Nations (UN) Security Council. Second, the bipolar international structure, which dominated the world's politics since the end of the World War II, has disappeared as well. Third, the elimination took place not due to dispersion of both poles, but because of the collapse of one of them. Since 1991—the year of the Soviet collapse—and until the early 2000s, the asymmetry between the two former poles continued to increase. In has happened not only due to Russia's decreasing influence, but also as a result of relative strengthening of political, economic, and military positions of the United States and the Western Alliance as a whole.

Since the Soviet collapse, the government in Moscow still controls half of the population of the dissolved country and a slightly bigger share of its economy. Deep economic crisis followed the collapse and led to a dramatic economic decline resulting in another halving of the national Gross Domestic Product (GDP). In 2001, Russia's GDP hardly exceeded $210 billion and, under market currencies exchange rate, comprised less that 3 percent of the U.S. GDP.

Such a dramatic decline affected the Kremlin's international influence and its military power. Until the late 1980s, Russia's forward defense line went across Germany. After the collapse, it moved by a thousand miles east and stopped a few hundred miles to the west of Moscow. It was a situation historically unprecedented since the late 18th century. Manpower of the Russian Armed Forces was reduced from 2.8 million in early 1992 to a million in 2000. While Soviet defense expenditures reached, under some estimates, an equivalent of $100 billion (in mid-1980s prices), in 2000 Russia's federal defense spending fell to less than $5 billion under the market exchange rate. Under the purchase capability, they were evaluated at $8 billion — still a minuscule level compared with level of the U.S. defense budget.

Another important characteristic of U.S.-Russian relations was that while the Cold War-type confrontation disappeared, they remained somewhere between noncooperative competition and partnership. On the one hand, in the 1990s Moscow and Washington cooperated in the area of nuclear safety and security and settling some regional conflicts. At the same time, the first post-Cold War decade illuminated deep disagreements on many other key issues—the NATO eastward enlargement, policy in post-Soviet space, and conflicts in the Western Balkans. As a result, old Cold War stereotypes were not completely overcome, and new grievances were added to them. If in 1992 it seemed that the United States and Russia would be capable of moving towards partnership or even allied relations, in 1999 prospects for returning to new forms of confrontation seemed more realistic.

Uncertainty in the sphere of political relations did not permit the sides to retreat from nuclear deterrence against each other. Moreover, in the 1990s Russia and the United States changed places. If during the Cold War NATO relied on nuclear weapons because of perceived inferiority of its conventional forces, since the USSR's end Moscow had to rely more on its nuclear arsenals vis-à-vis considerable and increasing NATO conventional superiority. In this sense, in the post-Cold War period the role of nuclear deterrence for Russia did not decrease, but instead grew.

However, it is important to mention that, despite changes in nuclear declaratory policy, Moscow did not make practical steps aimed at restructuring its forces and enabling them to conduct nuclear first use strategy. Nuclear deterrence against a large-scale conventional offensive requires possessing flexible and variable options for nuclear strikes. For that, high alert deployment of not only strategic, but also tactical nuclear weapons might be needed. However, in accordance with the 1991-92 U.S.-Russian Presidential Nuclear Initiatives (PNIs), Moscow has removed the majority of its tactical nuclear forces to central storage sites and promised their partial elimination. In the 1990s the Russians continued implementing PNIs.

All this means that in the 1990s a perception of vulnerability resulted from NATO's eastward enlargement, and unfavorable changes of the balance of power in Europe triggered actual and declaratory reactions in Moscow. This challenged opportunities for partnership. But deterioration of U.S.-Russian relations in late 1990s was not inadvertent. The paradox was that by the early 2000s, Russia, indeed, became an economic dwarf. At the same time, it was able to capitalize on the huge Soviet nuclear legacy. Deployment represents the cheapest phase of the lifetime of intercontinental ballistic missiles (ICBMs), the cornerstone of Russia's strategic nuclear deterrent. Their lifetime is also long, and can be prolonged by relatively inexpensive technical measures. This is why, despite the fact that the air and naval components of the Russian strategic triad experienced a decrease in their alert status due to economic constraints, the land-based forces still remained capable and combat ready.

In the 1990s, such a long ICBM lifetime helped Moscow to maintain an approximate strategic parity with the United States. This was greatly facilitated by START I signed in 1991 which required each side to reduce the number of its deployed strategic nuclear warheads from 10-11,000 warheads in 1990 to a 6,000 warhead level by 2001. This combination of natural performances of strategic nuclear forces with strategic arms control permitted Russia to maintain strategic parity with the much stronger United States for the whole decade.

However, the economic situation has greatly affected strategic nuclear modernization. In the 1990s the Russians developed one new single-warhead

ICBM, the SS-27 *Topol M*, and started construction of new *Borei*-class strategic nuclear submarines (SSBN). Construction of strategic bombers was halted in 1992, and the testing program of the new *Bark* submarine launched ballistic missiles (SLBM) was unsuccessful and cancelled in late 1990s. As a result, future development of Russian strategic nuclear forces was at stake. Without a new SLBM, there was a real risk for survival of the whole sea leg of the strategic triad.

The other problem was associated with arms control. In 1993, the United States and Russia signed the START II Treaty. It required elimination of all ICBMs equipped with multiple independently targeted re-entry vehicles (MIRV) by 2003; MIRVs were a cornerstone of the Russian strategic triad, the deployment of which could be inexpensively prolonged by several years, if not a decade. Rapid decommissioning and elimination of such systems could lead to a sharp decrease in strategic nuclear numbers, much lower than required by the START II ceilings — 3,000-3,500 strategic nuclear warheads.

Certainly commissioning new missiles could compensate such a rapid decline. But it was economically prohibitive to produce and deploy a large number of single warhead *Topol Ms*. In the late 1990s, their deployment rate was less than 10 missiles annually. This was clearly not enough to maintain the START II ceilings. Russia faced a realistic option to lose its strategic nuclear parity with the United States very quickly, and go down to probably less than a thousand deployed strategic warheads.

In 1997 the sides reached what at that time seemed like a deal. Moscow and Washington signed the Protocol to the START II, which delayed implementation of the Treaty reductions until 2007. The United States also agreed to discuss further nuclear reductions by negotiating the START III agreement. In exchange, the Russians accepted talks on controlling tactical nuclear weapons, which they had carefully avoided since the Soviet collapse.

However, very soon it became clear that the deal would not be implemented. The delay of the START II implementation permitted by the 1997 Protocol was too short to solve Russia's economic difficulties, and could save time only for producing just a few dozen *Topol M*s ICBMs to compensate for hundreds of MIRV'd missiles to be eliminated. A significant part of these MIRV'd ICBMs represented missiles, the lifetime of which could be prolonged by relatively cheap measures.

Regarding START III, during the consultations it was clear that the United States could not accept the very low ceilings proposed by the Russians. Washington was not able to go below 2,000 deployed strategic warheads because that would require significant restructuring of the U.S. strategic nuclear arsenals. The 1999 decision of the United States to amend the ABM Treaty to permit limited missile defense deployments further complicated the situation, and the whole Helsinki process had failed by the time the Bush administration came into power in early 2001.

The U.S. unwillingness to accept uncomfortable arms control measures could be explained by forecasts of future rapid degradation of the Russian nuclear might. Understandably, the United States was reluctant to make any sizable concessions to the Russians during a time when it expected that very soon the Russian strategic nuclear arsenals would degrade anyway, irrespective of any arms control agreements. Painful bilateral arms control dialogue in 1990s, which remained fruitless, further provoked disappointment in the United States on the formal negotiated arms control process, and increased preferences for informal light measures in this area.

In 1990s, Russian interest in arms control seemed to be motivated by conflicting interests. Generally, Moscow was ready to accept the lowest possible arms control ceilings in order to continue using strategic arms control for maintaining its shrinking arsenal on a par with the U.S. forces. That arsenal was needed not only for maintaining symbolic strategic nuclear parity, but also for keeping credibility for nuclear deterrence against predominant conventional forces. Such an objective could hardly be reached by much more inferior nuclear capabilities.

Simultaneously, the Russians faced problems with particular regimes, first of all, with START II. They effectively prevented implementation of economically feasible options for strategic nuclear modernization and maintained their ceilings close to the United States for the some period of time. Chances for solving the problem through bilateral deep reductions proved impossible due to the above-mentioned reluctance in Washington.

In the 1990s, the world still experienced nuclear bipolarity. Despite significant reductions, Russia and the United States possessed much larger arsenals than did the three other recognized nuclear powers — China, the UK, and France. The UK and France followed the U.S.-Russian example and unilaterally reduced their arsenals. The Chinese continued their nuclear modernization at a slow pace, and their arsenals remained relatively low, although some efforts were made to gain qualitative improvements. India and Pakistan held nuclear tests in 1998, and did not have time to weaponize their nuclear charges by the end of the decade. Israel also demonstrated self-restraint by deciding not to deploy strategic nuclear delivery capabilities.

Therefore, in the 1990s U.S.-Russian nuclear relations were motivated by a conflicting rationale. First, the confrontation was over, and nuclear issues were removed from the center stage of the bilateral agenda. However, remaining political disagreements did not permit the sides to renounce nuclear deterrence vis-à-vis each other. Moreover, it occupied a more important position in Russia's military thinking, while remaining high in the U.S. priorities despite Washington's increasing and unchallengeable conventional superiority.

Second, a dramatic economic and military gap emerged between Russian and the United States and affected the very base of the future bilateral nuclear relationship. The prospects for Russia's unilateral nuclear reductions and loss of nuclear parity with the United States in the early 21st century seemed inevitable. Simultaneously, strong inertia from sizable Soviet nuclear arsenals inherited by Russia and the long lifetime of key strategic nuclear assets allowed Russia to keep bilateral nuclear parity through the whole decade. Although the bilateral structure of international relations ended with the Cold War, in the nuclear realm it remained almost untouchable due to inertia of nuclear programs implementation and the fact that other nuclear nations started from low ceilings.

In the arms control area, there were the following consequences: Through the 1990s strategic nuclear discussions occupied an important place in the U.S.-Russian relations, although not as crucial as during the Cold War. On the very basic level, it could be explained by inertia in evolution of nuclear capabilities, including their international dimension. The dialogue did not transform into multilateral discussions, since other nations remained incapable of contributing to it. The bilateral structure of world nuclear relations did not change. While the UK, France, and even China had to demonstrate self-restraint in their nuclear modernization and deployment, they did that by unilateral decisions, not through arms control.

At the same time, the increasing gap between Russia and the United States led to expectations of the inevitable future decline and degradation of the Russian forces. This provoked U.S. reluctance to make uncomfortable decisions to gain Moscow's concessions. The perception was clearly growing in Washington that the concessions would be given anyway, and there was no need to pay any significant military and political price for them. This might explain why, despite intensive arms control dialogue between Moscow and Washington, it did not bring any significant fruit since 1993. Here, growing U.S.-Russian asymmetry played its role.

Stabilization in the 2000s.

Surprisingly, the 2000s brought rapid Russia's recovery. Instead of the decline of the 1990s, Russian GDP started to increase by an average 7 percent annually and by 2008 reached $1.2 trillion. This represented almost a six times increase in dollar terms since the beginning of the decade. Accordingly, the defense spending also increased up to $35 billion in 2007. By 2008 Russia passed a deep U-turn, and its economy returned to the size of the economy of the Russian Federation before the Soviet collapse. As a result of the ongoing but still unfinished military reform, the state of conventional forces was improved, and their combat readiness increased. However, despite rapid economic growth, Russia still occupies a quite modest position in the world. Its defense budget is compatible to those of medium European powers which enjoy a much safer neighborhood than the Russians. In terms of GDP size, Russia still lags behind the leading European Union (EU) nations with their much smaller populations.

On the other hand, the 2000s were quite divisive for the Western alliances. The United States and its European allies are still healing wounds inflicted by war in Iraq and the deteriorating situation in Afghanistan. NATO and EU enlargements did not strengthen them as expected. On the contrary, some believe that it affected the cohesiveness of these institutions. Some new dividing lines emerged inside them. Lack of attention to the Western Pacific helped the Chinese to consolidate their economic and political might, and Japan has started its controversial march to "normalcy."

Thus, in general geopolitical terms, the world became more fragmented, and the Western dominance, unchallengeable in the 1990s, has probably passed its peak. Like the 1990s, the decade was also characterized by an uneven development of U.S.-Russian relations. Immediately after the September 11, 2001 (9/11) attacks on the United States, they experienced an unprecedented rapprochement. Later, they again moved down and, like at the end of the Yeltsin administration, faced significant complications. While in the 1990s the ups and downs in the bilateral relationship were quite spontaneous and relatively short lived, in the 2000s observers started to speak of a gradual but steady divorce.

This again did not permit both sides to move out from nuclear deterrence in bilateral relations despite the declaratory willingness of some elements inside the Bush administration to do that. Also, like in 1990s, other nuclear powers did not challenge (willingly or unwillingly) U.S. and Russia's nuclear dominance. The world remains bipolar in the nuclear area. Although nuclear proliferation represented increasing concern, it still failed to affect the world nuclear picture dramatically. The Indo-Pakistani nuclear arms race remains contained by regional landscape, and so far has not influenced the global balance of forces. DPRK nuclear ambitions seem to be adequately managed, and Pyongyang's rollback looks quite feasible.

As expected, the decade started from partial collapse of the U.S.-Russian negotiated arms control. In December 2001, the United States decided to withdraw from the 1972 ABM Treaty. As a result, START II, ratified by the Russian Federal Assembly in 2000, did not enter into force. In fact, there was cooperative dismantlement of two pillars of the bilateral arms control regime. By withdrawing from the ABM Treaty, the United States gained a free hand in developing missile defense systems which the Republicans have sought for 20 years. For its part, the Russians got rid of the very uncomfortable START II, which blocked the most feasible strategic nuclear forces modernization. Having abandoned START II, Moscow made a natural decision to prolong the lifetime of a part of its MIRV'd ICBMs. This has prevented Russia's strategic nuclear triad from collapsing in this decade. The decline became slower, and left more time—up to 10 years—for compensatory deployments. The much better economic situation permits Russia to increase missile production to maintain strategic nuclear ceilings at least above 2,000 deployed warheads.

131

In response to the U.S. withdrawal from the ABM Treaty, the Kremlin commenced or accelerated several strategic nuclear programs. The major event was a 2007 successful flight test of new MIRV'd RS-24 ICBMs. The test demonstrated that the new MIRV'd ICBM is available for replacing older missile systems that will be gradually decommissioned during the 2010s. For maintaining the same level of forces, a smaller quantity of MIRV'd missiles is needed for compensatory deployments compared with the single warhead ICBMs.

Also, Russia has mainly solved an issue of maintaining its naval leg of the strategic triad. The *Sineva* SLBM (reportedly a modernized version of SS-N-23) has been successfully flight tested. Tests of the new solid fuel *Bulava* missile, designated for deployment on *Borei*-class SSBNs, were not very successful. Nevertheless, they could be deployed on new submarines, which could be commissioned until the end of the decade. In the 2000s, Russia also flight tested new warheads capable of penetrating through missile defenses.

Therefore, in the 2000s the Russians have quite successfully conducted strategic nuclear development and testing programs. The programs would determine composition of the forces in the next decade. However, the question of the forces' size remains open. The Russian authorities did not specify what force levels they would like to possess. President Putin only said that "we have grandiose plans in the area." On the other hand, the production rate of ICBMs in the 2000s remained at the same low levels as they were in the 1990s. It might demonstrate that Moscow's decision on those forces' ceilings have not been made yet. Its nature could be determined by the state of bilateral relations and future of strategic arms control.

Beyond cooperative dismantlement of two key elements of the bilateral arms control regime, in 2002 Moscow and Washington concluded the Strategic Offensive Reduction Treaty (SORT), also known as the Moscow Treaty. This document is unique in the history of U.S.-Russian strategic arms control. It consists of two pages and contains two figures. Under the agreement, the sides agreed to limit their overall strategic nuclear ceilings by 1,700-2,200 deployed warheads. However, the treaty does not contain verification provisions, counting rules, terms of definition, and all other technicalities without which the treaty can exist only as empty paper.

Moscow was not enthusiastic about the agreement, which in fact, codified internationally the U.S. Nuclear Posture Review, conducted by the Bush administration in 2001. Like in late 1990s in the case of the abortive START III discussions, the United States has decided not to restrict domestic nuclear planning by any arms control agreements. And contrary to the logic of the desired START III, the Russians decided to conclude SORT, most likely because this time painful restrictions of the START II were removed.

Between 2002 and 2006 there were only sporadic meetings of the U.S.-Russian institutions aimed at discussing strategic arms control matters. In this period, strategic arms control remained almost nonexistent. Only in 2006 did Moscow approach Washington to investigate its plans regarding the START I Treaty — the only still effective real bilateral strategic arms control agreement, which expires on December 5, 2009. As far as is known, that 2006 approach has led to U.S.-Russian consultations on the issue within the Kislyak-Joseph working group. Reportedly, the consultations were unsuccessful. However, in November 2007,

133

U.S. Secretary of State Condoleezza Rice and Russian Minister of Foreign Affairs Sergei Lavrov agreed that some sort of bilateral document should replace the START I. In the 1990s, concerns were expressed that abandoning U.S.-Russian bilateral arms control would deprive the sides with a permanent institutionalized channel of diplomatic interaction, which helped to maintain the relationship during the worst years of the Cold War. But effective nonfunctioning of this mechanism in the mid 2000s did not bring any immediate negative consequences for general bilateral relations. Nevertheless, longer term consequences might emerge in the next decade.

In the 1990s, the major paradox was that U.S.-Russian arms control survived the Soviet collapse and dramatic degradation of the Russian economy. There were intensive bilateral talks, but they did not bring expected results. In the 2000s, another paradox emerged. Arms control collapsed, partially because, based on the 1990s experience, there were expectations that arms control became obsolete, and results could be had without it. But this too did not happen.

THE FUTURE?

Although painful dialogue from the 1990s actually became an antidote against continuing arms control negotiations, both sides still maintain some motivations for doing so. First of all, Article VI of the NPT directly obliges them to conduct the talks. Absence of nuclear disarmament negotiations could become an argument for potential third world proliferators to divert international attention from their own misbehavior. Traditionally, the United States and Russia are considered as champions of bilateral dialogue, and they bear special responsibility for building universal support for nonproliferation norms. It would be hardly possible for them to do so, unless they settle the follow-on to START I. Dismantling the last substantive bilateral strategic nuclear arms control agreement might be a wrong message to non-nuclear participants of the next NPT Review Conference, which will gather a few months after the expiration of the START I in December 2009.

Without START I verification provisions the 2002 Moscow Treaty would become meaningless. According to its provisions, it largely depends on the START I verification and inspections regime. Thus, abrogation of the START I would also mean an effective abrogation of the SORT.

In the bilateral context, Russia still remains relatively economically vulnerable regarding entering costly strategic nuclear modernization programs, and might be interested in mutual arms control limitations. For its part, U.S. military planners also could be interested in establishing agreed limits on U.S. and Russian forces for better predictability. Testing new MIRV'd ICBMs hypothetically already permits Moscow to make considerable strategic deployments in the 2010s.

Ironically, solving the most urgent problems of Russia's strategic nuclear modernization opens more possibilities for a bilateral deal on force limits. Moscow's ability to maintain ceilings above 2,000 deployed strategic warheads would save the United States from making painful decision to go below this limit, which was so crucial in the U.S. debates in late 1990s. It makes future deals on the overall ceiling, maybe not as desirable as in the 1990s, but more feasible than then. Ideally, both sides share a motivation to continue observing part of the START I verification regime.

The regime creates the necessary transparency of each other's forces and would help both sides to be confident of avoiding surprises. The Russians believe that the START I verification regime is unnecessarily abundant and complicated. Therefore, it should become lighter and more streamlined.

Some analysts think that Russia is more interested than the United States in continuing the START I verification regime. The United States possesses much more advanced, sophisticated and widespread national technical capabilities for monitoring Russian nuclear developments. At the same time, similar Russian capabilities have been severely degraded since the Soviet collapse, and their reconstitution would require time and considerable spending. However, some other observers believe, that Russia, as a weaker power, might not be interested in intrusive transparency at all. Such transparency permits the stronger side to make detailed targeting lists. The lists might invite a disarming attack, which is considered destabilizing. They also undermine survivability of the weaker forces. The weaker side is relatively more concerned about survivability than the stronger one, since the former possesses less capable, smaller, and thus more vulnerable, arsenals. Such considerations could prevail if the sides fail to agree on imposing quantitative limits on their strategic nuclear forces.

START I is not the only arms control agreement whose fate is at stake. Since 2004 there were discussions in Moscow on the possible need to withdraw from the 1987 Intermediate-Range Nuclear Forces (INF) Treaty. This agreement has indefinite duration and requires complete elimination of land-based missiles with a range between 500 and 5,500 kilometers. The official explanation for the possible withdrawal rationale was that while the United States and Russia follow the ban, many other countries situated along Russia's periphery are developing such missiles. This discrepancy cannot last forever.

In September 2007, the United States and Russia distributed a joint paper in the UN General Assembly calling for multilateralization of the bilateral INF ban. In February 2008 Russia tabled in the Conference on Disarmament a draft proposal called "Main elements of an international legal agreement on eliminating intermediate and shorter range (land-based) missiles, open for wide international accession." Although chances for universal adherence to the document are close to zero, its appearance reflected that recently the debates on the INF Treaty in Russia have been diverted into a more constructive direction than unilateral withdrawal.

In early 2008, the Russians started to speculate on a need to multilateralize the talks on strategic stability which in the past were monopolized by the United States and Russia. Trends in nuclear development of other nuclear powers do not indicate that they entered a large-scale build-up of their nuclear forces, which would enable them to participate in multilateral traditional-type nuclear arms control negotiations. Such an option would hardly be possible in this and the next decade, if possible at all. Involving third countries in the strategic stability dialogue, first of all, requires defining what specific issues should be discussed there. The definition should be followed by selecting appropriate forums for the dialogue or establishing new ones. One also must be aware that in the foreseeable future such discussions could cover multilateral issues like the nuclear test ban, prohibition of producing weapons-grade nuclear materials, export control, various codes of conduct, etc.

Discussing issues of strategic stability in their traditional form is possible only between the states possessing an approximately numerically equal highly developed nuclear force and maintaining deterrence relations between each other. So far, only Russia and the United States meet such criteria. It is very unlikely that any other state could join them in the foreseeable future. The dilemma does not consist of whether to continue bilateral dialogue or to move to multilateral discussions. It is quite different: whether the sides will continue their bilateral interaction on strategic stability, or find it inappropriate either because of the requirement to depart from deterrence relations, or due to the increasing gap in their strategic nuclear capabilities.

ENDNOTES - CHAPTER 4

1. Dr. Alexander A. Pikayev is Director of the Department for Disarmament and International Security (IMEMO), Moscow, Russia, and a member of the International Institute for Strategic Studies, London, UK.

CHAPTER 5

TERMS OF ENGAGEMENT:
WEAPONS OF MASS DESTRUCTION
PROLIFERATION
AND U.S-RUSSIAN RELATIONS

Alexei Arbatov

The predictable result of the Russian presidential elections of March 2, 2008, ensures, at least for the next couple of years, a great measure of continuity in the main parameters of Russian non-proliferation policy. The same goes for Moscow's policy towards the United States.

This does not mean that serious positive breakthroughs are not possible in U.S.-Russian relations. The new Russian President Dmitry Medvedev would be quite willing to accomplish this. But a lot will depend on the policy of the new U.S. administration, whether it is Democratic or Republican. A more constructive attitude to reaching new agreements with Russia should be based not on purely American understanding of what "is good for both sides and everybody else," but on respect for the interests of the other side, even if differing from that of the United States; and on a genuine search for a compromise.

With respect to weapons of mass destruction (WMD) proliferation—chemical and biological weapons are prohibited by the Chemical Weapons Convention (CWC) of 1997 and Biological and Toxic Weapons Convention (BTWC) of 1972 respectively. The main problems with the first are financial costs and technical complexity of elimination, and with the second— verification and potential dangers of the revolution in

139

biotechnologies. If these problems are taken care of, the task of nonproliferation will be confined to inducing member-states to implement (and the outsiders to join) the two conventions, which may not be too difficult. Before that, chemical and biological weapons proliferation per se would hardly occupy a significant place on the agenda of U.S.-Russian relations (unless there is a case of hostile use of either of them).

It is quite a different case with nuclear weapons and ballistic missiles.[1] Unlike chemical or biological weapons, they are not prohibited and will not be for a long time. On the other hand, there is a Nuclear Non-Proliferation Treaty of 1970 and the Missile Technologies Control Regime (MTCR) and the Hague Code of Conduct, addressing directly the task of nonproliferation without prohibiting such arms. These problems have stayed at the forefront of U.S.-Russian relations after the end of the Cold War.

Besides nuclear proliferation to new states, of still more recent concern is the prospect of proliferation of nuclear explosive devices or materials to terrorist organizations. Preventing this horrible contingency implies cooperation between the two nations and other responsible countries regarding the twilight business of counterterrorist operations by special forces and secret services, as well as on very technical matters of export controls over nuclear materials and technologies.

However, the main channel of potential access of the terrorists to nuclear weapons would, most probably, lead through the new nuclear-capable states, which may serve as a source of nuclear weapons, materials, or critical technologies to terrorists either directly or through a pool of international "black markets" of the type initiated by Pakistani atomic industry officials.

Hence, this chapter is focused on the problems of U.S.-Russian interaction on nuclear nonproliferation, primarily with respect to new states and only indirectly to terrorist organizations.[2]

U.S. and Russian Asymmetric Nonproliferation Visions.

Dialectically, nonproliferation issues have shaped the major area of overlap of the security interests of the two nations even during the Cold War times, and still more after it was ended — and at the same time they have produced some of the major controversies between them during the last decade. These controversies, besides the mistakes of policymakers, have stemmed from some objective factors which must be understood and addressed in order to formulate the new rules of U.S.-Russian engagement on nuclear and missile nonproliferation.

Both powers officially emphasize the top priority of nuclear nonproliferation for their respective foreign policy and national security agendas. However, the reality is that they have different attitudes towards the threat of proliferation. During the Cold War decades, the United States learned, albeit with great difficulty, to live in a state of total vulnerability for the hypothetically devastating attack of Soviet strategic nuclear forces (SNF). This state of vulnerability (which was, of course, mutual) since the end of the 1960s came to be consistently managed through arms control negotiations and treaties. Neither substrategic nuclear weapons of the Union of Soviet Socialist Republics (USSR), nor nuclear arms of third nuclear weapons states (Britain, France, China, Israel, South Africa), threatened the United States since they were in the hands of reliable allies and friends or out of range of U.S. territory.

After the end of the Cold War and collapse of the USSR, the threat from Soviet SNF was greatly diminished and the principle concern was related to sustaining a robust control by Moscow over its nuclear forces. At the same time, acquisition of nuclear weapons and ballistic missiles by India and Pakistan and disclosed attempts to do so by Iraq, Libya, North Korea, and Iran quite understandably moved this new direct and purely physical threat to the forefront of U.S. security concerns. The September 11, 2001 (9/11) tragedy provided only too vivid an illustration of the possible human and material dimensions of such a threat, whether it emanated from new nuclear states or terrorists.

For the USSR and then Russia, the picture looked quite different. The Soviet Union had been vulnerable to the nuclear weapons of third nuclear nations for a long time: with respect to the United States, forward based substrategic nuclear arms, and nuclear weapons of Britain since the late 1940s and early 1950s; with respect to France and China, since the early and mid 1960s; with respect to Israel, since the early 1980s. For Russia, the acquisition of nuclear weapons and ballistic missiles by India and Pakistan and the prospects of further proliferation add some new elements to a familiar and old threat rather than creating a dramatic new one, as is the case for the United States. The USSR and Russia have learned to live with this threat and to deal with it on the basis of nuclear deterrence, some limited defenses (like the Moscow ballistic missile defense [BMD] system and national Air Defenses) and through diplomacy, which is used to avoid direct confrontation (and still better, to sustain normal relations) with new nuclear nations.

No doubt nuclear and missile proliferation is one of Russia's serious security concerns, all the more so because geographically it is within relatively easy reach of all existing and potential third nuclear weapons states (except Brazil, Argentina, and Indonesia). But on the other hand, Russia does not claim to be a global "policeman," does not deploy military sites or armed forces abroad (except in some post-Soviet states), and does not employ its forces in serious combat operations. In this way it avoids challenging other countries, including actual or potential nuclear and missile-capable regimes. Russia's vulnerability and lack of reliable security protection and commitments from other nations makes its nonproliferation stance much more cautious and flexible than that of the United States.

Besides, Russia's security situation after the end of the Cold War turned out to be incomparably weaker than that of the United States (at least before the U.S. failure in Iraq). This situation created many other, sometimes more acute security threats, perceptions of threats, or self-inflicted problems for Russia, besides nuclear and missile proliferation in the world. Among those are:

- The instability and bloody conflicts across the post-Soviet space and in the North Caucasus of Russia proper (which has a 1,000 km common border with the volatile South Caucasus).
- The North Atlantic Treaty Organization's (NATO) continuous extension to the east against Russian strong objections.
- Continuing stagnation of Russian armed forces and defense industries and Russia's growing conventional and nuclear inferiority to the United States and NATO.

- The threat of expanding Muslim radicalism in the Central Asia (7,000 km of common border with Russia).
- The scary growth of economic and military power of China (5,000 km of common border with Russia).
- Recently, the plan for the deployment of U.S. BMD sites in the Czech Republic and Poland, and the pressure from Washington in favor of accepting Ukraine and Georgia to NATO have moved to the forefront of Moscow's security concerns.

Official policy statements notwithstanding, in real decisionmaking all of the above threats and risks are higher on Moscow's scale of security priorities than that of nuclear and missile proliferation in the world. Moreover, there is a broad consensus in Russia's political elite and strategic community that there is no reason for their nation to take U.S. concerns closer to heart that its own worries — in particular if Washington is showing neither understanding of those worries nor any serious attempts to remove or alleviate them in resturn for closer cooperation with Russia on nonproliferation subjects.

Russia's Nonproliferation Posture.

As was mentioned above, the official documents and announcements of Russian leadership proclaim its dedication to the regimes of WMD nonproliferation and principally to the Nonproliferation Treaty (NPT). In an interview for the British Broadcasting Corporation (BBC) in June 2003, President Vladimir Putin emphasized: "If we are speaking about the main threat of the

21st century, then I consider this to be the problem of the proliferation of weapons of mass destruction." He spoke about the same subject at the session of the United Nations (UN) General Assembly on September 26, 2003.[3]

Control over foreign economic operations with nuclear materials, special non-nuclear materials and corresponding technologies, as well as dual-use goods and technology, is exercised in Russia principally as a component of the policy of nonproliferation. The Export Control Law, adopted in 1999, has locked in the term "Export Control" specifically for this sphere. In the 1995 Law on national regulation of foreign trading activities, Export Control was described as the full set of measures for the implementation of a "transfer procedure" for agreed-upon goods, technologies, and services. The 1999 law codified this term as "foreign trading, investment, and other activities, including production cooperation in the field of the international exchange of goods, information, work, services, and results of intellectual activities, including exclusive rights to them (intellectual property)." This means not only the export of goods and technologies abroad, but also their transfer to a foreigner within the territory of the Russian Federation. In January 1998, the Russian government introduced rules for "all-encompassing control" (catch-all).

The main threshold countries that elicit the greatest U.S. concern, Iran and the Democratic People's Republic of Korea (DPRK), are not seen in Russia as being potential enemies, just as the United States does not consider the nuclear forces of Israel and Pakistan to be a direct threat. In addition, Iran occupies the second or third place (depending on the year) among buyers of large lots of Russian arms, which helps the military-

145

industrial sector to survive in spite of limited defense orders for the Russian armed forces. Finally, Iran is an extremely important geopolitical partner of Russia's, a growing "regional superpower" that balances out the expansion of Turkey and the increasing U.S. military and political presence in the Black Sea/Caspian region, while simultaneously containing Sunni Wahhabism's incursions in the North Caucasus and Central Asia.

Yet another important consideration is that the shipment of nuclear energy technology and fuel abroad are much more important for Russia than for the United States, even though it lags far behind in sheer volumes of nuclear export. Among Russian exports (predominately oil, gas, and other raw materials) nuclear contracts relate to only a few types of high-technology products (beside arms sales) that are competitive on the global market. This is deemed an important high added-value component of the export structure and a matter of status of an advanced participant in the world trade.

The role of internal factors in Russian policy also must not be underestimated. Over the last 15 years or so, the Ministry of Atomic Energy (now the Federal Atomic Energy Agency [FAEA]) has been chronically underfunded for the purposes of maintaining, converting, and dismantling its nuclear legacy from the USSR. With "nuclear cities," nuclear warheads, and nuclear submarines being withdrawn from service, the income derived from foreign contracts has become an extremely important means for the survival of this colossal infrastructure of sites and people. The Nunn-Lugar-Domenici program, the "uranium deal," "plutonium projects," and a number of other cooperative measures on the part of the United States and other Western countries have undoubtedly been a great help. However, they did not fully cover the financial requirements of the FAEA. Extra-budgetary income from contracts with China, India, Iran, and other countries has become indispensable for life support of this immense social and technological organism. In turn, Rosatom[4] is playing an important role in the formulation of the technical and economic facets of Moscow's actual policy on nuclear nonproliferation and nuclear power plant construction contracts, in particular in Iran.

In light of the above, Moscow's real position in this area may be described as follows:

- Russia has an interest in enhancing the nonproliferation regimes, but this is not the main priority in its foreign policy or security strategy.
- Russia views with a lot of skepticism the global strategy of nonproliferation and counterproliferation declared by the United States, seeing in it a policy based in the practice of double standards and an attempt to veil other political, military, and commercial interests, including nuclear exports, with the goal of nonproliferation.
- Russia is not inclined to sacrifice its own economic and political interests in peaceful nuclear cooperation with other countries for the sake of the abstract nonproliferation ideal (especially in the U.S. unilateral interpretation). It will not initiate any further tightening of the regime (especially one associated with economic losses), while at the same time observing the letter of the provisions of the NPT, International Atomic Energy Agency (IAEA) safeguards, and agreed-upon norms for nuclear exports.

- Relations with the United States are of considerable significance for Russia (including cooperative threat reduction [CTR] and global nuclear energy partnering [GNEP] programs), and it is prepared within certain limits to take U.S. demands into account.
- At the same time Moscow will resist Washington's pressure to abandon its dealings with other countries that are legal from the standpoint of the NPT, even if these countries at this point in history are not to the liking of the current U.S. administration and even if there is suspicion about the military nuclear proclivities of Russia's foreign partners. In this sense, the continuation of the Bushehr project and its possible expansion have gained not only practical significance for Moscow ($5 billion in income), but a sense of principle and political significance as well.
- Russia will object, as will the majority of U.S. allies, to using force to resolve nonproliferation problems (although for political considerations, it has supported the Proliferation Security Initiative [PSI]), and will give preference to diplomatic and economic instruments in reinforcing the NPT. Russia has supported recent UN Security Council resolutions on Iran and DPRK but will resist "hard sanctions" (i.e., oil embargo, cutting communications, etc.) and will veto the use of force.
- Russia's nonproliferation policy (just as its defense and arms control postures) will probably stay passive and mostly reactive, except when promising direct economic benefits (as with the multilateral uranium enrichment plant in the

Siberian city of Angarsk). Without initiatives from outside, Russia would hardly initiate or readily endorse more strict export controls, embargoes on sales of nuclear fuel cycle components, or more intrusive IAEA guarantees. However, it may use nuclear and missile proliferation as a pretext for withdrawing from some treaties, foremost the intermediate-range nuclear forces and short-range nuclear forges (INF-SRF) Treaty of 1987, apparently motivated by other military and political reasons.

Nonproliferation among Other Great Powers' Priorities.

The United States, Russia, and other great powers, naturally, often have other, sometimes conflicting priorities beside nonproliferation, and these may often stand higher on their lists. Thus, for the United States, support for Israel is more important than the harm that its nuclear capacity inflicts on the nonproliferation regime, especially as Washington does not want to give Tel Aviv the formal security guarantees it extends to NATO members (or to Japan and South Korea), so as to avoid alienating oil-rich pro-Western Islamic countries.

Russia, for its part, also senses the economic and political advantages of collaboration with India and Iran more strongly than the losses they inflict on the cause of nonproliferation. This is just how it was for the United States regarding Pakistan. Of course, Russia, China, Japan, and South Korea are all worried by the DPRK's nuclear program and tests of nuclear weapons, but not so much so as to agree to U.S. military action that would bring unforeseeable consequences, especially after the experience of the 2003 war in Iraq.

To a larger extent, this is also true of Russia's approach to the Iranian nuclear problem, especially in view of the fact that, in contrast to Pyongyang, Tehran is declaring its adherence to the NPT. Western Europe's position regarding Iran is more flexible than that of the United States, but stricter than Russia's and China's.

Moreover, vicissitudes of global politics periodically change the major powers' attitudes to countries that are pursuing nuclear proliferation. For example, the United States encouraged Iran's nuclear program under the Shah, but now, 20-odd years after the 1980 Islamic revolution, the United States declares it one of the top threats to security. In the same way, Washington closed its eyes to Iraq's nuclear projects (while the former was at war with Iran in the 1980s) and was not terribly concerned about nuclear preparations in Pakistan, while at the same time, it strictly opposed India's nuclear program and its collaboration with Russia in the 1990s.

After the end of the Iran-Iraq war, Baghdad became the main enemy for the United States and the object of a 1991 military operation. Dubious suspicions concerning an Iraqi nuclear program served as a formal pretext for the 2003 war against Iraq. Towards the middle of the current decade, relations with Pakistan started to change for the worse, while relations with India sharply improved due to fears cultivated by the growth of Chinese economic and military might. Accordingly, Washington diametrically changed its attitude toward India's nuclear program and towards collaborating with the country in this sphere.

It is clear that the United States, Russia, and other powers in their real-world policies are far from indifferent about which countries actually or potentially threaten nuclear proliferation at any given moment.

Thus, a country's relationship with the major powers is not so much shaped by its conduct in nonproliferation; rather the reverse: The degree to which a country finds itself in cooperation or conflict with the leading powers determines the approach those powers take to its nuclear program. It would be naive to expect any other approach, but this political reality gives rise to serious problems.

That the leading powers do not always have the same partners or enemies at any given point in time, that they practice double standards regarding nonproliferation, and all of the other factors examined above, make it extremely difficult for the United States, Russia, and others to develop a common approach to strengthening the NPT, its mechanisms, and the regime when addressing the policies of particular nations. Moreover, the political swings of the major powers around countries that pose a threat to nonproliferation actually create significant freedom of movement for the latter, while pushing aside "law-abiding" non-nuclear NPT member states and undermining their desire to collaborate actively with the leading powers on nonproliferation.

The effect of differing geopolitical preferences is heavily exacerbated by the commercial competition in nuclear exports. The world market for nuclear materials and technology, promising billions in profits, became an arena of fierce rivalry, and what is still worse, not so much among the importers, but more among the exporters. This has led to two fundamental consequences, both of which have negative impacts on nonproliferation.

In the competition for markets, supplier states (and especially their private enterprises) were not inclined to be overly picky about customers' intentions and programs, the degree to which they upheld IAEA safeguards, the inadequacy of such safeguards (for example, in Iraq, the DPRK, Libya), or even the importer's nonparticipation in the NPT (as in cases of Israel, India, and Pakistan). Moreover, some of the leading exporters were themselves for some time not party to the treaty (including France and the People's Republic of China [PRC]). The exporters were not stopped from making deals with countries including Iraq, Iran, and Libya, despite the available information on their military developments.

The lack of mutual understanding among the supplier countries is another factor. Pressure from one supplier on another to stop supplies to a particular country is often seen not as concern for nuclear nonproliferation, but as an attempt to force a competitor out of the market and take its place. Thus, in 1994 the United States, South Korea, and Japan succeeded in pressing Russia to abandon its nuclear energy collaboration with the DPRK under the pretext that Pyongyang was seeking to acquire nuclear weapons. That done, they proceeded to sign a deal to build a nuclear power plant of the exact same type, but under their own control and supposedly subject to more effective IAEA safeguards. In the end, this project, the Korean Peninsula Energy Development Organization (KEDO), was frozen, and North Korea openly resumed its military nuclear program, withdrew from the NPT in January 2003, and tested a nuclear device in October 2006.

The Bushehr contract and other areas of cooperation with Iran (including arms supplies) are too attractive for Russia and its atomic and military industrial complexes. China and India are receiving up to 20 percent of their crude oil imports from Iran. As a result, Russia and the PRC, unlike the United States, do not see the development of uranium enrichment capacity—which makes it possible to build nuclear weapons but is not formally prohibited by the NPT—as sufficient grounds for the application of really tough sanctions against Tehran, to say nothing of the use of military force.

Great Powers' Strategic Juxtaposition.

One of the key conditions that enabled different countries with various interests to accept the package of agreements that form the Nuclear Nonproliferation Treaty is the subject matter contained in Article VI of the Treaty. In accordance with it, the states party to the Treaty undertake to "pursue negotiations in good faith on effective measures relating to cessation of the nuclear arms race at an early date and to nuclear disarmament, and on a Treaty on general and complete disarmament under strict and effective international control."[5]

As far as nuclear arms limitations and reductions implied by the first part of Article VI are concerned, the beginning of this process in the end of the 1960s and the following treaties until the signing of the third Strategic Arms Reduction Treaty (START-3) framework agreement in 1997 provided grounds for some optimism.

However, U.S. defense policy underwent significant changes at the end of 2000 and beginning of 2001. Washington announced its intention to withdraw from the Anti-Ballistic Missile (ABM) Treaty and adopted a new nuclear doctrine based on the deployment of a national BMD system and modernization of its strategic offensive arms, planning their employment in combination with high-precision conventional weapons, and also envisioning the use of nuclear weapons in preventive attacks against non-nuclear states.

The Bush administration justified its intention to discontinue strategic arms reduction talks with Russia, citing the end of ideological confrontation between the two countries and their steady progress towards strategic partnership (especially after 9/11). Washington proposed that each country develop its nuclear doctrine and program independently based on its own ideas of the national security threats it faced. But although it dismissed the arms control talks as a "Cold War" anachronism, Washington did not seem to feel that it was anachronistic enough to stop it and Moscow from keeping thousands of nuclear warheads aimed at each other and maintained in constant readiness for use (if only due to the lack of such a large number of targets in other countries).

Russia's determined support and the spirit of solidarity between the two countries following the 9/11 terrorist attacks led to the signing of the Strategic Offensive Reductions Treaty (SORT) in May 2002, which envisioned cutting strategic arms levels to 1,700-2,200 warheads. This new agreement was signed at the same time that the United States withdrew from the ABM Treaty and pulled out of START-2 and the START-3 Framework Agreements and the 1997 ABM delineation agreement. No counting rules or verification procedures for SORT were ever elaborated.

Overall, over the 2 decades following the end of the Cold War in 1991 (conclusion of START-1) and through to 2012 (the deadline for implementing SORT), the great powers, principally the United States and Russia, have reduced or plan to reduce their strategic and tactical nuclear warheads by about 80 percent, both in accordance with arms control treaties and on the basis of unilateral decisions.

This seems an impressive result, but there is still the question of whether the same will apply to the nuclear arms that still remain (around 10,000 combat-capable warheads in all the five nuclear powers taken together). Currently there are no further talks on more far-reaching nuclear arms reductions on the horizon. The great powers' open refusal to continue arms control talks is an unprecedented violation of Article VI of the NPT. Moves to openly bolster the role of nuclear weapons in defense policy and the repudiation of a number of past agreements are likewise flagrant violations of the Treaty spirit.

Sceptics and opponents of nuclear disarmament in Washington, Moscow, and other capitals deny the existence of any link between nuclear disarmament and nonproliferation. Supporters of arms control and reduction say, on the contrary, that more meaningful disarmament efforts by the nuclear powers would have had a significant impact on nuclear nonproliferation. Most of the non-nuclear-weapons states party to the NPT raise this argument at all the NPT review conferences and accuse the nuclear powers of not complying with their obligations under Article VI.

No doubt the incentives for states to acquire nuclear weapons are certainly a lot more varied and contradictory than the simple desire to imitate the nuclear powers. Most probably in the time the NPT has been in existence, Israel and South Africa's choice in favour of nuclear weapons had no link to the concept set out in Article VI of the Treaty. India's choice shows a clearer link because its decision to develop nuclear weapons was based not just on motives of international status and domestic prestige but also on its desire to deter China's increasing and unrestricted military, economic, and nuclear capability. Pakistan's decision to follow India's lead was mostly directed at countering India and thus was indirectly related to Article VI. Iraqi, North Korean, and Iranian programs obviously were not directly affected by the great powers' compliance with their NPT commitment.

However, a more thorough analysis shows that such a link did and still does exist, but it is far more complex and subtle. First of all, there is the general perception of the international security climate, in which all countries define their attitude towards nuclear weapons no matter what the concrete individual factors dictating this attitude at any given moment.

It is hardly just a coincidence that the biggest successes in enhancing the NPT system and regime happened at the same time as intensive nuclear disarmament talks and real reductions in nuclear weapons were taking place in 1987-97: the INF Treaty, START-1, START-2, the START-3 framework, the ABM delineation agreements, the Comprehensive Test Ban Treaty (CTBT), and unilateral reductions of tactical nuclear arms by the U.S. and the USSR/Russia. Add to this record some major non-nuclear treaties, foremost the conventional armed forces in Europe (CFE) and the CWC, this decade may be estimated as a "golden age" of disarmament. During the same period, around 40 new countries, including two of the nuclear powers, France and China, joined the NPT. The Treaty was indefinitely extended in 1995, and the IAEA Additional Protocol was drafted in 1997. Four countries abandoned their military nuclear programs or were forced to give them up through collective actions from outside (Brazil, Argentina, South Africa, and Iraq). Three countries that had nuclear weapons on their territory as a result of the break up of the Soviet Union joined the NPT as non-nuclear-weapons states after 2 years of negotiations (Ukraine, Belarus, and Kazakhstan). With 189 UN member states party to it, the NPT became an almost universal international agreement, with only three states (Israel, India, and Pakistan) remaining outside its framework.

If the great powers had followed a consistent policy of cutting back their nuclear arsenals and reducing the role of nuclear weapons in ensuring national and international security, the value of nuclear weapons as symbol of status, power, and prestige most likely would have decreased accordingly. Nuclear weapons popularity in the internal political life of many countries would also have declined.

Just as clearly, the directly opposite policy pursued by the great powers and by the three states that have not joined the NPT has, since the end of the 1990s, created a very fertile breeding ground for giving nuclear weapons greater appeal in the eyes of governments and public opinion in a growing number of countries. In fact, in contrast to optimistic expectations that set the background to nonproliferation during the 1990s, no treaty on nuclear disarmament was concluded or entered full legal force after the START-1 (signed in 1991 and joined by three post-soviet republics in 1994). The victims of this policy have been the START-2 and START-3 framework and delineation agreements, the CTBT, and the Fissile Material Cutoff Treaty (FMCT). As of now, there is no intention on the part of the United States and Russia to prolong START-1 after its expiration in 2009 or to provide SORT with counting rules and a verification system to make it a substantive treaty. This is perceived by most non-nuclear NPT member-states as a major failure to fulfil great powers' commitments.

Another point is that mutual nuclear deterrence of the United States and Russia has "frozen" hostile confrontation as the essence of their strategic relations (when thousands of nuclear warheads are targeting each other's territory and ready to be launched at any minute). It places strict limitations on developing the international cooperation between the great powers. The deadlock in nuclear disarmament talks only serves to fuel the mutual mistrust and suspicion of the political elites in these countries.

This applies more directly to nonproliferation, in particular to aspects such as sanctions against third countries, and reaching a common position in negotiations with third countries (e.g., the six-party talks with North Korea and the negotiations with Iran). It applies all the more directly to the possibility of joint military operations (as part of the PSI or in response to violations of IAEA safeguards agreements or plans to leave the NPT without valid grounds), and to the development of joint space warning systems and cooperative missile defense systems (which Russia and the United States agreed on in 1998 and 2002 respectively).

It is exactly in the context of mutual nuclear deterrence and the absence of further talks on nuclear arms reductions that the U.S. plan to deploy BMD sites in Central Europe against Iran is seen by Russia as a threat to its defense and security. This misperception and conflict have presently moved to the foreground of U.S.-Russian relations instead of cooperation on nonproliferation. In fact, in the context of mutual nuclear deterrence nonproliferation, steps of some nations may turn into a subject of major strategic controversy and a new round of arms race between the great powers.

The link between nuclear disarmament and nonproliferation is even more direct in some areas. This relates above all to the CTBT, signed in 1996 but not yet brought into force, and the FMCT, on which talks at the Geneva Disarmament Conference have entered a complete deadlock. Implementing these very important nuclear disarmament measures and having the great powers exert pressure to ensure that all of the NPT participants and the three "outsiders" join them would automatically create additional barriers to nuclear proliferation. If the United States had not withdrawn from the ABM Treaty and not blocked the CTBT and the FMCT, North Korea (and potentially Iran in the future) would have had not just one barrier but three to cross in its quest for nuclear weapons (the NPT, the CTBT, and the FMCT). This would have made their acquisition much more difficult and would have met with far tougher and more united resistance from the great powers, the UN Security Council, and the international community in general.

Finally, nonfulfilment of the obligations under Article VI of the NPT has become a bone of contention between the great powers, above all the United States, and many non-nuclear and fully law-abiding states party to the NPT. The latter consider it a violation of the understanding reached when the Treaty was indefinitely extended in 1995, and of the agreement on 13 points of nuclear disarmament reached at the NPT Review Conference in 2000. The fiasco of the Review Conference in 2005 showed just how deep these divisions go. This situation undermines the great powers' political capacity to advance a whole range of measures for bolstering the nonproliferation regime, including measures discussed at the 2005 conference.

These measures include making the 1997 IAEA Additional Protocol universal, introducing more stringent procedures and conditions for withdrawing from the NPT according to Article X.1, tightening export control rules and conditions through the Nuclear Suppliers Group (NSG), abandoning national nuclear fuel cycle programs in favour of international fuel cycle centers, giving a foundation in international law to the PSI, and so on. It is very difficult to impose these measures on the non-nuclear parties to the NPT, which already bear the main burden of restrictions and control systems under the Treaty's provisions, in a situation where the nuclear powers give themselves almost complete freedom of action in their military nuclear activities, in legal and contractual constraints, and in control and transparency.

The link between nuclear disarmament and nonproliferation can be formulated as follows: Fulfilling disarmament obligations in accordance with Article VI is not in itself a guarantee against nuclear proliferation given the diversity and complexity of the motives inciting countries to obtain nuclear weapons. Preventing proliferation would require numerous additional measures to strengthen and develop the NPT and its provisions and mechanisms. But nonfulfilment of the disarmament obligations contained in Article VI practically guarantees further nuclear proliferation and makes it extremely difficult to strengthen the nonproliferation regime and system. The only remaining option left open is a resort to armed force to settle problems, often outside the boundaries of international law. As the 2003 war in Iraq has shown, this "cure" can be worse than the "disease" and can have the opposite effect from that intended, including with regard to nuclear nonproliferation.

New Rules of Engagement on Nonproliferation.

The dynamics of U.S. and Russian interaction over nonproliferation issues provide abundant matter for learning lessons for the future and making recommendations for new rules of engagement for strengthening the nonproliferation regime and system throughout the world.

The **first** rule is that regime change and preventing nuclear proliferation should not be mixed. Placing the nature of the regime and the political relations with it above the interests of nonproliferation is short-sighted and ultimately counterproductive. Regimes change, and the great powers change their attitudes accordingly, and even the great powers themselves and their interests are not exempt from transformation. But nuclear technology and countries' nuclear ambitions usually stay, and what seemed harmless in the past can become a threat in the future. The United States made this mistake in its time with regard to the nuclear programs of Iran, Pakistan, and Iraq (during the Iran-Iraq war), and is perhaps repeating it today with India. The Soviet Union made the same mistake in the past with regard to China and North Korea, and could be doing it again now with regard to Iran.

Moreover, a subjective approach to nonproliferation issues makes it difficult for the great powers to coordinate a common policy, as they often have different and periodically changing allies and partners. This, in turn, weakens the role and capabilities of the UN Security Council, which is the only institution authorized by international law to take measures to enforce maintenance of the nuclear nonproliferation regime. The Security Council's passive stance either incites "threshold" countries to violate the NPT, or pushes the great powers into taking unilateral action outside the boundaries of international law.

The **second** rule is that external threats to a regime's survival can increase its desire to obtain nuclear weapons as the final means of self-preservation. Nonproliferation policy should be based on the idea that the threat to a regime's survival should come precisely from the desire to obtain nuclear weapons, and not the contrary — when obtaining nuclear weapons looks like the absolute guarantee of survival.

The **third** rule is the importance of not overestimating the capacity of external economic, political, and military pressure to enforce the nonproliferation regime. Priority should be given to diplomacy, with the IAEA playing the leading role.

The **fourth** rule is that, although countries, including the great powers, obviously have many foreign policy, economic, and military interests other than nonproliferation of WMD, there can be no continuing the current situation, in which the great powers officially declare that nonproliferation and the fight against international terrorism are the supreme security policy priorities; while at practical level, they pursue foreign, military, and economic policies based on completely different geopolitical and commercial interests. Even worse is when they act ostensibly in the name of nonproliferation to pursue these interests, thereby discrediting the very nonproliferation concept and undermining cooperation between the NPT parties (as was the case of the military operation in Iraq in 2003).

The **fifth** rule is the need to lower the level of competition between supplying powers by developing a collaborative project (such as an international consortium for nuclear fuel supplies), and by strengthening the rules of export control and creating a legally binding framework to govern this sector of international trade.

Relying on the above general rules of engagement, the two powers and their allies should implement some joint actions, directly addressed to nonproliferation problems and concerns. The first involves *raising the effectiveness of IAEA safeguards*, and requires several major steps:

- It is essential to ensure that all countries, especially countries carrying out nuclear activities of any kind, join the 1997 Additional Protocol on safeguards. A state's refusal to abide by the Additional Protocol should be seen as a "presumption of guilt" and be considered valid grounds for the imposition of sanctions.
- The nuclear states-parties to the NPT should encourage this process by signing the Additional Protocol themselves and applying it not only to their international cooperation but to the totality of their peaceful nuclear activities, including their nuclear fuel cycle activities (uranium enrichment and plutonium extraction). This will also help to improve the prospects for achieving the FMCT.
- The NSG should adopt a common guideline making joining the Additional Protocol an obligatory condition for receiving imports of nuclear materials, equipment, and technology.
- With regard to states which have joined the Additional Protocol, the IAEA should step up work to introduce the practice of integrated safeguards, which make safeguards more effective and also more economic and cost-effective.

- The scientific, technical, and financial base for the IAEA safeguards activities needs to be reinforced.

The second area of action for strengthening the mechanisms of the NPT involves *improving the export controls system*. In particular, this implies more intensive harmonization of national export control systems, creation within the NSG framework of a multilateral mechanism for exchanging information on the end-users and end uses of exported goods. Moreover, it is high time to start work on a new universal document (for example, a convention on export controls on nuclear materials and technology), which would delineate the obligations of states in this area and the obligatory accounts, methods for the control, and verification of this information, as well as procedures for examining violations detected and imposing sanctions, including referring the case to the UN Security Council. This is all the more necessary since it directly relates to the task of countering nuclear terrorism.

The third area of action for strengthening the NPT regime over the coming years involves introducing *strict formalities for and raising the political significance of procedures to withdraw from the Treaty*. The fact is that all NPT outsiders are nuclear states, and hence all other potential nuclear powers will have to withdraw from the Treaty in a legal way in line with its Article X. Although it is impossible to deprive them of this right, non-nuclear member-states should be denied an option of easy withdrawal to use the benefits of membership in the NPT for creating nuclear weapons.

The fourth area involves concluding and bringing into force a *number of additional multilateral agreements* that would help to bolster the NPT and create additional barriers to countries seeking to violate it or withdraw from it. This is related foremost to the CTBT and the treaty prohibiting the production of fissionable materials (above all weapons-grade uranium) for military purposes, the FMCT.

If the great powers are to gain a strong moral and political position to enforce the above steps, they must make *consistent progress towards fulfilling their nuclear disarmament obligations under Article VI of the NPT*. This is all the more necessary in that the closer cooperation that the great powers need to develop in order to respond to new threats and challenges is impossible so long as they remain stuck in Cold War-era mutual nuclear deterrence. This constitutes the fifth area for action to strengthen the NPT, and in this area the following specific steps are a priority:

- In the short term, the five nuclear powers — the United States, Russia, the United Kingdom, France, and China — should reduce the priority given to nuclear weapons in their national security strategies, and this conceptual decrease in priority should be reflected in their main doctrines and programs. An important measure is that these five countries should also bind themselves without reservation to a policy of no-first-use of nuclear weapons against any state that is party to the NPT.

- The United States and Russia should move rapidly to agree on verification procedures and warhead counting rules in implementing the SORT of 2002. The conflict over the planned U.S. deployment of BMD sites in Poland and the Czech Republic should be settled by an agreement on joint use of the radar in Azerbaijan (and possibly in Ukraine and the

Czech Republic) and on nondeployment of U.S. antimissile interceptors in Poland until and unless Iran tests medium-range ballistic missiles of its own. In the meantime the infrastructure of the base in Poland may be built.

- The two sides should start preparation for and begin negotiations on SORT-2 with the aim of reducing strategic nuclear arms to around 1,000-1,200 warheads by 2017, and should agree on verified lowering of their level of launch-readiness through various technical and operational methods.
- Moves should be made to expand objectives and technologies for joint reaction to missile threats. With this aim in mind, the Moscow Centre for data exchange on the launches of missiles and space-launchers should be revived, and in the mid-term its functions should be further developed and expanded to cover other links in the missile early-warning and information systems.
- Steps should be taken to activate dialogue on long-term development of a joint strategic missile defense system in accordance with U.S.-Russian official obligations of May 2002. Joint development of Russian-NATO theater BMD should proceed in advance of strategic defense and serve as its starting point and test field.
- The main powers involved in space programmes should begin negotiating a Code of Conduct in outer space (in the medium term) to be followed by negotiations on preventing a race in space weapons (in the long term). Eventually MTCR should be turned into a legally binding international convention.

- Multilateral nuclear consultations should begin on involving the United Kingdom, France, and China in nuclear arms reductions and on adopting some control and confidence-building measures.
- The participants in the PSI should develop procedures for keeping the Security Council rapidly informed on their plans and activities. Russia and other states should intensify their cooperation within the PSI framework. Action to prevent the illicit transfers of WMD, their delivery means, and related materials, including through inspecting cargoes, is not only acceptable but necessary so long as the provisions of international law are respected.

States that are loyal to the NPT should receive material incentives in the form, above all, of guaranteed access to the products and services of the international nuclear fuel cycle centres which are proposed to be developed over the medium term, and in the long term, they should be involved in developing safe new-generation nuclear technologies and materials.

The wide-ranging spectrum of new rules of engagement and concrete measures proposed for strengthening the NPT provisions and mechanisms implies the need for the United States and Russia to seriously rethink their current policies. If the necessary change in thinking takes place, it will be possible to resolve economic, military, technical, and other matters with time, despite their many complexities.

ENDNOTES - CHAPTER 5

1. Besides nuclear, chemical, and biological weapons, the fourth type of WMD is a radiological weapon. It is usually given much lower priority since its proliferation is virtually impossible to prevent, but the consequences of its potential use are much easier to contain than with the other three types.

2. This chapter borrows some ideas from Alexey Arbatov and Vladimir Dvorkin, *Beyond Nuclear Deterrence: Transforming the U.S.-Russian Equation*, Washington, DC: Carnegie Endowment for International Peace, 2006; Alexei Arbatov, ed., *At the Nuclear Threshold: The Lessons of North Korea and Iran for the Nuclear Non-Proliferation Regime*, Moscow, Russia: Carnegie Endowment for International Peace, 2007; Alexei Arbatov and Vladimir Dvorkin, eds., *Nuclear Weapons After the Cold War*, Moscow, Russia: Carnegie Endowment for International Peace, 2006 (in Russian). An English version will be published in 2008 by the Carnegie Endowment for International Peace, Washington, DC.

3. Russian Federation President Vladimir Putin, interview by the British Television and Radio Corporation (BBC), June 22, 2003, available from *www.kremlin.ru*, accessed December 30, 2004.

4. The Rosatom Nuclear Energy State Corporation is a State Corporation in Russia, the regulatory body of the Russian nuclear complex. It is comparable in function to the U.S. Nuclear Regulatory Commission. It is headquartered in Moscow, Russia.

5. "Nuclear Non-Proliferation Treaty," in Vladimir Orlov, ed., *Yadernoye nerasprostraneniye*, Vol. 2, Moscow, Russia: PIR-Center, 2002, pp. 26–27.

CHAPTER 6

PROSPECTS FOR RUSSO-AMERICAN COOPERATION IN HALTING NUCLEAR PROLIFERATION

Stephen J. Blank

Introduction.

In view of Iran's continuing defiance of the United Nations (UN) on its nuclear program, North Korea's retention of its nuclear weapons, the continuing existence of A. Q. Khan's network (albeit without Khan's supervision), and the global proliferation of cruise missiles, the urgent need for Russo-American cooperation on proliferation remains obvious.[1] In the wake of the progress achieved during 2007 regarding North Korea's nuclear program, and the December 2007 National Intelligence Estimate (NIE) saying that the U.S. intelligence community judges with "high confidence" that Iranian military entities have not resumed the program under government direction to develop nuclear weapons and that it stopped the program in 2003, we could easily argue that proliferation is no longer so urgent a threat or that Russo-American cooperation against that threat is also no longer urgent or even necessary.[2] The NIE also assesses with moderate confidence that if Iran sought to produce highly enriched uranium (HEU), it would do so through covert sites as it appears to have been actively trying to do through 2003 but has apparently not resumed since. And it judges with high confidence that Iran will be technically incapable of producing and reprocessing sufficient plutonium for a weapon before 2015.[3] However such an argument about Russo-American cooperation would be tragically and perhaps even lethally myopic for the following reasons:

First, as Director of National Intelligence (DNI) J. Michael McConnell recently testified, the NIE stated only its assessment that Iran had halted weaponization and warhead design along with military uranium conversion and enrichment–related activities. Declared enrichment activities that facilitate production of fissile material, which is the most difficult challenge in nuclear production, continue. So, too, do Iran's efforts to perfect long-range ballistic missiles that can reach Europe, Russia, and even America.[4] These missiles have recently, and finally, evoked even Moscow's dismay.[5] Moscow should also remember that, as Duncan Lennox wrote in 2006, "No nation has developed intermediate (over 1,000Km) range ballistic missiles [IRBMs] without the intention of fitting them with nuclear warheads."[6] And recently Foreign Minister Sergei Lavrov publicly urged Iran to desist from uranium enrichment as he saw no economic need for continuing with it. That argument represented a new point in Russia's posture vis-à-vis Iran.[7] Therefore, there is good reason for concern about Tehran's intentions, and both the NIE and the DNI assert that Iran is at a minimum keeping open the option of developing nuclear weapons.[8]

Similarly , the DNI assessed with moderate confidence (and the reality to date would bear this out) that it will be difficult to persuade Iranian leaders to forego eventual development of nuclear weapons since they see so many links between developing those weapons and attaining Iran's key national security and foreign policy objectives.[9] Therefore, even if Iran is less inclined to develop nuclear weapons than was previously assumed, the NIE's assessment attributed the halt in the weapons program primarily to international pressure. For those reasons, such pressure is likely to continue to deter or dissuade Iran from going the nuclear weapons route. Indeed, the NIE implies that this pressure might be the most effective way to deter or dissuade Iran from going nuclear. Second, this pressure is essential because Iran is still developing centrifuges.[10] Indeed, since the NIE, we have learned that it is now testing advanced centrifuges.[11] And in April 2008 it announced that it was tripling the number of its centrifuges to 9,000. We can be skeptical of such announcements, but any acceleration of Iranian nuclear capability is a matter of utmost danger.[12]

The DNI further observed that despite the halt in weaponization and warhead design in 2003, Iran resumed its declared centrifuge enrichment activities in January 2006. Furthermore, even if one assesses that Iran may not have a weapons capability by 2010 or 2015, the DNI's assessment about the halted Iranian programs is sobering enough to warrant continued pressure on Iran. The DNI stated that,

> We judge with high confidence that in fall 2003, Tehran halted its nuclear weapons design and weaponization activities, as well as its covert military uranium conversion and enrichment activities, for at least several years. Because of intelligence gaps, DOE [Department of Energy] and the NIC [National Intelligence Council] assess with only moderate confidence that all such activities were halted. We assess with moderate confidence that Tehran had not restarted those activities as of mid-2007, but since they comprised an unannounced secret effort which Iran attempted to hide, we do not know if these activities have been restarted.[13]

In this light, the reasons for Russo-American cooperation on halting Iranian and other proliferation

171

remain highly relevant. As high-ranking Russian defense officials have told U.S. analysts, if Iran gets 3,000 centrifuges, as the International Atomic Energy Agency (IAEA) now admits Iran has, it could have the required nuclear material for a bomb in 18 months.[14] Since Iran's centrifuge program is continuing along with uranium enrichment which is critical to making a bomb, it does not seem that Iran has stopped its quest even if its weapons designs have stopped. Indeed, the resumption of enrichment in 2006 and Iran's continuing defiance of the UN and international community suggests very strongly that Tehran is building a bomb. Furthermore, in building a bomb, the hard part is developing the bomb, i.e., enrichment, not the warhead.[15] Thus Iran's seeming restraint in desisting from progress on building the warhead is of relatively little importance. We might remember that it only took 3 weeks from the first American tests at Alamogordo, New Mexico, in July 1945 to the actual dropping of the atomic bomb on Hiroshima and Nagasaki, Japan, in August 1945. As Secretary of Defense Robert Gates has emphasized, Iran's ongoing missile program, which now includes a 2,000 Km IRBM (the *Ashura*, the *Qadr-1*, and alleged smart bombs), makes little or no strategic or economic sense if it is not to carry nuclear warheads.[16]

Therefore, we cannot be too confident that Iran has really stopped its program for attaining a nuclear bomb, especially inasmuch as the NIE concedes that the most likely route for Iran is through centrifuge enrichment, a program that makes no sense if it is for civilian energy given Iran's natural energy endowment.[17] Indeed, as critics of the NIE point out, there is no fundamental difference between the civilian and military nuclear program, and the former has always been considered the main threat for proliferation.[18] Third, the NIE also admits the continuation of Iran's programs for uranium enrichment, which likewise make little or no economic sense given its natural energy endowment.[19]

Fourth, while the NIE assesses with moderate confidence that it will be difficult to persuade Iran's leaders to forego nuclear weapons development, such a decision is easily and inherently reversible.[20] Fifth, the NIE confirms that Iran lied to the international community and IAEA and successfully concealed a military nuclear program from 1985-2003 and retains the capacity to resume it, leading to a weapon in 5 years' time.[21] Sixth, the IAEA, not an organization known for a priori hostility to Iran, remains more skeptical than does the NIE concerning Iran's capabilities and intentions.[22] Seventh, as Israeli expert Gerald Steinberg observes,

> Israeli analysts have long warned their U.S. counterparts about the potential for a parallel "black" Iranian weapons program, based on a small nuclear reactor producing plutonium, and following the North Korean model. Indeed, Iran is known to be constructing just such a reactor at Arak, leaving room for another undetected facility.[23]

Eighth, in November-December, 2007 it began to appear that North Korea may be backtracking on its treaty obligations to list all of its nuclear facilities and disable them by the end of 2007. Indeed, it missed that deadline.[24] Certainly North Korea is persisting with the development of nuclear-capable intercontinental ballistic missiles (ICBMs) as well as short-range ballistic missiles (SRBMs) and intermediate or medium range solid fuel missiles, and Washington remains uncertain as to its full commitment to de-nuclearization despite

Chinese claims that the Yongbyon nuclear facilities had been almost completely dismantled by the end of 2007.[25] Likewise Secretary Gates has stated that North Korea transferred a missile with a 2500Km range to Iran, so presumably other deals and technology transfers, including perhaps bomb-making capabilities, are taking place.[26] Worse yet, North Korea has now announced that it has said all that it is prepared to say about its nuclear program—thereby refusing to discuss the possibility of a covert uranium program to manufacture nuclear weapons. And it has announced that it will boost its war deterrent, a term that has often been used to signify its nuclear weapons program.[27] As a result, there is considerable and possibly growing concern in Washington, if not elsewhere, that the entire 2007 agreement is in danger and that North Korea will not, under any circumstances, give up its nuclear weapons or the program for building them. While great strides have been made in dismantling the nuclear reactor at Yongbyon, the administration insists on a full accounting of all the elements of North Korea's nuclear program before going forward. Especially North Korea must account for its plutonium installations and the amount of weapons-grade material it has; and disclose any nuclear material it may have passed on to third parties, the number of warheads it has, and the purchase of aluminum tubes that could be used for converting uranium gas into nuclear fuel.[28]

So even if the NIE is correct—and here we should remember that it is only an estimate, not a conclusion, and one hedged with numerous reservations concerning the level of confidence its authors have in different aspects of Iran's intentions and capabilities—there is no reason for retreating from the quest for Russo-American cooperation (and also Chinese participation in that process) against proliferation. This is especially true if one takes at face value the numerous statements by government officials and leading military figures about the threat to Russia from proliferation and nuclear weapons. Indeed, given the salience attached by Russia's military and government to that threat, as well as the importance of that threat to American policymakers, such cooperation is in both countries' highest interest.[29]

The Current Situation in U.S.-Russia Relations.

Therefore the urgency of bilateral U.S.-Russian cooperation on proliferation threats (if not trilateral or multilateral cooperation with China and the European Union [EU]) has not abated. Indeed, the fact that in 2008 both the United States and Russia underwent presidential successions creates possibilities for reviewing the entire agenda of U.S.-Russian relations with a view toward developing further cooperation. That agenda is currently in a state of serious disrepair to the extent that pundits and even Russian officials openly warn about a revival of the old Cold War antagonism.[30] Likewise, on both sides military moves that are currently underway look ever more like a response to perceived military threats of the other side.[31] And there are signs of a growing disposition to resort to the postures and perceptions of nuclear enmity that disfigured world politics for almost 50 years and raised as well the threat of nuclear proliferation.[32]

For example, in his press conference before the annual G-8 conference in Heiligendam, Germany in June 2008, Russian President Vladimir Putin told reporters that Russia and the West were returning to the Cold War and added that,

Of course we will return to those times. And it is clear
that if part of the United States' nuclear capability
is situated in Europe and that our military experts
consider that they represent a potential threat then we
will have to take appropriate retaliatory steps. What
steps? Of course we must have new targets in Europe.
And determining precisely which means will be used
to destroy the installations that our experts believe
represent a potential threat for the Russian Federation
is a matter of technology. Ballistic or cruise missiles or
a completely new system. I repeat that it is a matter of
technology.[33]

Since then some Russian ambassadors and generals
are calling for the positioning of new missiles in
Belarus whereby they can then fulfill this threat of
targeting Europe.[34] But such possibilities for future
nuclear rivalry are equally potentially present on the
American side. Thus the recent Report of the Defense
Science Board on Nuclear Capabilities stated openly
that nuclear reductions agreed to in the Moscow treaty
of 2002 and recommended in the Nuclear Posture
Review (NPR) of 2001 pointed to a new and benign
strategic relationship with Russia after the end of
the Cold War and the desire to forge a new bilateral
strategic relationship that no longer was based on the
principles of Mutual Assured Destruction (MAD). This
presumption may not be as justified today as it was in
the past.

Today, the Report observes, that presumption
of a new benign strategic relationship with Russia is
increasingly open to doubt. Certainly the Russian
military and government seem to want to return to
MAD, to a relationship based on deterrence and the
starting presupposition of an adversarial relationship
on strategic nuclear issues with America, and to a

176

demand for Russian nuclear parity with America, even though doing so would destroy the foundations of Russian security because the Russian economy cannot afford to keep pace with U.S. nuclear and conventional capabilities.[35] This U.S. doubt about Russian intentions, written by the Defense Science Board even before the recent calls for parity and for continuing with a MAD relationship, appears to be heading in an analogous direction by observing that, "Although United States relations with Russia are considered relatively benign at the moment [December 2006], Russia retains the capacity to destroy the United States in 30 minutes or less." Moreover, Moscow's reliance on nuclear weapons to compensate for a weakened conventional military has led it to emphasize nuclear weapons for purposes of maintaining superpower status, deterrence, and potentially warfighting. Russia's regression from democracy and rivalry with America over European and Commonwealth of Independent States (CIS) security, as well as Iraq, Iran, and Central Asia (other issues may well be added since then to the mix — author) suggest that the assessment of 2003 that nothing had changed since 2001 to justify revising the NPR's presumption of a benign strategic relationship with Russia needs to be revised.[36]

Therefore the Report recommends the creation of a permanently standing assessment Red Team "to continuously assess the range of emerging and plausible nuclear capabilities that can threaten the United States and its allies and friends with potentially catastrophic consequences."[37] This team would monitor Russian, Chinese, and North Korean developments because,

Despite the desire for improved relations with Russia, the direction, scope, and pace of the evolution of U.S.

177

capabilities must be based on a realistic recognition that the United States and Russia are not yet the reliable, trusted friends needed for the United States to depart from a commitment to a robust nuclear deterrent. Intentions can change overnight; capabilities cannot.[38]

Other examples of a growing wariness about Russian intentions can also be cited.[39] Thus there is a real danger that these perceptions can grow on both sides into self-fulfilling threat perceptions that will drive conventional and nuclear defense acquisitions, and foreign policy decisions as well, until they influence formal doctrinal and strategic pronouncements.

Under these circumstances, efforts to retrieve a working consensus on any major security issue appear quite unpromising. This unhappy situation is no less visible at present with regard to issues of nuclear proliferation (the most strategic and immediately urgent form of proliferation) as it is to other issues. And as a result of the linkage between the missile and nuclear threat from Iran with the issue of placing missile defenses in Poland and the Czech Republic, the proliferation problem has now become tied to both sides' strategic competition in Europe and Asia and the threat of a breakdown of both the arms control and proliferation regimes inherited from the past. As Lavrov has said,

The first problem is that we differ in our assessment of the threat of missile proliferation which is the target of the global system of anti-missile defense. . . . We have agreed that experts will focus on working out a common understanding of the present threat. And the second problem is that for the joint work of Russian and American experts to become more effective, it is necessary to "freeze" the new plan for the deployment of the new installations in Europe.[40]

Thus, for example, despite mounting concern over the fate of the six-party accords on North Korea, Moscow claims to be unconcerned by the delays in North Korea's de-nuclearization.[41] In this context, the NIE will certainly be used by Russia to cast further doubt on the veracity and accuracy of U.S. threat perceptions and ensuing justifications for these components of a European missile defense system. Indeed, Lavrov used the NIE's findings to say that Russia has no evidence that Iran was conducting research for a nuclear military program before or after 2003 as Washington had previously asserted.[42] The NIE thus provides further justification for Russia to pursue a policy toward Iran that seems to be driven more by anti-Americanism and desire for great power standing and allies in the Middle East than by a realistic assessment of Iran's potential threat.[43] Even though Moscow now urges Iran to cease enrichment and heed the mandate of the IAEA, it still falsely claims that Tehran is undertaking such cooperation. Thus Russia and Iran are, according to President Putin, stepping up cooperation; Lavrov reportedly offered Iran a strategic partnership in November 2007 that would include lifting of all sanctions and prevention of new ones, and a treaty on arms sales plus cooperation in economics, energy, and even space. Furthermore, such partnership would mean that Russia views any encroachment on Iran's interests as constituting an encroachment upon its own interests.[44]

Despite Russian denials, there is apparently a plan to upgrade Russian arms sales to Iran of S-300 anti-air missile defense systems to make any foreign air strikes on Iran more difficult. Meanwhile it has begun sending nuclear fuel to the reactor at Bushehr as part of its policy to gain nuclear footholds throughout the Middle East, claiming that the fact that Iran is buying this fuel and is supposed to return spent fuel to Russia shows that Iran has no "objective need" for generating its own nuclear fuel. Even so, Iran merely pockets the fuel and moves forward.[45] Indeed, Iran's Foreign Ministry lauded Russia and China for creating splits between the United States and the Europeans on one side and Russia and China on the other.[46]

Russia's policymakers seem to have decided to use support for Iran as a kind of equivalent of a Swiss army knife, i.e., as a policy response that can answer any policy from the West that it does not like. Thus Russia privately threatened Washington and the North Atlantic Treaty Organization (NATO) that if they went ahead with a Membership Action Plan (MAP) for Ukraine at the 2006 NATO Riga summit, it would drastically retaliate, including arming Iran against the United States. Conversely, if Washington suspended the offer of membership, Russia might then become much more friendly on the Iranian issue.[47] This example underscores the fundamentally shortsighted and self-seeking Russian policy towards Iran and towards proliferation threats more generally. Leon Aron recently captured the evolution of Moscow's Iranian policy,

> The evolution of Moscow's Iran policy is particularly troubling. Until about a year ago, the Moscow-Tehran quid pro quo was straightforward. Russia defended Iran in the U.N.'s Security Council, while Iran refrained from fomenting fundamentalism and terrorism in Central Asia and the Russian North Caucasus, and spent billions of dollars on Russian nuclear energy technology and military hardware, including mobile air defense missiles, fighter jets, and tanks (At the request of the U.S. Boris Yeltsin suspended arms sales to Iran in 1995). Then

180

Russia's strategy changed from moneymaking, influence peddling, and diplomatic arbitration to a far riskier brinksmanship in pursuit of a potentially enormous prize. The longer Moscow resists effective sanctions against an Iran that continues to enrich uranium—and thus to keep the bomb option open and available at the time of its choosing—the greater the likelihood of the situation's deteriorating, through a series of very probable miscalculations by both the U.S. and Iran, toward a full-blown crisis with a likely military solution. As Iran's patron, Moscow would be indispensable to any settlement of such a conflict as was the Soviet Union when it sponsored Egypt in the 1973 Yom Kippur War. And through that settlement it would get its prize. In one fell swoop, Russia could fulfill major strategic goals: to reoccupy the Soviet Union' position as a key player in the Middle East and the only viable counterbalance to the U.S. in the region; to keep oil prices at today's astronomic levels for as long as possible by feeding the fears of a military strike against Iran (and see them go as far as $120-$130 a barrel and likely higher if Iran blocks the Strait of Hormuz and disrupts the flow of oil from the Persian Gulf) and to use the West to prevent the emergence of a nuclear-armed Iran a few hundred miles from Russia's borders.[48]

The Reasons for Cooperation.

Nevertheless, and perhaps directly because of Moscow's self-seeking myopia, the effort to forge a viable and durable consensus between Moscow and Washington regarding nuclear proliferation is as urgent as ever. Despite the NIE, there are several reasons why this is the case apart from the obvious one that Iranian and North Korean nuclear and conventional missiles as well as horizontal and vertical proliferation elsewhere in Asia, e.g., the Middle East and South Asia, threaten international security as a whole as well as the vital interests of both Russia and America. Indeed, not even this seemingly obvious statement resonates in Moscow as it does among U.S. policymakers as Lavrov's remarks indicate. While proliferation certainly is perceived in Europe as it is in America, a deeper and more objective understanding of Russia's genuine national interests suggests that Moscow's current assessment may be misconceived.

Certainly no objective assessment of Russian national security should overlook the seriousness of the threat posed by terrorists who might gain access to Russian nuclear materials or even weapons. To be sure, Russian officials periodically invoke this threat.[49] But none of them expresses the seriousness of purpose captured by Gordon Hahn in his recent analysis of the threat posed by Islamic terrorists. As he writes,

> Proliferation specialists are nearly unanimous in regarding security at Russia's WMD [weapons of mass destruction] sites as woefully insufficient, underfunded (including underpaid scientists and other workers), and weakened by corruption and a lax security culture. . . . [T]he already mentioned June 2004 terrorist attack against the MVD building in Ingushetiya showed that Muslim terrorists are capable of successfully seizing sensitive objects. However, there is no need to actually seize a site. Three or four consignments of nuclear weapons are transported by rail across Russian territory every month. Also there is no need for such a massive assault or high-profile seizure, which would surely set Russian forces and [the] international community on the terrorists' trail. Using a "micro" approach, exploiting widespread corruption and lax work on security cultures to access small amounts of material at Russia's many WMD sites, could garner terrorists sufficient materials for a damaging attack such as one utilizing a "dirty bomb."[50]

Furthermore, Russian sources confirm that terrorists have carried out reconnaissance on Russian nuclear sites and transport trains. Nearly 100 trespassers were caught in 2004 at restricted areas. In 2003 there were at least 12 reported cases of trafficking in nuclear, radiological, and dual-use materials originating at a Russian site. And similar incidents were reported in 2004-05.[51] And then there are the numerous reports of smuggling from Russia to other states on its poorly guarded border.[52] Indeed, in 2007 alone Russia reported foiling 120 nuclear smuggling attempts.[53] The recent case where a Russian man was caught smuggling weapons-grade uranium from Russia into Georgia, but where Moscow refused to cooperate with the investigation, exemplifies both the scale and nature of the problem and the ambivalence of Russian authorities that hinders effective responses to the threat of such smuggling.[54]

Such ambivalence is decidedly not the case in Europe. For example, the 2003 European Security Strategy of the EU openly states that, "Proliferation of weapons of mass destruction is potentially the greatest threat to our security." It goes on to highlight the role of the Middle East as a potential flashpoint and the possibility that advanced biological and/or chemical weapons can also pose greater threats to security than previously was the case.[55] Indeed, in the Iranian case, the urgency of stopping nuclear proliferation is ever more compelling because Iran believes it can stonewall negotiators and because it appears that privately many key European political figures including the EU's Foreign policy *supremo*, Javier Solana, and former French President Jacques Chirac, are resigned to Iran acquiring nuclear weapons.[56] In the North Korean case, by contrast, nobody supports the idea of North Korea remaining a nuclear power. There are also the increased dangers of Iran developing an indigenous space capability; of North Korea continuing to proliferate missile if not nuclear technology to Iran, Syria, and other states, e.g., Myanmar (which also evidently benefits from the transfer of nuclear technology from Russia); and the continuing threat of Iranian-sponsored missile proliferation. These trends underscore a murky triangular relationship between Pyongyang, Damascus, and Tehran.[57]

Admittedly Moscow seems unwilling to accept the significance of these trends for its own security and to draw the required conclusions despite its numerous invocations of the threat posed by nuclear proliferation. President Putin recently observed that Russia had no certain proof of Iran developing a nuclear program and his government has repeatedly indicated its intention (along with China) to block any further effort to impose sanctions on Iran or use force against it.[58] Instead Moscow insists that only the IAEA, which Iran has repeatedly and successfully stonewalled and deceived, should deal with Iran's nuclear program despite the abundant evidence of its inability to monitor that program.[59] Notwithstanding this fact, Russia's consistent line has been that the IAEA should be the only agency that pressures Iran, and that this pressure should only aim at inducing Iran to follow the IAEA's guidelines and requirements.[60] The experience of the IAEA in Iraq suggests that Moscow's and Beijing's argument that it alone should monitor Iranian nuclear activities amounts essentially to an abdication of responsibility. Iraqi scientist Khidir Hamza noted that "the understanding that gradually emerged from a closer relationship to the IAEA was how weak and manipulated the agency was."[61] Further, if an inspector came to be perceived as too aggressive or antagonistic, few states would let him inspect their facilities. "Overall, the IAEA proved extremely useful to the Iraqi weapons program in obtaining nuclear technology."[62]

Thus the Iranian issue highlights Moscow's divergences from Washington over proliferation as did the North Korean issue where Moscow achieved a reputation for being the most sympathetic of the negotiating parties to North Korea's position.[63] Nonetheless, despite this highly discouraging situation, a robust dialogue with Moscow (and Beijing) over proliferation is essential. That dialogue is essential not just because Russia has so many nuclear bombs and so much nuclear and fissile material that may conceivably become a target for proliferators; even if Russia is obstructing U.S. policies against proliferation, without that dialogue America has literally no option with which it can successfully stop, dissuade, or deter proliferators other than the unilateral use of pressure culminating in force. And we have seen how difficult it is to rally support for such a course of action and how unsatisfying an option or result that is. Indeed, in many quarters that approach has come to be seen as fundamentally illegitimate. Moreover, as the recent North Korean example and the previous record of 1987-96 show, cooperation is by no means impossible. Nor has bilateral cooperation completely stopped. Indeed, despite the growing enmity in East-West relations, substantive programs in both arms control and proliferation cooperation are currently taking place between Washington and Moscow. These programs include but go beyond the Cooperative Threat Reduction program (CTRP) that is de-nuclearizing no longer usable Russian weapons and sites and the cleanup of chemical weapons sites.[64] Thus both sides signed a recent agreement on enriched uranium.[65] Another reason for the necessity of dialogue is that otherwise the Russian military's and government's relative impermeability to outside influences will lead it back into the hermetic shell that characterized much of Russia's Cold War approach.[66] As we have seen above, movement in that direction has already begun.

This dialogue must, *inter alia*, bring home to Russia and China just how isolated they are on the contemporary issues of proliferation, and how much of a threat it poses to them. There is no doubt that the EU sees proliferation much as the United States does (as its 2003 Security Strategy indicates). Therefore, in any such dialogue, it is more likely than not that the EU or most of it will adopt positions closer to Washington than to Moscow.

The Urgency of a Growing Proliferation Threat.

The growing urgency of the proliferation threat is therefore the first, and arguably the most, compelling reason for restoring Russo-American cooperation with regard to all forms of proliferation and especially nuclear proliferation. An estimated 40 states now have a nuclear capacity, and ever more governments are seeking it. Thanks to Iran's increasingly undisguised military nuclear program and conventional rearmament, 13 Sunni Arab nations are seeking some form of nuclear power.[67] Moreover, Russia is ready, willing, and able to provide many of them with nuclear reactors and know-how.[68] That fact alone should galvanize efforts to reach out to Russia to forestall further proliferation in the Middle East. The implications of both a potential nuclear drive throughout the Middle East at a time of profound instability and accompanying, ongoing conventional rearmament of local states and nonstate and terrorist movements are all too obviously negative, or should be, for both Russia and America.

Certainly the prospect of states like Turkey, which may now be friendly to Russia but has a history of troubled ties to it, going nuclear should not be welcome to Russia. Yet there are signs that Turkey, among others, is hearing the siren call of nuclear power in response to the Iranian threat.[69] After all, Turkey has long lived in the shadow of a growing Iranian missile threat.[70] Furthermore, Middle Eastern states which are participating in the current arms race like Israel and Iran are developing an indigenous space reconnaissance capability that could then lead to development of space-traversing or space-based weapons or Command, Control, Communications, Computers, Intelligence, Surveillance, and Reconnaissance (C4ISR) capabilities, thereby adding a new dimension to regional tensions and threats.[71] Given Russian opposition to further militarization or weaponization of space, one would logically expect it to manifest more concern about these developments rather than abetting them as it has done in Iran's case.[72]

Adding to the urgency of this region's proliferation potential is that it is again proliferators who are now beginning to conduct so-called secondary or tertiary proliferation whereby states who are themselves proliferators, like Pakistan and North Korea, are evidently selling reactor technology, e.g., to Syria. Historically, the only way to arrest such proliferation in the Middle East has been through unilateral acts of force such as Israel's attack on Osirak in 1981, its demolition of the Syrian reactor in September 2007, and most obviously the U.S. invasion of Iraq. Whereas Israel's raids at least bought time for it and the world with regard to Iraqi and possibly Syrian proliferation, the U.S. adventure in Iraq has been an unmitigated fiasco for U.S. policy and may have stimulated Iran and North Korea, if not others, to move faster towards nuclear capability.

Beyond these facts, the technological improvements that are already being made to both ballistic and cruise missiles should evoke much more concern from the established great powers. Indeed, Dennis Gormley, a leading expert, talks of an "epidemic" of cruise missile proliferation.[73] Meanwhile technological improvements to missiles also facilitate an enhanced nuclear and missile proliferation threat. As Lennox wrote in 2006,

> Solid-propelled ballistic missiles are beginning to replace the liquid propellant weapons, as solid propellants can be prepared for launch in minutes, not hours, and do not require the ten or more support vehicles associated with liquid propellants. Low-cost multiple-launch, unguided rocket systems are being upgraded with guidance and control systems, to make more accurate short-range ballistic missiles (SRBMs). There are three new countries reported to be planning or developing solid-propellant submarine launched ballistic missiles (SLBM): these are India, Iran, and Pakistan. If we add to this list the increasing number of cruise missile development programs, with ranges in excess of 150Km, then we need to think carefully about the threat that could be posed by ship-launched missiles.[74]

Lennox also points out that Russia, India, Israel, China, Iran, and the United States are all developing SRBMs with the capability to maneuver in both the boost and terminal phases making interception and prediction of the impact point even more difficult. Research in America and Russia also aims to provide reentry vehicles (RVs) for ICBMs with similar capabilities. When one juxtaposes these trends to improvements in cruise missile capabilities, especially at high altitudes and high speeds and including the introduction of ramjet powered missiles, then ballistic and cruise missiles are coming closer together in terms of capabilities. Once the multiple staging techniques for these weapons are mastered, their ranges could dramatically increase. Since it is likely that the requisite technology or know-how will migrate abroad, countries like India, Iran, North Korea, and Pakistan could have missiles with ranges of 6-10,000 Km by 2015. Similarly, developments in RV capability will allow those kinds of launches to resemble satellite launches. And since all these countries are developing space launch vehicles (SLVs), their missile launches could evade detection and be mistaken for regular peaceful satellite launches.[75] For example, satellite photos recently revealed the existence of a secret Iranian base about 230Km southeast of Tehran where Iran is building its long-range (6000Km) missiles. And the published accounts of this base strongly suggest that Iran is emulating North Korea's path of pursuing a space program that facilitates the acquisition of expertise in long-range missile technology.[76]

Other reasons for concern about cruise missiles relate to developments like the Ukrainian revelation in 2005 of illicit missile transfers of the Kh-55 cruise missile, a long-range nuclear-capable cruise missile (NATO designation AS-15 *Kent*) to Iran and China, and the Indo-Russian joint *Brahmos* project. The Kh-55 has a range of 2-300Km at subsonic speed with high precision, and represented Irano-Chinese access to a higher level of technological sophistication than was previously the case. The *Brahmos* (PJ-10) is a supersonic anti-ship ramjet-powered cruise missile and has a 300Km range and identical configuration for land-sea, and sub-sea launching platforms.[77] The spread of these systems and the fact that countries as diverse as Sweden, France, China, and Taiwan were working on advanced cruise missiles in 2005, underscore the porosity of existing anti-proliferation regimes, including the Missile Technology Control Regime (MTCR), and the ensuing rising threat from missile proliferation which has continued without letup since 2005.[78]

Furthermore Gormley's evidence of trends in cruise missiles proliferation and improvements to them underscores the danger of missile and nuclear proliferation from another angle. According to his evidence, "signs of a missile contagion abound."

Pakistan surprised the world by test launching *Tomahawk* look-alike cruise missiles. India, together with Russia, is developing the *Brahmos* supersonic cruise missile, which will have the capability to strike targets at sea or over land to a range of 290 kilometers. In East Asia, China, Taiwan, and South Korea are rushing to develop and deploy new Land Attack Cruise Missiles (LACMs) with ranges of 1,000Km or more, while Japan is contemplating the development of a LACM for "preemptive" strikes against enemy missile bases. In the Middle East, Israel was once the sole country possessing LACMs, but now Iran appears to be pursuing cruise missile programs for both land and sea attack. Iran has also provided the terrorist group Hezbollah with unmanned aerial vehicles (UAVs) and sophisticated anti-ship cruise missiles, one of which severely damaged an Israeli vessel and killed four soldiers during the 2006 war in Lebanon. In April 2005, Ukraine's export agency unveiled plans to market a new LACM called *Korshun*. The design of this new missile appears to be based solely on the Russian Kh-55, a nuclear-capable, 3,000Km-range LACM, which

Ukrainian and Russian arms dealers had illegally sold to China in 2000 and Iran in 2001.[79]

When we bear in mind what Lennox had to say about the impact of the illicit Kh-55 transfers, the dangers of that particular missile or its Ukrainian "clone" become quite real. Furthermore, as Gormley points out this "epidemic" or "contagion" could not have happened without the willing participation of other parties. Thus, Chinese fingerprints are all over Pakistan's newly tested LACM, while Russian engineering is known to have enabled China to produce a workable propulsion system for its new LACMs. Russian technical assistance, formalized in a joint production agreement, has helped India to produce and deploy its first cruise missile, the supersonic *Brahmos*. Iran's three new cruise missile programs depend heavily on foreign-trained engineers who honed their skills in France, Germany, Russia, China, and North Korea. Thus while the flow of technology components is necessary, it is not sufficient to enable cruise missile proliferation without the critical support of a small and exceptionally skilled group of engineering practitioners.[80]

Certainly such trends raise the question of missile defenses, but they should also stimulate greater cooperation against missile and nuclear proliferation. And it is not only a question of missile defenses. As we shall see, in South and East Asia, for example, states and governments are also trying to counter their rivals' offensive missile programs by developing their own "superior" programs whereby both sides rely on a purely offensive missile capability race against their rivals. Moreover, the universality of these trends makes clear that it is not only in the Middle East that we must worry about proliferation.

For example, we find this competitive offense model in East Asia. Because of its concerns about the consequences of the DPRK's proliferation, Washington, in 2001 persuaded Seoul to accept a 300Km range and 500Kg payload limit on ballistic missiles as a condition of South Korea's entry into the MTCR. Yet Washington allowed Seoul to develop LACMs with no conditions. The consequences were not long in coming, especially as South Korea, mindful of Chinese pressure, the costs involved, and its own strategic vulnerability to North Korea, has rejected participation in the U.S. missile defense system and the U.S. proposals to sell it the *Patriot* missile defense system. As Gormley notes,

> Shortly after Pyongyang's October 2006 nuclear test, South Korean military authorities leaked the existence of three LACM programs, involving ranges of 500Km, 1,000Km, and 1,500Km. The South Korean press took immediate note of the fact that not just all of North Korea would be within range of these missiles, but also neighboring countries, including Japan and China. Nearly simultaneously Seoul's military rolled out a new defense plan, involving preemptive use of "surgical strike" weapons, including its LACMs, against enemy missile batteries.[81]

The same kind of dominance of the offensive based on mutual deterrence, an inherently hostile posture between two states armed with missiles, not to mention nuclear missiles, is occurring in Taiwan. Although Washington has successfully persuaded Taiwan to steer clear of ballistic missiles, faced with China's relentless buildup of conventional missiles against it, Taiwan bought *Patriots* but demurred from buying the latest U.S. hit-to-kill missile defense due to the Chinese buildup and the cost of the U.S. system. Instead, it started developing its own LACMs in 2005, originally with a range of 500Km, but with the intention of ultimately deploying 500 of them with ranges of 1,000 Km on mobile launchers. Taiwanese military leaders spoke increasingly of a "preventive self-defense" strike option, to disrupt China's plans. And recent evidence suggests that Taiwan also now has started a ballistic missile program.[82]

South Asia.

As the foregoing analysis strongly argues, the urgency of reviving great power cooperation on proliferation and the enhanced capability of missiles and regimes is not confined to the Middle East or Northeast Asia where nonproliferation appears to have succeeded to some degree vis-à-vis North Korea. Indeed, there is a distinct spillover of proliferation trends or events from Northeast Asia to South Asia and vice versa. The North Korean-Pakistani reciprocal supply relationship of missile and nuclear technologies is an outstanding example of such spillover. At least in part due to this relationship, pressures for not only proliferation but also missile defense programs are growing in both Japan and India. In turn, those programs could ultimately have transformative strategic implications across Asia.[83] Both Russia and China have already registered their strong opposition to Japan's missile defense program and its strengthening of its alliance with America as a result of that program.[84] Were India to be added to this relationship, the consequences throughout Asia and world politics would be immense and profound.

In the context of that DPRK-Pakistani relationship, we need to remember that the single biggest proliferator in the last generation has been Pakistan through the A.

Q. Khan operation that has been extensively described at least as regards its public record.[85] Khan (whom it is difficult to believe was not working with the knowledge and consent of Pakistani military and political authorities) sold centrifuge and other technologies to North Korea and Iran as well as to other proliferators like Libya.[86] As noted above, India and Pakistan are expanding the number, range, and type of their nuclear weapons and missiles, e.g., moving to submarine-based systems and developing the capability for strikes across a greater distance with conventional missiles, e.g., the *Agni* missile.[87] Both states are also developing new and advanced conventional weapons that could be used in a bilateral or proxy war between them or between one of them and the other's proxy. Indeed, recently there have been charges that Pakistan continues to sell nuclear technology and that Khan's former middlemen are still trying to acquire those technologies.[88]

Thus the danger of a conventional war between India and Pakistan or proxies acting in their behalf presents the real possibility of an escalation first to missile war and then nuclear war. Indeed, as the stability-instability theory tells us, the possession by both sides of nuclear war capability paradoxically "makes the region (or the world) safe for conventional war" in the belief that the other side will be deterred due to the aggressor's possession of a nuclear capability. Thus stability at the nuclear level creates the paradox of giving openings to governments or even to terrorist groups to trigger instability at lower levels of conflict. Those crises could then spiral out of control into bigger wars. The many crises in the region, the last one being in 2001-02, indicate just how precarious regional stability is, and Pakistan's continuing ambivalence about supporting terrorist and Islamist military forces in Kashmir and against Afghanistan provide ample opportunities for such a war to break out.

Thus Pakistani President Musharraf's characterization of the *Babur* LACM as undetectable and incapable of being intercepted suggests its potential for use against India. That statement may have been intended as an *ex post facto* counter to India's doctrine of "Cold Start," unveiled in 2004 where precision long-range strikes, including the *Brahmos* missile, would feature in an Indian effort to conduct lightning strikes across the Line of Control in Kashmir before Pakistan could respond. Once Musharraf uttered his remarks about the Babur LACM, Indian strategists evidently approached Russia to obtain certain "restrictive technologies" to match or even greatly exceed the *Babur's* 400 km range, considerably more than the *Brahmos*.[89]

At the same time, the risks of such proliferation are apparent from another, equally urgent regional threat. Pakistan's spiraling internal instability has more recently raised as well the question of the security and control of its stockpile.[90] The links between its intelligence service, the Inter-Services Intelligence (ISI), and terrorist groups, as well as the mounting instability there, heighten the danger of terrorist forces gaining some measure of control over that stockpile, or of actual weapons. This danger is so great that Washington has secretly been working with the Pakistani government to maintain security and control over the stockpile.[91] However, anxieties about Pakistan's nuclear capabilities only begin here. As a recent article argues, the credibility of Islamabad's claims about the safety and security of its stockpile are open to serious doubt.

Instituted in 2000, Pakistan's nuclear command and control arrangements are centered on the National Command authority, which comprises the Employment Control Committee, the Development Control Committee, and the Strategic Plans Division. Only a small group of military officials apparently have access to the country's nuclear assets. However, these command and control arrangements continue to be beset with some fundamental vulnerabilities that underlie the reluctance of the Pakistani military to cede control over the nation's nuclear assets to civilian leaders. It is instructive to note that of all the major nuclear states in the world, Pakistan is the only country where the nuclear button is in the hands of the military. It is not at all comforting when former civilian leaders — including former Prime Minister Benazir Bhutto and Nawaz Sharif — make it clear that even at the height of various crises, the Pakistani military kept the civilian authorities out of the decisionmaking loop on the crucial issues of nuclear weapons.[92]

Beyond this, the Pakistani military's track record is no less disturbing. It is not merely a question of support for terrorism in India and Afghanistan or the instigation of previous crises, serious as those considerations are. Beyond that support, there are other strategic considerations in this region that should impel the major world actors to greater concern for halting nuclear and missile proliferation. For example, a second point is that in the event of the fall of the current Pakistani government, it is not at all clear that the armed forces could safely continue to exert control over Pakistan's nuclear assets, especially as there are multiplying signs of demoralization, fraying loyalties, and loss of cohesion, e.g., the growing Islamization of younger officers and the existence of links to terrorist groups in Pakistan, Afghanistan, and Kashmir. The number and location of those nuclear assets remains a closely guarded secret, and Pakistan has long resisted U.S. efforts to find out more about them lest Washington target them or remove those assets in case of a real threat to them.[93] Not surprisingly, Pakistan has now come out with a campaign to reassure all onlookers concerning the safety and reliability of its controls over its nuclear arsenal.[94] Although Washington has suggested that contingency plans are in place to deal with the threat of Pakistan's weapons falling into the hands of militants, it remains very unclear what could and will be done should such a crisis occur.[95]

Third, in South Asia it is also the case that the other nuclear powers have clearly helped India and Pakistan move forward with their conventional and nuclear arsenals. We need not revisit the details of the decades-long weapons programs of Russia, China, and the United States to these countries except to observe that they are continuing and, if anything, growing as the United States seeks to become a major seller of weapons to India. Certainly there is enough evidence as well of Russo-Chinese proliferation to India and Pakistan as well as to other states.[96] But in the current South Asian context, the new U.S.-India agreements of 2005-06 are of particular importance. On the one hand, these accords open the way for assimilating India into the global nonproliferation regime and ending the absurd and counterproductive isolation of India from these global structures. The agreements also provide a measure of control over Indian nuclear activities, precisely the reason why nationalists and evidently pro-Chinese Communist Party elements there oppose it and brought Parliamentary approval of these accords to a standstill.[97] However, American opponents of these agreements strongly argue that they legitimate India's defiance of these regimes by its nuclear testing reward. They argue that such behavior provides incentives for other states to behave in the same way to gain such rewards, and in general undermine the nonproliferation regime by showing that America essentially plays favorites and hews to a unilateral line where national interests trump the principle of treaty observance.[98]

Despite this agreement's importance, it is impossible to conclude which side has the better argument. This author supports the agreement because it brings India into the nonproliferation regime and is recognized as doing so by the IAEA, and other powers like Russia and maybe even China and Australia who wish to sell India reactors.[99] Ten years after India's tests, it is foolhardy to deny that it is a nuclear state and exclude it from the Nonproliferation Treaty (NPT) regime. In fact, once the Congress voted the necessary amendments to U.S. law and allowed the accords to go through, Australia, France, Japan, and Russia supported the transfer of civilian nuclear technologies to India, and Great Britain began discussions with India about such transfers.[100] Indeed, one analysis of the Indo-American deal called it an enabling agreement for (*inter alia*) the resumption of Indo-Russian civil nuclear cooperation despite the concerns it raised in Washington.[101] And while China has supported further technology and weapons transfers to Pakistan as could be expected and argued by the agreement's opponents, it has supported the de-nuclearization of North Korea and voted twice for sanctions on Iran. At the same time, recognizing India's partnership with Washington and Moscow and its other foreign policy priorities elsewhere, China has entered into an entente with India and is endeavoring to devise a cooperative relationship with India on nuclear energy, even to the point of discussing similar reactor sales to it.[102] Nor is it clear that U.S. foreign or nuclear policy is the determining factor for states which wish to go nuclear although they certainly do have some influence on proliferators' policies.[103]

Although opponents of the deal have pointed to the adverse implications it might have for the Iranian and North Korean calculations, it should be noted that both these states pursued nuclear weapons long before this deal. States pursue nuclear weapons on the basis of their own calculations of security interests, and both Iran and North Korea seem to have made a choice that they need nuclear weapons for their security. In a world where states have to fend for their own security, there is no better deterrent than a nuclear weapon. Nuclear weapons may not be popular with public opinion in the West, but all major states that have nuclear weapons know their importance and therefore have no intention of giving them up. It is the regional imperatives that will, in the ultimate analysis, drive other states toward nuclear weapons. The two regions with the greatest likelihood of witnessing nuclear proliferation in the near future are East Asia and the Middle East. States in these regions are unlikely to be influenced by the kind of deal the United States strikes with India. They will be driven by what happens to their own regional security environment.[104]

Yet the opponents of this view of the deal, like China, have already cited it as providing a bad example for other countries.[105] Thus, China has agreed to provide Pakistan with 6-8 reactors as part of its traditional policy of enhancing Pakistani capabilities to contain Indian power in South Asia. It should be pointed out here as well that this long-standing Sino-Pakistani cooperation long predates the Bush-Singh agreements of 2005 and also acts to constrain India's ability and desire to play a key role in South Asian nonproliferation, especially by military means, so one of this partnership's consequences is the escalation of the Indo-Pakistani arms race in South Asia.[106] Meanwhile, China demands as a condition of its support for cooperation with India on civilian nuclear energy that it be free to pursue its interests with Pakistan and that Washington allow other countries besides India to benefit from modifications to U.S. law on nuclear technology.[107] Similarly, North Korea has called upon America to treat it like India.[108] Meanwhile, Iran, too, complains that it is singled out unfairly. Critics thus derided this accord as breaching and undermining the NPT regime. They also argued that,

> A significant increase in India's nuclear arsenal could only increase the pressure on Beijing to abandon its strategic self-restraint. The U.S. action also undoubtedly lessened Beijing's inclination to do America's bidding with regard to North Korea and Iran. America's selective and high-handed treatment of the nuclear issue is likely to intensify Chinese efforts to realign the overall structure of the international system. As its influence grows, China will increasingly see itself as a major global player that will not be bound by rules of the game largely invented in an era of American supremacy.[109]

Finally, India in the past apparently also broke American law in attempting to obtain missile technology.[110] These trends, even if one accepts the utility of the Indo-American agreement, oblige us to confront the arguments against this deal and the policies it could then justify or lead to.

Thus the foregoing analysis underscores the urgency of confronting the rising tide of proliferation and the threats to the nonproliferation regime and more broadly to regional and international security across Asia. The urgency of dealing with these dangers and threats should alone suffice to regenerate a serious Russo-American dialogue about mutual cooperation to avert these threats together and where possible with other nuclear states like China, France, and England, if not the EU acting as a corporate European voice. But beyond these existing threats, which comprise the first and most compelling reason for such cooperation, there are many other reasons for reviving this dialogue.

Other Reasons for Cooperation.

The second reason for such cooperation has to do with the war in Iraq. The U.S. Government invaded Iraq because of its proliferation (which turned out to be nonexistent). The resulting fiasco bogged the United States down in a war, imposed substantial costs upon its overall international position and interests, discredited its standing across the globe, and continues with no clear end in sight. As a result of this war, Iran's position in the Middle East has been greatly strengthened to the point where it is believed to be the dynamic force in the area and a threat to almost all the other regional governments there. This war has given Iran both the time and opportunity to go full steam towards nuclearization and weaponization along with concurrent missile and space programs.

Likewise, Russo-American cooperation that began in earnest after the attacks of September 11, 2001 (9/11) steadily broke down due to America's unilateralism and Russia's perception that America simply disregarded its interests. This process has led to ever greater bilateral estrangement which has impeded progress on a host of international issues, not least Iranian proliferation. As a result, virtually every Arab state is now contemplating the possibility of developing its own indigenous nuclear energy sources.[111] As noted above, Russia is also eager to help them in the misplaced belief that doing so gives it revenue and standing in the Middle East even if the barriers to further proliferation are thereby lowered.[112] Thus one of the most tragic ironies of Iraq is that a war conducted in the name of nonproliferation and democracy has led to anarchy and civil war. Arguably as well, due to the war in Iraq, Iran's authoritarian regime has been strengthened and the possibilities for region-wide proliferation heightened.

This new strategic situation imperils the interests of all the local governments as well as those of Moscow and Washington. While the Russian government may pretend publicly that it has no evidence of a nuclear weapons program in Iran, it knows full well what Iran is up to and by selling it air defense and other weapons and transferring know-how and technology, it has abetted that process. Thus, Moscow's own analysts and Russian officials, like Deputy Prime Minister and former Defense Minister Sergei Ivanov and Chief of the General Staff General Yuri Baluyevsky, acknowledge it.[113] Commenting on Iran's launch in early 2007 of a sub-orbital weather rocket, Lieutenant General Leonid Sazhin stated that "Iran's launch of a weather rocket shows that Tehran has not given up efforts to achieve two goals — create its own carrier rocket to take spacecraft to orbit, and real medium-range combat missiles capable of hitting targets 3,000-5,000 miles away."[114]

Although he argued that this capability would not fully materialize for 3-5 years, it would also take that long to test and deploy the American missile defenses that are at issue. Equally significantly, Major General Vitaly Dubrovin, a Russian space defense expert, said flatly, "now Tehran has a medium-range ballistic missile, capable of carrying a warhead."[115] Although both men decried the fact that Iran appears intent on validating American threat assessments, facts, as Nikita Khrushchev was wont to say, are stubborn things.[116]

Since they wrote in February 2007, Iran has now announced that it has developed the *Ashura* IRBM with a 2000Km range.[117] Iran has also announced that it has produced its first nuclear fuel pellets for use in the Arak heavy water reactor that is under construction. This reactor, which began construction in 2004, concerns foreign governments because spent fuel from a heavy water facility can produce plutonium that can then be used for a nuclear weapon.[118] Nor has Iran ever come clean to the IAEA about its activities, even in the most recent report of its activities to the IAEA in November 2007.[119] Both Russia and China have recognized this and still urge Iran to do so in order that they may be able to protect it against sanctions.[120] Conversely, Iran fully understands that Russo-American cooperation, e.g., in jointly operating a missile defense station based in Gabala, Azerbaijan, checkmates its political basis for going nuclear and threatening all its interlocutors. Indeed Putin's proposal for joint use of Gabala implicitly acknowledges the validity of the U.S. threat perception concerning Iran. As one Iranian newspaper wrote in September 2007,

> Meanwhile, the change of stance by Russia regarding the anti-missile defense shield, from criticizing it and rejecting it to proposing the use of an alternative site for that system, could be regarded as a remarkable development that indicates the serious threats posed by that project. . . . [T]he implementation of a "joint missile defense system" and the installation of intercepting

radar systems in our neighboring countries—the Republic of Azerbaijan, Turkey, Iraq, or Kuwait—would include the intensification of American threats against our country.[121]

This reason for cooperation, growing out of the transformed post-Iraq strategic situation that threatens Moscow as well as Washington, also pertains to the overall question of the growing utility of nuclear weapons as both political and military (i.e., warfighting instruments) for all or most nuclear powers. Although specific American policy may not be determinative for proliferators, it does have some influence upon their calculations. Second, the rising tendency of states to utilize nuclear weapons for the pursuit of tangible political gains or as warfighting instruments undoubtedly creates pessimism about the durability of a nonproliferation regime or the utility of adhering to it.[122]

Thus, the debate about U.S. nuclear policy is instructive here. On the one hand, the Bush Administration has explicitly attempted to marginalize the use of nuclear weapons in American military strategy in its 2002 NPR.[123] However, outside observers have nonetheless made many charges against the United States: that Washington relies excessively on nuclear forces; that the United States is either not reducing nuclear forces or doing so fast enough; that the United States is building new and more dangerous nuclear weapons; that the United States is lowering the threshold for nuclear weapons use by emphasizing preemption; and that these failures and the supposed failure to sign new arms control treaties are encouraging proliferation. Washington's attempts to argue that these charges are myths have failed, convincing neither domestic or foreign audiences.[124] Instead, for some time every existing and potential nuclear power, including Russia and America, has been moving to operationalize their nuclear weapons, assert a broader range of missions for them, and develop credible first and second-strike capabilities despite Russo-American reductions in strategic nuclear weapons.[125]

America, Russia, and France are the most visible examples of this trend, as evidenced by the new French nuclear doctrine, statements by the new French President that France must be prepared to use nuclear weapons if necessary, enhancement of those weapons, Russia's reliance upon lower thresholds for nuclear use, talk of first-strike use even in limited wars, the Bush administration's addition of dissuasion to the list of functions intended for its nuclear arsenal, and rumors of potential deployment or use of nuclear weapons against North Korean threats.[126] Critics of the Bush administration see these and associated policies as efforts not just to dismantle the existing arms control regimes, but also as efforts to dismantle the nonproliferation regime and to obtain complete unilateral freedom of action by the United States in nuclear affairs.[127] We also see growing pressures to preempt proliferators, and not just by the United States.[128] Finally, even new nuclear states like India will probably export nuclear technology, ensuring continuing proliferation.[129]

These global trends predate the Bush administration. Instead, at least to some extent, they derive from abiding forces operating in world politics and contemporary strategy, and find reflection in the deteriorating Russo-American strategic relations. The rising number of threats to these regimes and the alleged nuclear taboo highlight the threats to those regimes and their possible unsuitability vis-à-vis deep-seated contemporary strategic trends favoring development and possible use of nuclear weapons for political, if not military, gains.[130] Unless arms control, nonproliferation, and counterproliferation campaigns can account for real trends in contemporary warfare and politics, they will fail.

What do these trends imply and how do they affect and how are they affected by Russo-American strategic relations? Many authors argue that Russo-American strategic relationships exert significant influence upon states' decisions whether or not to proliferate.[131] They regard 1987-96 as a golden age of arms control and nonproliferation when Soviet and Russian-American agreements fostered major reductions in superpower arsenals, and created a climate wherein many states—South Africa, the post-Soviet successor states, Argentina, and Brazil—stopped or revoked their nuclear programs.[132] Yet simultaneously, the range of missions and threats answerable by nuclear weapons expanded, and India, Pakistan, Iraq, and Iran intensified their proliferation. Clearly that strategic landscape permitted nuclearization as well as nonproliferation and possibly remains so today as Russo-American relations visibly deteriorate.

In this context, Iranian proliferation represents one of the main, if not the main, challenge to these arms control and nonproliferation regimes. (This would also hold true for North Korea if it breaks the 2007 accord and does not denuclearize). Apart from the implications of a nuclear Iran for the Middle East and Caspian basin, Iranian nuclearization spells the real, if not formal, end of a viable global nonproliferation regime. It would also probably render an equal blow to the structure of the arms control and strategic regime between Moscow and

Washington that has been and remains the paradigm and foundation of both regimes because it would increase the pressure on Moscow to leave treaties like the Intermediate Nuclear Forces (INF) treaty. Indeed, Russia already argues publicly and privately that every other major state has such weapons except for it and America. Therefore it demands, as its price for remaining in the INF treaty regime that this treaty be globalized, i.e., expanded to many other states.[133] Thus Moscow's threat to jettison the INF treaty of 1987, due for renewal in 2008, is rightly believed in Washington to be motivated by China's missile program and the threat of Iranian proliferation, not U.S. missile defense and NATO buildups as is regularly charged.[134] Even so, this does not deter Russia from making spurious and hysterical charges that these defenses jeopardize the Conventional Forces in Europe (CFE) treaty (which, in any case, Russia wants to dismantle) and could become the future basis for a first-strike against it.[135]

As a result, Russia itself now represents a new challenge to existing arms control treaties. In fact, and in no small measure thanks to Russian, Chinese, North Korean, and Pakistani help, the threat of Iranian, Chinese, North Korean, or Pakistani missiles is all too real. But it is too ironic a commentary on Russian foreign policy for Moscow to admit that its friends and customers, Iran and China, constitute the main and growing threat to its security. Observers may be correct therefore when they charge that Russian nonproliferation policy in the Middle East is confused, to put it mildly.[136] But Russian charges and threats also suggest that Moscow, like other nuclear states, is merely responding to contemporary strategic trends, not the least being proliferation (for which it too is partly to blame) and the rise of China and Iran. Certainly Russia is not interested in multilateral cooperation any more than is Washington, otherwise it would not have spurned earlier offers of cooperation with Washington in building missile defenses in Eastern Europe, another sign that there is no real defense threat from those systems.[137] Yet it is precisely this situation in Russian policy that necessitates continuing proliferation and arms control dialogues with it, lest its threat perceptions congeal and become drivers of a new arms race that would again have global repercussions, including further vertical and horizontal proliferation.

The North Korean Case and Proliferation.

A third reason for the necessity of Russo-American cooperation regarding proliferation can be seen in North Korea's case. Although North Korea has begun to de-nuclearize as called for in the February and October 2007 accords, Moscow as well as Beijing, Washington, Tokyo, and Seoul all acknowledged that a North Korean nuclear weapon or weapons represented a threat to their vital interests. Hence their cooperation in the six-power talks that led to these accords. Now as a result of those agreements a new process has begun that could lead to a new balance of power and cooperative regional order in Northeast Asia among the six parties to the talks.[138] This case shows what can happen when tenacious and cooperative diplomacy among the major players works in a concerted fashion towards a consensus objective, although it took an immense effort to overcome American demands for total North Korean surrender and the resulting mistrust among the parties.[139] Nevertheless, the fact remains that due to its own determination and a divided and frankly incompetent response from among the other five powers, North

Korea has become a nuclear power and is continuing to facilitate missile, if not nuclear proliferation abroad. And as noted above, it may be having second thoughts about complying with the February and October 2007 agreements. Other states can follow in this course, especially if they, like Iran, perceive their interlocutors to be divided and irresolute. Dialogue leading to a more or less united front is essential to prevent a recurrence of this example so that others do not get the idea that they can exploit great power differences in their quest for nuclear weapons. But beyond that, should this agreement break down, so will efforts at inter-Korean reconciliation and at devising a viable multilateral security order for Northeast Asia. In that case, the way would then be open to regional polarization and arms races, especially as Japan already has missile defenses and is tying them into the U.S. network, trends which have aroused strong Russo-Chinese condemnation.[140] It already is the case that North Korea's missile and nuclear tests were very influential in pushing Japan to decide irrevocably for missile defenses after 2002 and in overcoming its previous ambivalence about those defenses which are incurring the costs mentioned above and that Japanese planners could anticipate.[141] But it also is true that Japanese analysts, e.g., retired Army General Yoshiaki Yano, directly cite Russo-Chinese passivity and unwillingness to sacrifice anything to stop North Korean nuclearization as a reason for Japan not only to have missile defenses, but to go nuclear itself.[142] Indeed, some Japanese analysts believe that because Moscow is covertly actually helping North Korea develop its nuclear and missile program, this response is appropriate.[143] In other words, if Moscow (and Beijing too) want to decrease the likelihood of an arms race in East Asia, they need to do more to stop North

Korea from nuclearizing because the consequences of such a trend not only harm U.S. interests, but their own interests also. Dialogue leading to a more or less united front is essential to prevent a recurrence of this example. But beyond that, should this agreement break down, so will efforts at inter-Korean reconciliation and at devising a viable multilateral security order for Northeast Asia.

The fourth reason why Russo-American (if not Russo-American-European-Chinese) cooperation is necessary grows out of the lessons of these two cases. They show quite conclusively that discord between Moscow and Washington creates possibilities for proliferators to move forward based on the notion that Moscow will resist Washington's pressure and even give them both material and intangible or diplomatic assistance in developing their programs and gaining political cover for them. The same lesson applies as well to China, which has clearly taken the opportunity to support Iran and continue its support (albeit under the guise of economic colonization) of North Korea.

Washington, on its own, lacks the means for achieving its objectives without replicating the Iraqi scenario. The more either the United States or Russia resists the international cooperation needed to achieve a workable and durable international nuclear order, the more other players will act to impose such an order or at least such cooperation upon them. And that new order will inevitably be less favorable to U.S. and Russian interests than the one they could have had had sounder policies been pursued. This is what Iran, and behind it Russia and China, are doing in the Middle East to the United States. Indeed, Russia now manifests alarm about Iran's activities in the Middle East.[144] Similarly, China seized upon great power rivalries in Northeast

210

Asia to exploit North Koran proliferation and modify the regional order to its taste. Unilateralism actually creates a series of perverse incentives and processes for other powers to act unilaterally in defense of their own interests to obstruct Washington from achieving its goals and fosters the resulting loss of American capability and legitimacy around the world. Or, once one or another state has acted to upset the strategic status quo, others fearing U.S. abandonment or weakness, or believing that "the gloves are off," will take their own unilateral steps or at least argue for them. In turn, those outcomes open up possibilities for creating new and less congenial regional or even global orders. As we have also noted regarding Iranian activity in the Middle East, the same logic applies to Russian unilateralism and to the ensuing damage that is then done to Russian interests. Therefore it is eminently in the vital interest of both Russia and the United States to achieve real cooperation regarding nuclear and other forms of proliferation lest an inferior order be imposed upon either or both of them.

Another point is of importance here. Experience with successful resolution of proliferation issues strongly suggests that to induce proliferators to desist, it is necessary to address their regional security agendas as well as to do so in a way that strengthens the existing nonproliferation regime.[145] As John Simpson wrote, "The evidence from the past suggests that the most effective demand-side non-proliferation mechanisms are those which resolve interstate conflicts. . . . The long-term solution to security threats is almost always a political one."[146] Such processes are inherently multilateral given the number of key actors both inside and outside of any given region who must guarantee such settlements and who must also sustain the global nonproliferation regime. If they cannot reach consensus on either the regional or global dimensions of any such nonproliferation agreement, it is doomed to failure in advance. And potential or real proliferators will then draw the appropriate conclusions from that failure.

Therefore a fifth reason for cooperation is that Washington no longer can and therefore certainly should not try to impose its own views on this issue upon other countries. Today Washington, to achieve its nonproliferation objectives, must persuade others in the rightness of its assessments, intelligence, and objectives, not to mention its methods and tactics. America's earlier and misconceived policies have given space for states that define themselves in opposition to American interests, including Russia and China, to increase their power and standing in world politics to the point where they must be reckoned with. Because Washington cannot merely impose its will, it must gain international legitimacy from other governments for whatever it now seeks to do and not only in regard to proliferation. Consequently, no solution to a proliferation problem is either viable or perceived to be legitimate without the stamp of approval of the major powers to include Russia, China, and, in Iran, the EU.

A sixth reason for the urgency of cooperation is that as the nonproliferation regime is steadily being compromised, if not threatened, it bids fair to undermine Russo-American arms control regimes and cooperation, e.g., the INF treaty and the Strategic Arms Reduction Treaty (START) accords, as well. Here we should remember that Russian officials' statements from President Putin on down all indicate that Moscow wants to leave the INF Treaty of 1987 because its neighbors to the south and east, i.e., Iran and China, are busy producing ever more missiles.[147] These examples of both vertical proliferation (development of ever more capabilities by a single nation to go from nuclear bombs to missiles and launchers) and of horizontal proliferation (transfer of technology, weapons, or capabilities from one state to another) could undermine both European and Asian security, including the vital security interests of both Russia and the United States.[148]

There is little doubt that withdrawal from the INF treaty, as Russian experts have predicted, would not afford Russia any more security than it now has. If Moscow withdrew from the INF Treaty, NATO could then station INF missiles in the Baltics and Poland. That withdrawal would also lead China and Iran to step up their production of intermediate range missiles as well. Furthermore, it is by no means clear that Moscow could regenerate production for both IRBMs and ICBMs as their plant for such production systematically misses production goals. Thus withdrawal from the treaty could actually further diminish Russian security, not enhance it.[149] Yet Moscow dare not admit that the enemy of America is also its enemy lest its domestically based foreign and defense policy that postulates partnership with China and Iran be seen to be inherently contradictory and even dangerous.

Indeed, withdrawal from the INF Treaty makes no sense unless one believes that Russia is genuinely--and more importantly--imminently threatened by NATO, or Iran and China, but most of all by U.S. superior conventional military power, and cannot meet or deter that threat except by returning to the classical Cold War strategy of holding Europe hostage to nuclear attack to deter Washington and NATO. Similarly with regard to China and Iran, absent a missile defense, the only applicable strategy would be to use nuclear weapons to deter them, but this means admitting that these supposed partners of Russia actually constitute a growing threat to it. Since it is by no means clear that Russia can or should reply to any such threat by producing IRBMs, the desire to leave the INF Treaty and reactivate missile production of IRBMs represents only the interests of the defense and defense industrial sectors, not necessarily Russia's true national interest.

Nevertheless, Moscow's response to call for universalizing the treaty lest it withdraw to pursue what amounts to a strategy of deterrence against its supposed friends contains elements within it that reinforce our arguments for greater bilateral and multilateral cooperation against nuclear and missile proliferation. It is clear that proliferation is endangering previous arms control regimes because it is enabling purely regional actors to develop capabilities that can threaten the vital interests of the nuclear members of the Security Council or of their allies. Iran's threat to Israel and to Russia is a case in point. Thus a German commentary observes that limited nuclear wars and nuclear terrorism are now quite possible at the regional level even if superpower nuclear conflict is on the way out. The multiplicity of actual or potential nuclear players eclipses efforts to subsume them in any old-style arms control treaty, something borne out by the Russian and American approach towards unilateral force development programs and movement into space.[150] Other analyses concur as well that the superpowers have done little to prevent this demolition of the old arms control regime and treaties. But until and unless the relations between Moscow and Washington improve or the overall arms control process is multilateralized to bring in the new players (i.e., states, not nuclear terrorists), then there is not much to hope for in the way of Russo-American cooperation on such issues as ballistic missile defense (BMD) or on existing proliferation cases.[151]

The threat of proliferation to regional actors makes it also possible to launch nuclear strikes, particularly in a first-strike mode, using smaller launch vehicles and missiles across shorter distances. Those ranges might be considered "operational-tactical" by NATO and/or Russia, but they could easily have devastating strategic consequences, e.g., in an Indo-Pakistani war that could drive an equally devastating but still in some measure "proportionate" response.

Thus one of the major dangers of nuclear proliferation is the possibility of lowering the threshold of decisive attacks against a state's armed forces, political leadership, command and control system, or economy without requiring weapons of intercontinental or even intermediate range. In addition, contiguous nuclear wars, as opposed to nuclear exchanges between distant powers like the United States and Russia or the United States and China, allow comparatively shorter times for the defender for launch detection, processing of information, and decisionmaking prior to the impact of a first strike. Realizing this, contiguous states, fearing the opponent's prompt launch or preemption, might be driven toward hair triggers that bias their options towards preemption in first use or first strike.[152] Surely the great powers should have little interest in fostering this kind of strategic environment that threatens to entangle them as well in these webs of regional rivalries.

The seventh compelling reason for the necessity of cooperation is the lesson of contemporary history. The period of greatest Russo-American cooperation, 1987-96, is not by accident the period of the greatest global progress in arms control and proliferation.[153] The range and scope of the agreements that were achieved then were due in no small measure to the bilateral efforts of both sides in regard to arms control and nuclear disarmament and to the convergence of their views regarding outstanding proliferation issues.[154] During this period, such cooperation provided immense legitimacy to American interventions abroad like Operation DESERT STORM precisely because of great power consensus. Indeed, not only did this cooperation and the breakdown of the Soviet Union, and along with it the end of the Cold War, remove the specter of nuclear conflagration between Moscow and Washington that could have come about due to any number of conflicts in Europe, Asia, or even the Third World, it also opened up new possibilities for a more viable and enduring international security order.

The prospect for a new world order brought about advances in nonproliferation whereby Iraq was stopped by force after its aggression against Kuwait from further developing its weapons of mass destruction (WMD); South Africa's security threat, and with it its justification for going nuclear, disappeared; Brazil and Argentina scaled back their nuclear programs; and Ukraine, Belarus, and Kazakhstan were persuaded to abjure nuclear weapons even though they had inherited many with the collapse of the Soviet Union. Moreover, the United States benefited in other ways from the advent of this new order, and the end of the nuclear arms race not only facilitated multilateral arms control and nonproliferation, America gained the uncontested ability and greater scope to project its conventional forces abroad, among other things to prevent proliferation and to do so with international legitimacy.[155] That ability has died in the sands of Iraq, but it could be revived through meaningful great power cooperation on nonproliferation. This age was not a panacea for other states, e.g., India and Pakistan intensified their nuclear quest as we have seen, but they still did so under the constraints imposed by this Russo-American cooperation. While not perfect, this period's record is much better than what has followed it since 1996.

Thus in the past decade when such cooperation broke down, there have been examples of successful proliferation: India, Pakistan, and North Korea, and Iran's accelerating but still incomplete program, all of which have repercussions that put not just these countries' regions, but also international security at risk. Consequently, it is clear that failure to find a basis for mutual cooperation adds substantially to the risks and threats to the international order as a whole. Arguably those states that remain outside the NPT regime or are threatening it—India, Israel, Iran, Pakistan, and North Korea—were not only nonsignatories or violators of the NPT but also were states that existed outside of or broke free from the two reigning Cold War alliance systems led by Washington and Moscow. China in 1964 when it tested its nuclear bombs and declared its strategic independence from the "Sino-Soviet bloc" is also an example (until it joined the NPT) of this process. As these states were outside of any alliance system, they had to help themselves in an anarchic and threatening world. Neither could they rely on economic or trade blocs that overlapped with these alliances so they had to fend for themselves in economics as well. Indeed, there is some evidence suggesting that it was the U.S. security relationships with Egypt and Saudi Arabia that held them back from developing WMD.[156] Given such results, and in the light of existing Russo-American programs of cooperation, it is clear that if

217

a basis for meaningful cooperation on proliferation issues can be found, real progress in stabilizing the overall international order can be achieved.[157]

The eighth reason grows out of this historical record. Bilateral agreements are no longer sufficient to revive the prospects for effective cooperation across a broad range of issues affecting the global order, including nonproliferation. Neither is American unilateralism sufficient or effective. In other words, it is high time to strive to multilateralize the arms control process so that it is more adequate to the contemporary strategic realities, e.g., China's rise and the EU's growing consolidation as a nuclear actor and negotiator in its own right. Obviously as part of that process, improved Russo-American ties are necessary to gain that bilateral aspect of nonproliferation and to establish the confidence necessary to move to the next or multilateral step. One reason, among many, for the collapse of the 2005 Nonproliferation Treaty Review Conference was America's insistence on its agenda directed at Iran and North Korea and refusal to discuss other parties' concerns that America is not denuclearizing as they interpret the NPT's Article VI to require. Therefore we could not develop any multilateral consensus to leverage developments in Iran and North Korea.[158] This stance was shortsighted and counterproductive because it ignored the realities of power by assuming too much strength on the U.S. part and because it overlooked the positive gains, including greater legitimacy, that multilateralism offered and still offers America. As Clifford Kupchan writes,

> The multilateral policies of a dominant power should both prolong the hegemonic order and increase the chances that it will attain a specific goal. Multilateralism alleviates weaker states' fears of hegemonic power and

reduces their motivation to balance, because it gives those states some voice and role in setting the policy of the hegemon. Multilateralism increases the dominant power's chances of prevailing in specific difficult cases because it brings additional influence and resources to bear.[159]

In a contemporary environment where such agreements must be multilateral in nature, Kupchan's admonition has been proven. It is no longer possible to speak of a Russo-American consensus on proliferation and/or arms control issues as sufficing to reduce nuclear threats although such cooperation remains a necessary element of any real progress towards that end. As noted above, and as shown in the Iranian negotiations, the EU has insisted on playing a robust role in the negotiations, and earlier it sought involvement in the North Korean nuclear issue. But equally importantly, China can no longer be ignored. Chinese participation and leadership were instrumental in bringing the North Korean issue to what could become a satisfactory resolution. Likewise, China is a key factor in the South Asian nuclear equation and any diminution of one or both sides' nuclear programs must correlate to the balance of threat between China and India, for we should remember that the initial justification in some key quarters for the Indian nuclear tests in 1998 was the Chinese threat. Obviously then, China must be part of any resolution of South Asia's nuclear equation as it is perceived as being in some way responsible for the overt nuclearization of the subcontinent. Similarly, China's voice on the Iranian issue is ever more important. Although China certainly materially aided Iran's missile and nuclear programs, it now is urging Tehran to accept IAEA and UN resolutions.[160] Apparently it has also given the UN information on Iran's nuclear program.[161]

But China's importance goes beyond acknowl-
edgement of its importance as a contributor to regional and global security balances. Given the
complexity of those regional balances, any Russo-
American cooperation that does not include substantive discussions with China as an equal partner could
easily be overturned by Chinese resistance to the outcomes devised by Moscow and Washington. Zbigniew
Brzezinski has already argued that,

> A significant increase in India's nuclear arsenal could only
> increase the pressure on Beijing to abandon its strategic
> self-restraint. The U.S. action [e.g., the Indo-American
> agreements of 2005-06 — author] also undoubtedly
> lessened Beijing's inclination to do America's bidding
> with regard to North Korea and Iran.[162]

Brzezinski further observes that a high-handed and
selective U.S. (or implicitly U.S.-Russian) approach to
proliferation and arms control, will probably prompt
China to redouble and intensify its efforts to reorder
the international system's structure. China increasingly
will (if it is not already the case) see itself as a major
global power which will resist being bound by rules of
the game from which it has been excluded. And there is
sufficient evidence that Chinese foreign policy analysts,
if not leaders, are increasingly ready to assert Beijing's
prerogatives across the entire international agenda.[163]
In this context, no Russo-American agreements can
long endure without Chinese participation. Indeed,
the prevailing Russo-Chinese tendency to unite in
a very robust form of strategic partnership, if not
alliance, against American policies makes it all the
more imperative that these three states and the EU
face each other in any future proliferation dialogue.
This would prevent such behind-the-back alliances

from materializing and maximize American leverage in situations where China and Russia along with America are forced to confront both their common and diverging interests.[164]

There is considerable evidence to suggest that while Chinese and Russian perspectives will make it difficult for American policymakers to achieve their stated goals, the exclusion of states will make it all but impossible to realize those goals, thereby confirming Kupchan's remarks. For example, despite China's unwillingness to press North Korea in the six-power talks, it appears that Russia rather than China achieved a reputation for being the most sympathetic of the negotiating parties to North Korea's position.[165] But ultimately this opposition to America's position had to give way to the cooperation process generated by Beijing. Had either or both China and Russia been excluded from the process, they may well have been available to Pyongyang as potential spoilers of any agreement negotiated exclusively with Washington and its allies. Indeed, we see what China might be predisposed to do in regard to the Indian Parliament's debate on ratifying the Indo-American nuclear agreement. Thus a number of Indian analysts are questioning whether or not China's close ties to the Communist party of India (Marxist) (CPI[M]) helped that party block adoption of the Indo-American accords.[166] While this cannot be proved, a U.S. analyst observes that,

> The CPI (M)'s intervention with the Singh government to thwart the U.S.-India nuclear deal greatly benefits Beijing. If the deal had continued to move forward, China would have confronted a difficult choice when the issue of opening nuclear trade with India came before the Nuclear Suppliers Group. Since the group operates by consensus, China, in effect, would have

had the opportunity to veto the deal by voting against lifting the group's 15-year embargo on nuclear trade with New Delhi. That step, however, would have forced Beijing to directly and openly oppose the United States. At least for the moment, the CPI(M)'s ostensibly independent initiative freezing the deal achieves the same result, without the potential risks for Beijing of a stark confrontation with Washington.[167]

It also is the case that such a Chinese veto would have greatly set back China's relationship with India which is a relationship—due to China's focus on domestic development and Taiwan, and its partnership with Moscow and India in a "strategic triangle"—that possesses considerable international importance for Russia, China, and India. A more open multilateral process thus led to the attainment of an outcome acceptable to Washington in Korea, whereas China's rivalry with India and nonparticipation in the U.S.-India deal (which is often advertised as part of a larger relationship to check China) may have contributed to the frustration of an important U.S. policy goal with significant nonproliferation implications.

The exclusion of China from such fora also constrains efforts to stop proliferation in key areas like South Asia. A. Vinod Kumar, in advocating a more robust Indian counterproliferation policy writes that,

For many years, China tacitly assisted Pakistan in building up its nuclear infrastructure and missile systems. Although both countries have denied this, there is abundant proof that Pakistani nuclear and missile systems have clear Chinese origins. After the 1998 tests, China reportedly curbed this relationship but is now providing support for Pakistan's nuclear ventures. China has also declared its reservations on the Indo-US nuclear deal, arguing that it legitimizes India's weapons status outside the NPT system. As such, there are possibilities for China pushing for a similar deal with Pakistan to legitimize its nuclear status, and also to put a legal stamp on their cooperation. Despite China being India's rival, the military asymmetry posed by a China-Pakistan partnership constrains the scope of an Indian military response to deal with proliferation and terrorist threats emanating from Pakistan. Under such circumstances, India's anti-proliferation strategy has to address the China factor through credible strategies that would contain this partnership without vitiating the strategic stability in the region.[168]

A ninth reason for the desirability of a robust bilateral dialogue leading to cooperation is that both sides have material and prestige interests involved in resisting the proliferation of nuclear weapons. Many commentators have observed that for the United States, nonproliferation is important because the spread of nuclear weapons reduces our ability or willingness to project power abroad — the historic character of the extra-continental deployment of U.S. military power — in defense of American interests and/or allies. Moreover proliferators can then not only "fence off" key areas of the world where they can threaten our interests or allies, they can also, as in Iran's case, threaten to extend deterrence to terrorists, transfer to them weapons for the conduct of mass terrorism, and engage in nuclear blackmail. Iran has already threatened to extend deterrence to Hezbollah and shipped them thousands of short-range rockets for use as terror weapons.[169] Pakistan's nuclear capability in effect does the same for both its regular forces and those terrorist groups it has sponsored. This pattern could easily be replicated elsewhere in the Middle East or for that matter in Central Asia and the Caucasus if Iran had a nuclear capability with which it could threaten and deter others.

If we take into account that the main mission of American forces since 1945, at least in operational terms, has been the long-range projection of U.S. military power to distant theaters and countries, it quickly becomes clear that states which develop credible nuclear capabilities or even possibly credible precision-guided munitions capabilities can deter or dissuade U.S. authorities from conducting operations against their countries.[170] At the same time, the end of the Cold War has left America in a condition of clear nuclear primacy which it is determined to maintain. As a result, its efforts to tailor U.S. strategic forces to counterproliferation, deterrence, and dissuasion missions have exacerbated Russian and Chinese suspicions, paradoxically making it more difficult for Washington to prosecute its antiproliferation policies successfully.[171] Cooperation with both Moscow and Beijing would reduce the burden on our nuclear forces while also alleviating international tensions and making consensus on achieving nonproliferation more likely.

Beyond that, it has also been repeatedly argued that one of the most effective nonproliferation instruments has been the American alliance guarantees in Europe and Asia that have extended deterrence to allies and have been instrumental in persuading them to forego nuclear weapons. Were those alliances to be devalued by the proliferation of nuclear weapons to ever more states, many of which are hostile to those allies, they would find themselves under increased pressure, as happened with Japan and to some degree the Republic of Korea (ROK) in the wake of North Korean proliferation, to consider going nuclear on their own.[172] Such an outcome would be decidedly inimical to Russian as well as American interests. Indeed, the prospect of

Japan participating in the U.S. missile defense system was heightened by the North Korean tests to the point where Japan successfully tested an interceptor missile in December 2007.[173] Because such developments are neither in Russian nor Chinese interests, they have protested the U.S.-Japan alliance's work towards a joint missile defense even though China's reaction to the Japanese test was unexpectedly mild.[174] Indeed, in October 2007 Russian Foreign Minister Sergei Lavrov warned Japan that Russia fears this missile defense system represents an effort to ensure American military superiority, and that the development and deployment of such systems could spur regional and global arms races. Lavrov also noted that Russia pays close attention to the U.S.-Japan alliance and was worried by the strengthening of the alliance triangle comprising both these states and Australia.[175] He observed that "a closed format for military and political alliances" does not facilitate peace and "will not be able to increase mutual trust in the region," thereby bringing about reactions contrary to the expectations of Washington, Tokyo, and Canberra.[176]

Since Moscow clearly hoped that a successful nonproliferation outcome in North Korea would invalidate Washington's arguments for missile defenses in the Asia-Pacific region, Lavrov's complaints show what happens when bilateral cooperation breaks down and, as a result of proliferation, overall regional tensions increase, in this case in Northeast Asia.[177] Thus the North Korean case shows both the need for cooperation in advance of proliferation and ultimately what can happen when tenacious and cooperative diplomacy among the major players works in a concerted fashion towards a consensus objective, although it took an immense effort to overcome American demands for

225

total North Korean surrender and the resulting mistrust among the parties.[178]

For its part, Russia, in this context, also has strong reason to want to restrict the number of nuclear states as a general principle, not just because the most recent proliferators are on its borders or close to it. Alexander Lukin's observations below about the impact of the North Korean nuclear tests of 2006 are instructive in this regard.

> There is a general understanding in Russia that it runs counter to the fundamental interest of the country. Currently, only a few countries have nuclear weapons, and Russia and the United States have many times more than any of the other nuclear states. If the current structure of the United Nations guarantees Russia special status among other countries as one of the five permanent members of the Security Council, then the nuclear nonproliferation regime is at the base of Russia's position as one of the world's two most powerful countries. This means that weapons proliferation seriously devalues Russia's influence in the world. The more nuclear states there are, the less Russia's comparative military strength might become. This is a purely pragmatic consideration, to which can be added a number of other negative consequences from further nuclear proliferation such as increased probability of nuclear conflict, and threats to national security in the Far East.[179]

Another reason for cooperation relates to the regional rivalries between Moscow and Washington (the same can apply as we shall see to Beijing). Today, as during the Cold War, we see intensifying regional rivalries between America and Russia throughout Asia from the Middle East to the Pacific Ocean. Both these states tend to support governments which have, by their proliferation activities, intensified tensions, e.g., America's support for Pakistan and Russia's earlier support for North Korea and present support for Iran. The reasons for this support often have to do with quite classical concepts of national interest which in Russia's case relate to material interests, recovering its great power status, and checking American power. For example, Gleb Ivashentsov, then Director of the Second Asia Department of the Russian Foreign Ministry, told a Liechtenstein Colloquium on Iran in 2005 that,

> Iran today is probably the only country in the greater Middle East that, despite all of its internal and external difficulties, is steadily building up its economic, scientific, technological, and military capability [what about Israel? — author]. Should this trend continue, Iran — with its seventy million population, which is fairly literate, compared to neighboring states, and ideologically consolidated, on the basis of islamic and nationalist values; with a highly intellectual elite; with more than 11 percent of the world's oil and 18 percent of natural gas reserves; with more than 500,000 strong armed forces and with a strategic geographic position enabling it to control sea and land routes between Europe and Asia — is destined to emerge as a regional leader. This means that the Islamic Republic of Iran will be playing an increasing role in resolving problems not only in the Middle East and Persian Gulf area but also in such regions that are rather sensitive for Russia as Transcaucasia, Central Asia, and the Caspian region. This is why dialogue with Iran and partnership with it on a bilateral and regional as well as a broad international basis is objectively becoming one of the key tasks of Russia's foreign policy.[180]

Unfortunately such support for regional partners, if not allies, often ends up (as in 1914) with the greater power being drawn into the smaller partner's conflicts because it fears it cannot afford to lose its partner or ally to the other side. The result is often heightened conflict, and today those crises often revolve around proliferation. Thus when Israel bombed an alleged

North Korean-built reactor in Syria in September 2007, it reflected what could happen when states like Syria and North Korea strike out on their own in the belief that they can rely on a protector like Moscow or in Israel's case, Washington. As Yitzhak Shichor writes,

> Most likely, Pyongyang had failed to consult with either Moscow or Beijing prior to its decision to engage in some kind of "illicit" strategic or nuclear cooperation with Syria, although both may have become aware of this activity at a certain point of time. This failure reflects not only North Korea's inflated nationalism but also its belief that whatever misunderstandings and disagreements it has with Russia and China—quite a few are known— both will continue their commitment and support and the same goes for Syria.[181]

Furthermore, as Shichor notes, such crises are likely because such states often have no other way to pursue their vital interests other than by interesting great powers in their survival. While such support may preserve these states, it hardly advances their overall cause of changing the status quo. "Unable to use diplomacy and not allowed to hold negotiations, apparently the only way open to settle their respective conflicts is by using threats, sponsoring terrorism, and building up the infrastructure for future violence."[182] If there were more effective great power cooperation on both regional security and nonproliferation, then the scope for such provocative behaviors would be correspondingly restricted.

But since there is presently no such effective cooperation either on regional security or nonproliferation, Russia also values the Iranian connection because its support for an anti-American Iran helps Moscow restrain U.S. power in the Middle East, makes it a player or "great power" in the same region, and allows it to gain influence with other Gulf states who see it as having influence on Iran. Thus, during Putin's Februry 2007 tour of Saudi Arabia, Jordan, and Qatar, he offered all these states major energy deals, arms sales, and even nuclear power, ostensibly for peaceful purposes, but in reality signifying his efforts and theirs to balance what they all realize is Iran's refusal to stop its nuclear program and put it under effective IAEA supervision.[183] In fact, Russia is offering up to 13 Arab states nuclear technologies of one sort or another. Russia is even launching Saudi satellites and undertaking major business initiatives with Saudi Arabia, even as it assists Iran's space program.[184] This posture once again reflects Russia's wholly instrumental approach to questions of proliferation of nuclear technologies, discerning no real threat from the spread of nuclear power in the Middle East if it checks Iran and makes it remember who its patrons are. The many reports speculating about possible Saudi nuclear ambitions evidently have made little impression upon Putin and his subordinates.

Furthermore, the support for Iran and its anti-Americanism parallels attiutudes toward the Middle East that had deep roots in Russian foreign policy even before Ivashentsov justified the Russian policy above. Already in the 1990s, Russian observers agreed that the Middle East's continuing proximity to Russia impels it to resist any foreign military presence, particularly an American presence, and especially nuclear arms. Therefore nuclear weapons technology transfers should be strictly controlled even though conventional arms may be sent in abundance to rescue the beleaguered defense industry and strengthen potential friends of Moscow like Iran, Syria, the new Iraq, and the Palestinian Authority.[185]

Lest one believe that Iran's nuclearization might drive or have driven Russia away from Iran, since Moscow knows full well that Iran is pursuing a nuclear bomb, Russian analyses even then performed an astonishing feat of casuistry, e.g., in the Russian Foreign Intelligence (SVR) 1995 report on proliferation threats, authored by Evgeny Primakov, SVR's then director: Fully recognizing that nuclear proliferation in the Middle East threatened Russian security and the CIS, and could force the revision of Russian defense policy, the report nonetheless argued that the West was unfairly singling out Iran for undeserved reasons as it was not conclusively pursuing a military nuclear option. So while Iran was already regarded as a problematical partner or ally, actually the United States was persecuting it to exclude Russia from Iran and the Gulf.[186] As long as Iran keeps the "bomb in the basement" and does not jeopardize other key Russian interests, partnership with Iran was and is very much in Russia's interest and could actually serve as an example of how to conduct nonproliferation.[187]

Russia saw Iran as a partner in ending regional conflicts in Central Asia, controlling the Caspian's oil and gas flows, and in stabilizing the Caucasus.[188] In 1995 Valery Manilov, Deputy Secretary of the Security Council, stated that in regard to Iran, interests based on economic competition and great power competition for spheres of influence had intruded into (and presumably superseded) concerns of nuclear proliferation. Manilov claimed that Russia has strictly evaluated Iran's nuclear program and was convinced that it did not represent a threat since everything Iran does is under IAEA supervision. Russia understood its responsibility to prevent nuclear proliferation, but its program with Iran would facilitate both regional and global stabilization.[189]

Russian analysts also recommended partnership, if not more, with Iran, clearly believing that to do so would not only suppress Russia's and the CIS' internal Islamic threats, but that Iran did not support those threats. Russian authorities had fully grasped Iran's potential capability for threatening Central Asia and the Caucasus by 1992 and sold it weapons then partly to deter that threat.[190] Nonetheless, Moscow's continuing disclaimers that Iran does not sponsor terrorism reflects its persistent belief that Iran presently does not represent a threat to it or its neighbors.[191] Thus this strategic partnership also belies or at least neutralizes Iran as an avatar of the Islamic threat often used in the Russian media and by Russian elites to justify every Russian policy from Chechnya to Tajikistan. Iran is simply not regarded as a genuine threat despite whatever might be said about Islamism in general. In fact, many policymakers recommend dealing with Muslim societies, specifically Iran, to engage Islamism and divert it from threatening Russia, a solution that Primakov had previously espoused.[192] Andranik Migranyan, an advisor to President Boris Yeltsin and an unapologetic defender of Russian primacy in the CIS, then told Iran News in 1995 that,

> In many areas Iran can be a good strategic ally of Russia at [the] global level to check the hegemony of third parties and to keep the balance of power. . . . Russia will try to further cooperation with Iran as a big regional power. We will not let the West dictate to Russia how far it can go in its relations. Of course, we will try at the same time not to damage our relations with the West.[193]

Similarly, at a 1995 Irano-Russian roundtable,

> The speakers alluded to the quest by Iran and Russia for an identity and to Russia's political determination to prevent any country from dominating the region

231

[Central Asia and the Caucasus]. It was stressed that Iran and Russia are natural allies with distinctive natural resources and the predominance of any third power should be prevented. This is related to the manner in which the two sides define their strategic objectives. It was also stated that Russia's influence in Central Asia and the Caucasus should be treated with respect and if domination is not the objective cooperation is possible.[194]

Every word of Manilov's and Migranyan's precepts (including the uncertainty as to whether or not Iran is actually capable of building a nuclear weapon— an axiom dear to those in the military and political leadership who want to pretend there is no justification for missile defenses against it[195]) could be said today without any change up to and including Migranyan's implication that Russia would consider jettisoning Iran if that partnership became too great an impediment to its relations with the West, or a threat to Russia. As noted above, the peerception that Iran is crossing that red line may be influencing current Russian policy.

Finally, there is an 11th reason why Russo-American cooperation is so desirable which applies with particular force primarily to the United States, namely the greater goal of integrating Russia into a peaceful Euro-Atlantic or Eurasian order. As stated in 2000 by Zbigniew Brzezinski,

The progressive inclusion of Russia in the expanding transatlantic community is the necessary component of any long-term U.S. strategy to consolidate stability on the Eurasian mega-continent. The pursuit of that goal will require patience and strategic persistence. There are no shortcuts on the way. Geostrategic conditions must be created that convince the Russians that it is in Russia's own best interest to become a truly democratic and European post-imperial nation-state—a state closely engaged to the transatlantic community.[196]

Insofar as key military-political Russian elites believe that proliferation is the biggest new threat to Russia or at least one of the most critical threats it faces, the ground for reigniting and sustaining a vibrant Russo-American dialogue on this subject is possible as well as desirable.[197]

Pathways to Cooperation.

These eleven reasons should provide compelling justification for future efforts to regenerate that consensus concerning not only proliferation but also other issues as well. Here again the Chinese example is useful because China's growing aspiration to be seen as a responsible world power which upholds international security along with its evolving perception of its national interest has led it to join nonproliferation regimes and to become more sensitive to nonproliferation issues than had previously been the case.[198] While its behavior may not yet reach the ideal of support for nonproliferation as a general principle, nobody else's does, and the signs of its evolving outlook, e.g., in regard to North Korean nuclearization, are unmistakable.

The necessity for a multilateral dialogue on nonproliferation that embraces Russia and America, as well as China and the EU, is, under the circumstances outlined above, as urgent as before the NIE. The experience of the last 20 years shows that such cooperation is a prerequisite for any progress on issues of regional security as well as adherence to global arms control and nonproliferation regimes. The alternative, as we see, is a regional race to either the nuclear bottom or to a new period of intractable rivalries among both great and small powers. And that insight applies equally to the Middle East, South Asia, and Northeast Asia.

Nevertheless, the problems facing the realization of such cooperation are enormous, and they are aggravated by the very clear Russian effort to make relations with the U.S. Government seem worse than they are. For example, the Russian media took a speech in October 2007 by U.S. Ambassador William Burns wholly out of context and published a headline charging him with saying that tensions in bilateral relations are more acute than they have ever been.[199] Moscow in other ways also seems intent on being as provocative as possible, e.g., by selling nuclear fuel to Iran for the reactor at Bushehr even as it admits that Iran does not need it, and in continuing to block efforts to impose UN and IAEA controls on Iran.[200] Given Russia's constant invocation of the UN as an international authority on security questions, these efforts to hamstring and obstruct it and its component bodies like the IAEA reflect Moscow's own double standards and double bookkeeping.

Even so, if there is to be more meaningful cooperation between Washington and Moscow, both sides must change their foreign and defense policies and their perceptions of the threats they face. Because the U.S. presidential election will result in a new cast of policymakers and they will quite likely repudiate much of the Bush administration's heavy-handed and ineffective unilateralism, such a change is more likely to occur in American policy than in Russian policy. This is especially the case since there is no sign of personnel change in Moscow or in the structure and balance of the Russian government which grants disproportionate power to the hard-line Siloviki (even under a Medvedev presidency) and to a foreign policy that in many critical cases seems driven by anti-Americanism rather than by any mature concept of the national interest. This is not to say that there is no cooperation on nonproliferation between Moscow and Washington. Indeed, the record shows that there is considerable cooperation on several aspects of the problem.[201] Nonetheless, this cooperation is faltering and insufficient, and the likelihood of further proliferation is likely growing due to North Korea's nuclear program, proliferation to other countries like Iran, Syria, and Myanmar and apparent backtracking on its most recent agreements. Abroad, the greatly increased instability in Pakistan was aggravated further by the December 27, 2007, assassination of former Prime Minister Benazir Bhutto; Iran's defiance of the Security Council also contributes to the urgency of resuming this cooperation. Despite expressions of common concern on all or most of these issues, Russo-American cooperation is decreasing. Therefore the balance of this chapter focuses on what needs to be changed, first in American policy and then in Russian policy.

Changing U.S. Policies.

There are several reasons why we need to change our policies. And they would be justified even if the December 2007 NIE had not knocked the ground out from under American rhetoric about Iran.[202] Experts generally concur that under all circumstances,

> The United States is uniquely now the driver of international nuclear policy. This is not just because of America's preeminent military and economic power, its control of roughly half of the world's nuclear arsenal, or its disproportionate influence among world powers. It is also because the United States has, at virtually every juncture, shaped the international rules and norms of the nonproliferation regime and led the negotiations to form the NPT and the Nuclear Suppliers Group.[203]

For example, it should now be clear that we cannot achieve our basic and primary strategic aim of strengthening the nonproliferation regime by tying Iranian and North Korean nonproliferation to externally imposed regime change or the threat of it by unilateral American military action. Our power and understanding of what needs to be done over both the short and long term in such cases are both limited, thanks to Iraq. Moreover any such efforts, in the absence of forceful provocation by those or other states, will enjoy no support anywhere, further overtaxing the resource base for American power and limiting our capacity to preside over any kind of security order in the relevant region.

If our fundamental objective is nonproliferation, our resources should be focused on achieving that goal since the effort to link it to coerced regime change in Northeast Asia or the Gulf enjoys no support by the other negotiators and cannot be reached in any satisfactory way by any unilateral means available to the United States now or anytime soon. Objectionable as these regimes are, we have neither the means, nor the legitimate international authority to change them by force, nor the international support needed to achieve a legitimate order in these areas afterward by unilateral action.

Furthermore, by decoupling this demand for regime change from our demands for proliferation, we actually gain more flexibility to send a robust message to Iran, Syria, and North Korea should they then proliferate because then they no longer have even the semblance of a justification for their position. Even if the invasion of Iraq may have given them a supposed justification for proliferation and sponsorship of terrorism, the fact that they will subsequently be held to account on the basis of existing international agreements to which they are parties to desist from proliferation and sponsorship of terrorism creates a sufficient justification for the use of pressure or the threat of force and releases us from the position of making threats that cannot currently be carried out.

If we can change the international behavior of these regimes, by political means preferably but by force if absolutely necessary, then their current foreign and domestic policy behavior will gradually be rendered increasingly dysfunctional, forcing change upon them from within, not from outside. To the extent that they cannot then mobilize domestic or foreign support against the Bush administration, they will be compelled by force of circumstances and superior Western power to adjust their behavior over time. Admittedly this is a slow process, but Iraq shows what happens otherwise. That lesson should induce behavior change in Washington first before we seek to persuade other key interlocutors of the soundness of our position.

Once the threat of proliferation is uncoupled from the objective of regime change, it becomes much easier to fashion both a strong negotiating coalition against the former and to do so strictly on the grounds of international security and international treaties that must be observed. This allows us and the other treaty signatories to create a different security environment around proliferators, complete with binding accords, supervision, and inspections that safeguard their internal security, but which also contributes to rendering proliferators' form of rule even more dysfunctional than is now the case. But most importantly, it facilitates the reaching of verifiable agreements on these states' nuclear programs. That is the key point.[204]

Therefore to effectuate domestic political change

within Russia and other challenging states, we must change the external environment within which they operate by means of engaging them politically. Indeed, careful examination will show that there is no other realistic alternative. Despite all the inherent traps and snares in a dialogue between Pyongyang and Washington or between Tehran and Washington, we cannot compel their de-nuclearization by our refusal to talk to them. In fact, quite the opposite is true. Neither can we induce Russian liberalization by refusing to deal with Moscow on issues of common concern. Indeed, doing so only strengthens the negative features of today's Russia. Here we cannot hide behind multilateralism because international and domestic pressure to talk directly to Iran without preconditions is also rising. Avoiding such dialogues and clinging to ringing but empty rhetorical positions only deepens our internal divisions and disputes with our negotiating partners and allies while failing to achieve de-nuclearization. If anything, the threat of coerced regime change powerfully accelerates these countries' nuclear programs which enjoy tacit or covert support from Moscow and Beijing precisely because they are joined in rejecting any further unilateralism by Washington.[205] While it would be satisfying to punish these states, e.g., Iran for its actions in provoking a war in Lebanon, our actual capabilities are more circumscribed and limited.

Consequently we need a strategy that will force these proliferators to change their behavior over time by mitigating their and our security dilemmas. Doing so would then render their current behavior even more dysfunctional than is presently the case until it is no longer feasible to carry it out. Furthermore, such an engagement will work over time to dissolve the bonds linking China, Russia, and in the Korean case, South Korea because neither Moscow, nor Pyongyang, nor Seoul wants China to be the deciding voice in Northeast Asia, whatever their criticisms of Washington. Endless statements from Beijing and Moscow reiterate the identity of these states' views about Korea and much else because we have done everything possible to drive them together.[206]

Indeed, Russian scholars now state that Russia works with China to coordinate their proposals in the Korean nuclear negotiations, and numerous communiqués cite an "identity" of views on this topic.[207] Removing many of the reasons for their shared positions regarding either North Korea or Iran helps erode their unified position in these and other issues. As experts have argued that a working Russo-Chinese alliance is the greatest security threat we could face, a negotiating strategy designed to uncouple these two potential rivals against us but also against each other, makes perfect sense.[208]

This policy's wisdom would also be underscored by the fact that an examination of the historical record strongly suggests that a precondition for effective nonproliferation is mutual cooperation between Moscow and Washington, as happened in 1986-96 and which has since evaporated due to Russian domestic regression to autocratic rule, American unilateralism, and the perception thereof abroad.[209] Without the ability or rationale to justify threat-based programs in the absence of a threat, these states must then deal much more urgently with economic and political questions at home for which they have no answer and for which their structures are woefully inadequate, if not illegitimate. And since contemporary scholarly research suggests that proliferation policies are the product of various coalitions of domestic interest groups in these states, a policy that transforms the playing field on which these coalitions maneuver has a much greater chance of success than does unilateral rhetoric, which in reality cannot be implemented except at ruinous cost.[210] That process, as was the case with Moscow in 1986-91, will generate change that will be all the more powerful for being domestically generated rather than externally coerced.

More specifically recent research shows that proliferation policies in both the Middle East and Northeast Asia are tied to the ways in which states have organized their political survival and macroeconomic policies among the elite blocs or coalitions that make up these states.[211] In particular,

> Systematic difference in nuclear behavior can be observed between states whose leaders or ruling coalitions advocate integration in the global economy, and those whose leaders reject it. The former have incentives to avoid the political, economic, reputational, and opportunity costs of acquiring nuclear weapons because such costs impair a domestic agenda favoring internationalization. Conversely, leaders and ruling coalitions rejecting internationalization incur fewer such costs and have greater incentives to exploit nuclear weapons as tools in nationalist platforms of political competition and for staying power.[212]

Thus arguably the nuclear proliferation crises of our time, Libya, North Korea, Iraq, and Iran, were driven more by apprehensions for regime security, or even the personal security of the ruling dictator, than by concerns for state security (i.e., Iran's security rather than that of the Mullahs and their system of rule).[213] In proliferating states, ruling coalitions have generally been what Etel Solingen calls backlash or inward look-

240

ing coalitions (these are ideal types rather than specific cases) that are suspicious of extensive foreign relations with external powers, economic internationalism, and export-driven rather than import-substituting policies. They espouse bureaucratically-directed and autarchic economic programs rather than economic policy based on market-based logic. Therefore, their economic and national security policies are oriented toward nationalist, protectionist, military elites who benefit the most from such bureaucratic and closed economies. As Solingen argues,

> Inward-looking political survival entails policies that are mutually enhancing or synergistic across domestic, regional, and global levels. *Nuclear aspirants are more likely to emerge from domestic political landscapes dominated by inward-oriented coalitions than from their alternatives.*[214] (Italics in original)

From a policy point of view, this means that we can affect the domestic balance of power in these states in a nonproliferation context not just by isolating and sanctioning them — a process that often results in strengthening precisely those coalitions that we do not wish to see in power — but also by actually negotiating viable nonproliferation accords with those governments. Once the security justifications for going nuclear and the associated material or intangible pay-offs to interested elites from going nuclear diminish, these coalitions must find a new basis for exercising power, reach out to other groups with different agendas, or gradually lose relative power at home. In time, if we are patient, admittedly something that goes against the grain of U.S. politics, we will see regime change or a struggle for it beginning in these countries. Even where it is very difficult to reach out to such alternative coalitions that would benefit from nonproliferation accords, there are signs that such trends may be possible, even in North Korea.[215] Furthermore, as Solingen concludes, new mass technologies have enabled us to reach out to elites and masses in both Iran and now in North Korea and we have begun to do so.[216]

Espousing an approach to nonproliferation that concentrates strictly on the proliferation of WMD and utilizes all the considerable armory of American national security policy save the threat of preemptive strikes to effectuate regime change would be a much harder program for Russia to resist. As we shall see below, Russian approaches to the nonproliferation issue do not fixate on the nature of the regimes but on whether or not there is an actual threat, and they prefer to resolve these issues as in Ukraine in the 1992-94 period, in the North Korean case, and clearly in the Iranian example by political means, not military threats. The dead end that we have reached in Iraq, as well as the NIE, have essentially taken military means out of policy consideration for the Bush administration.[217] And its successors will hardly be willing to launch preemptive strikes against either Iran or North Korea without enormous provocation as long as we are embattled in Iraq and Afghanistan.

Towards more Genuine Russo-American Cooperation.

If we are to achieve lasting and effective U.S.-Russian cooperation on proliferation, it is inevitable that it will also impinge on the possibilities for cooperation on arms control and regional security issues. This was the way things worked out in the Gorbachev and Yeltsin periods, and it is logical to expect that this is a precondition for future success as well. In other words, such cooperation must be part of a program that is supremely political in content and form, and bilateral (if not multilateral to encompass China and the EU) in nature. To realize even part of this overall agenda, we must understand the following requirements for success:

First, we must understand the bases on which past cooperation resided as well as the structure of contemporary world politics and how it applies to the problem of generating bilateral, if not multilateral cooperation against proliferation of WMD. A recent article by Danish scholar Sten Rynning insightfully cites the work of Lassa Oppenheim, the founder of the school of positive law, on these points.

As Rynning writes, Oppenheim argued that, "International law can operate only under certain conditions, the two most important of which are *a balance of power and a shared conception of politics.*"[218] (Italics in the original) Rynning further argues that the supply of WMD will be the focal point where these two conditions are met because "a shared conception of power within a working balance of power makes for satisfied or conservative great powers." These powers are uniquely empowered because of their size and reach to control the flow of the resources needed for WMD in the international system. And during the Cold War, the NPT came into being exactly when they both became fully conscious of their mutual interest in controlling nuclear weapons.[219] The ensuing regime was supposed to bolster mutual deterrence, but it also enhanced bilateral communication and restricted nuclear weapons diffusion to other members of their alliance systems that helped counter the outbreak of new threats.[220]

However, today's world is rather different. Even if

America has lost ground under the Bush administration, it still remains by far the greatest power and master of the strongest global alliance system. Thus a fundamental asymmetry or imbalance of power exists. Yet Washington cannot simply insist upon its demands and get its way as current proliferation crises show us. Under the circumstances, we can either follow the logic of imbalance or strive to uphold the old balance in unfamiliar environments. As Rynning observes,

> If none of Oppenheim's conditions are met, if power is asymmetrically distributed and ideological conflict predominates, we encounter cases of *revisionist demand*; revisionists demand nuclear weapons as deliberate instruments of expansion, because they wish to check hegemonic power and enhance the scope for their own values and desires. What happens when an order designed to control supply and counter misguided demand — by nature a generalized, universal order — encounters cases of revisionist demand? Gerry Simpson is in no doubt: legalized hegemony and antipluralism will move to the forefront of the international debate. Legalized hegemony denotes the hegemon's attempt to secure for itself special privileges justified on the grounds that it is policing the order; anti-pluralism denoted the political effort to delineate the ideas and ambitions that will earn some states the title of "outlaw" and cause their exclusion from the society of nations. The implication is that status quo powers cannot merely uphold the old order. They can either seek to *reshape* the old order to make it relevant and sustainable or they can more simply, but also dramatically seek to *replace* it with something new.[221] (Italics in the original)

Washington, in this case the hegemon, sought to reshape the order through both the UN Security Council Resolution 1540 and the Proliferation Security Initiative (PSI) to create a universal regime allowing for the maritime or aerial interdiction of prohibited cargoes usable for WMD. But it also sought to replace the old order by its preemptive invasion of Iraq and its creation of an exemption for India which violated the NPT.[222] Furthermore, the U.S. nuclear weapons policy and overall nuclear unilateralism has stimulated Sino-Russian fears of U.S. intentions and capabilities as well as considerable criticism abroad of Washington's supposedly cavalier attitude towards arms control treaties.[223] Indeed, not only are North Korea and Iran examples of revisionist demand, so too is Russia, given its strong opposition to U.S. nuclear weapons policies, missile defenses, and nonproliferation policy. There is good reason to see in Russian policy for the last several years a move towards the revisionist demand posture that "Demands nuclear weapons as deliberate instruments of expansion, because it wishes to check hegemonic power and enhance the scope for its own values and desires."[224]

This conjuncture of all these nuclear issues is not accidental. As Stephen Cimbala writes,

> The possible emergence of a nuclear armed Iran shows how the issue of cooperative security in Europe and the Middle East is directly linked to the US-Russian problem of post-Cold War nuclear stability. Russian political support is necessary inside and outside of the UN Security council in order to contain Iranian nuclear ambitions. To obtain this cooperation, the [United States] must reassure Russia that it has no interest in nuclear superiority with the intent of coercing Russia or using NATO as a vehicle for undermining the Russian regime. Missile defenses, if deployed, cannot have their Cold War flavor of competition for nuclear superiority, but must emerge from an environment of US-Russian security cooperation.[225]

However, we are far away from that environment of

concord and evidently moving farther and farther away. Even if we discount the various remarks cited above by Russian Foreign Minister Lavrov, it is clear that Russia cannot and will not base its approach to the United States on any foundation other than the one of mutual suspicion embodied in Mutually Assured Destruction. As he stated in February, 2007,

> Our main criterion is ensuring the Russian Federation's security and maintaining strategic stability as much as possible. . . . We have started such consultations already. I am convinced that we need a substantive discussion on how those lethal weapons could be curbed on the basis of mutual trust and balance of forces and interests. We will insist particularly on this approach. We do not need just the talk that we are no longer enemies and therefore we should not have restrictions for each other. This is not the right approach. It is fraught with an arms race, in fact, because, it is very unlikely that either of us will be ready to lag behind a lot.[226]

Thus Lavrov puts his finger on the fact that in an atmosphere of political mistrust and where both sides' deployments are still based on the philosophy of deterrence and mutual assured destruction, strategic unilateralism is both unacceptable and indeed dangerous to all because it stimulates arms races across the world. In other words American unilateralism is inherently a threat to Russia wherever it appears because Russia cannot but proceed from the a priori assumption of hostile American interest, i.e., what the German philosopher Carl Schmitt called "the presupposition of an enemy."

Thus the problem and the threats that we face as this relationship erodes are not due to Russia's military modernization but rather to the overall deterioration of Russo-American relations or to the failure to break out of past cognitive paradigms. And here Russia, precisely because it has reverted to previous policies, structures, and mentalities is as much to blame as is the United States. Whereas the United States is moving or claims that it has sought to move toward a strategic relationship based on partnership with Russia, defense against and dissuasion of enemies, and lessened reliance on nuclear weapons and deterrence vis-à-vis Russia and other states, Russia cannot let go of the past.[227] It remains committed to a strategy and posture of deterrence that postulates an inherent adversarial relationship with the United States.

In regard to nuclear issues the argument that Washington has also operated on the basis of the same Schmittian presupposition of enemies and a determination to retain nuclear primacy since 1991 can also be made.[228] And simultaneously Washington has also striven to ensure its unchallenged conventional superiority and ability to intervene undeterred in foreign countries so that the projection of American conventional military power abroad can take place at minimum risk. The collision of these two strategic worldviews is all but ensured to heighten regional, if not global tensions. Thus neither Washington nor Moscow can escape from the gravitational pull of mutual deterrence by unilateral actions like each side's effort to start withdrawing from arms control treaties in a unilateral fashion. Even if one accepts Cimbala's arguments that missile defenses need not destabilize the bilateral contemporary relationship, it is clear that they are doing so right now because there is, as Lavrov suggested, a deficit of trust, and Russia's internal structure precludes it from conducting any kind of foreign and defense policy other than one based on Schmitt's presupposition of enemies. Therefore mutual deterrence must remain intact as the foundation of bilateral cooperation until a comprehensive political agreement (possibly in the form of new arms control and nonproliferation treaties) takes hold.[229]

What specific points those treaties must contain is a matter for negotiation, but American policymakers should have learned by now both the necessity for genuine, if arduous, negotiation with Moscow on arms control and nonproliferation and the importance of a supremely political act in creating a legitimate international order with respect to all nuclear issues, not just proliferation. As George Kennan's famous X article in Foreign Affairs said in 1947,

> It is a sine qua non of successful dealing with Russia that the government in question should remain at all times cool and collected and that its demands on Russian policy should be put forward in such a manner as to leave the way open for a compliance not too detrimental to Russian prestige.[230]

Besides this admonition, it should be clear that the U.S. position on proliferation issues must be a unified one across the government and advance American interests. The Bush administration's position violated both these tenets with visible and predictable results. On Korea, it was so internally divided that for a long time it could not come up with a credible negotiating posture in the six-party talks. In turn, this led to a conclusion that may be unstable today, but which also goes far towards substituting a multilateral arrangement for one in which the U.S. position was quite secure and relatively uncontested.[231] And more broadly, as Robert Litwak has argued,

> The unresolved tension over the objective of U.S. policy toward rogue states—behavior change versus regime change—frustrates the effective integration of force and diplomacy. Major constraints on the use of force that preclude the application of the "Iraq model" in the ongoing crises with North Korea and Iran create the conditions for a pragmatic turn in U.S. policy—a shift from a strategy of regime change and preemption to the alternative of deterrence and the reassurance of regime survival.[232]

While there is an evident turn towards pragmatism on North Korea, it may yet prove unsuccessful, while our Iran policy, even before the NIE, was increasingly ineffective, not in small measure due to Russian noncooperation.

If one thinks about the forthcoming requirements for future U.S. success in achieving nonproliferation in the widest possible strategic terms, the problem of securing Moscow's (and Beijing's, not to mention the EU's) support should be a high priority issue meriting the most serious thought and analysis. U.S. and Western analysts remain divided (as are no doubt policymakers) over the continuing relevance of deterrence against Moscow, and possibly Beijing, as the foundation of Washington's arms control and nonproliferation strategy. There are those like Robert Litwak and before him Michael Howard who underscore the centrality of a twin policy of deterrence and reassurance concerning the utility of nuclear weapons use as the basis of arms control and nonproliferation policy. This school of thought argues against threats of regime change and counsels security guarantees and robust diplomacy on a coalition basis to confront the problem, and is confident that the deterrence relationship will in and of itself deter and maybe dissuade proliferators.[233]

The second school believes that deterrence has failed and will certainly fail at some point in the future. Therefore a robust counterproliferation strategy involving missile defenses and even a willingness to run risks of a potential military nature—possibly including preventive war if sufficient justification can be advanced—is justified.[234] The Bush administration has clearly inclined in its overall strategy to the latter point, even to the point of including dissuasion as a part of its nuclear strategy and in seemingly (at least according to its critics) advancing to the creation not only of missile defenses but arguably of first-strike superiority as well.[235] And that consideration includes the administration's arguments that since it is no longer adversarial to Russia, neither Washington nor Moscow needs to be bound by arcane counting rules, verification procedures, etc., and can build whatever they need for their nuclear forces.[236]

No single study is going to resolve the dilemma or persuade policymakers of one or another stripe to jettison their existing approach to these issues. But the necessity of taking our partners' points of view into account on these issues, even if they are disagreeable partners, is inescapable and absolutely necessary given the decline in relative U.S. power since the invasion of Iraq. At the same time, it should also be clear to American policymakers that, as this author has previously written, we must first dispel several myths and obstacles that obstruct coherent U.S. and Western policymaking. The first obstacle is the widely accepted myth that we, or the West as a whole, have little or no leverage upon Russian policy and therefore must adjust to it or tolerate it silently.[237] This, of course, is a highly self-serving tactic when stated by Russians who love to insist that the United States or the West cannot sway their policies and that foreign motives towards Russia are invariably hostile and self-serving. Or else they argue that such criticism is pushing to a return of the Cold War.[238] In the West this precept amounts to a self-denying ordnance that paralyzes efforts to advance Western political objectives when it has the stronger hand in every dimension of international power. Moreover, obtaining such a condition of Western paralysis or admission of defeat is actually the goal of all of the bad behavior displayed by Moscow in the hope that foreigners will assume nothing can be done. Therefore the Russian media is all too happy to report frequently that the West "accepts" the nature of Russia's "special democracy."[239] Indeed, at one point Lavrov even asserted that after a Putin-Bush summit meeting in 2004 "no concern was sounded" about the lack of democracy in Russia by the American side.[240]

But when uttered in the West, this observation represents a bizarre failure of applied political intelligence. We need not argue that American or Western power is unlimited or that its authority, legitimacy, and virtue are absolute—neither of which is true—to realize that the strongest power in the world and the strongest alliance in the world do not lack the resources with which to influence Russian policy and that Russia has frequently adjusted to meet firm American policies. After all, George Kennan's containment strategy was just such a strategy that sought to compel an eventual "mellowing" of Soviet domestic and foreign behavior by applying political and other external pressures abroad. Similarly the judicious application of the total weight of the instruments of power available to the West in world politics would surely frustrate or at least blunt the imperial drive and the restoration of autocracy that underlies so much of today's Russian foreign policy and force domestic changes as a result. As Heinrich Vogel writes,

> This logic of "mutually assured dependency" (the political dimension of interdependence) implies a world of rational choices. In this world the structural deficiencies of the Russian economy and its integration and interdependence with the international community restrict Moscow's ability to be uncooperative or engage in spoilsport behavior in international crisis management.[241]

Arguing that we have no leverage is not only bizarrely misguided but also reduces the Western pursuit of a viable Russian policy to incoherence.

But beyond realizing that we have leverage and the right, if not the duty, to use it both on our own and in tandem with our allies to advance our interests, we need to overcome the second obstacle to a sound Russia policy. Namely, we must devise and implement a coherent strategy, first of all within our own government, and then together with our allies, in order to deploy that leverage to its most efficacious use. This strategy must be implemented in regard to key issues: Iran, the Middle East, the Western presence in the CIS, the sanctity of treaties signed by Russia, energy, arms control, and Korea, to name only a few. Doing so requires first that we overcome the fact that on numerous key issues, including apparently policies toward Russia, and in regard to at least some of these aforementioned issues, our policy process has been and is still broken. Any attentive reader of the newspapers can quickly discern that there exist major divisions among the players in Washington that inhibit unified and coherent policy formulation and implementation.[242] Until and unless we can overcome those problems, any approaches to our European and other allies regarding these issues will be compromised from the start.

Russian Policy.

For the United States to achieve legitimacy and authority with regard to nonproliferation accords in which Russia is involved so as to redress the balance broken by power asymmetries, a clear understanding of priorities and interests must exist. It may well be the case that Iran's potential proliferation represents a threat not just to regional security (which in the Middle East is bad enough) but to global security as a whole and opens up the prospect of future nuclear use in the Middle East.[243] Moreover, if Iran continues to be intransigent and can rely on Moscow and/or Beijing to give it cover for its nuclear activities, then it will also continue to defy the UN until it acquires nuclear weapons. As Iranian proliferation raises issues that go far beyond the threat raised by North Korean proliferation (as seen in the different U.S. policy responses to each phenomenon), failure to gain Russian cooperation and to arrest Iran's progress may truly leave us with unacceptable political options and unpalatable military ones for dealing with the prospect of a nuclear Iran. This outcome cannot be dismissed as a possibility. For example, Lavrov has said that North Korea's nuclear weapons are a threat to international order whereas Iranian nuclearization would not be such a threat.[244] Some believe that Moscow really does not believe this about Iran.[245] But this may accurately reflect Russian policy even though Russia has often said publicly that it opposes Iran's nuclearization. Although Putin, as late as the fall of 2007, kept repeating that he had no evidence of Iranian nuclearization, in fact Russian generals and officials, e.g., Baluyevsky, Ivanov, Sazhin, and Dubrovin all cited above, have told us something different.[246]

In other words, we have yet to fully understand what drives Russia's nonproliferation policy. In early 2002 Sergei Ivanov told us what those motive forces are, i.e., Russia scrupulously adheres to its international obligations in the sphere of nonproliferation of WMD, means of their delivery, and corresponding technologies. The key criteria of Russian policy in this sphere are its own national security, the strengthening of its international positions and the preservation of its great power status.[247]

Russia evaluates proliferation issues not according to whether the regime is democratic or not, as in America, but on the basis of whether a country's nuclearization would seriously threaten Russia and its interests.[248] With that criterion in mind, and given analyses like Ivashentsov's and Lavrov's remarks in Japan cited above, it is not difficult to see why North Korea ranks larger as a threat. Indeed, Moscow is offering nuclear technology to 13 Middle Eastern states to make money and gain influence there. Thus in commenting on the June 2007 proposal by Putin to let the Americans jointly manage the Russian missile defense radar at Gabala, Azerbaijan, Baluyevsky stated that Washington's claim that Russia now admitted to an Iranian threat was a misinterpretation. While Russia never denied a global threat of nonproliferation of missiles and nonproliferation, "we insist that this trend is not something catastrophic, which would require a global missile defense system deployed near Russian borders."[249] Certainly Moscow has tended to view American policy towards nonproliferation in jaundiced fashion, displaying a visible *schadenfreude* (joy at another's sorrow) when North Korea tested missiles and then a nuclear weapon in July and October 2006.[250] Or alternatively, Russian officialdom views Washington's insistence on nonproliferation controls as merely or mainly an effort to pressure competitors in the nuclear and arms markets.[251] A recent analysis of Russian reactions to the February 13, 2007, six-party agreement on North Korean de-nuclearization strongly suggests the continuation of this misanthropic view.

Moscow's reasoning on the February 2007 deal conflicts with that of the Bush administration believing that: (1) It came about as a result of the United States correcting its past mistaken diplomacy; (2) It is likely to fail because the United States will not fulfill its commitments; (3) The talks serve as a model of multi-lateralism, applying pressure only in extreme need through unanimous UN Security Council resolutions and encouraging diplomacy in which officials having good ties to all parties play the decisive role; and (4) At fault is a U.S. worldview that demonizes the North Korean regime in order to justify a strategy of global hegemony. Given this line of reasoning, Russians are inclined to interpret ambiguities in the timing of mutual steps in carrying out this deal as U.S. attempts to gain one-sided advantage.[252]

This analysis duly suggests, then, that if the United States is to elicit Russian cooperation on non-proliferation, it has to do so not by offering to stop the critique of the rush to authoritarianism in Russia. That would be a step that would then merely be pocketed and lead to no concessions on nonproliferation. Rather the carrot that should be offered to Moscow and which would boost its prestige and let it boast about its great power if it likes (nobody outside the Kremlin will be convinced by it in any case) has to do with arms control, not democratization. If the problem in our relations is the growing though unjustified Russian sense that America is a mounting miltiary and political threat, as appears to be the case, then moves to reduce military and specifically nuclear tensions must be offered as part of the bargain. At the same time, it should be made clear to Moscow that if it persists in denying the validity of American threat perceptions from Iran and behaving irresponsibly by offering everyone nuclear technology, then Washington will see fit to go it alone with its allies and leave Moscow to face the Iranian music alone. Putin and company may harrangue their audiences with dark tales of American unilaterlaism and malfeasance, but as of 2007 the reality, as stated by former Ambassador Robert Blackwill, is that,

> Let me be very clear. President George W. Bush and State Secretary Condoleezza Rice are deeply committed to trying to solve this problem with Iran through multilateral diplomacy. They understand that multilateralism, which in the past was regarded by some as a diplomatic alternative for the United States, has now beome a compelling foreign-policy requirement. They genuinely seek to a void a binary choice by an American president either to attack Iran or to acquiesce to Iran's possession of nuclear weaons.[253]

The multilateralism, for example, is surely discernible in American policy towards North Korea since 2006 if not before.

Thus beyond the explicit renunciation of the inclination towards regime change, there needs to be a commitment towards Russia to reexamine mutual arms control issues seriously. The fact is that Russia, in its growing emphasis on nuclear weapons since 1993 and its emphasis on the perception of an American threat, is also an example of revisionist demand as cited by

Rynning.[254] Likewise, the current Russian government, with this threat perception and its authoriarian and somewhat autarchic domestic policies, perfectly embodies Solingen's backlash or inward-looking coalitions. Consequently, a similar logic applies to dealing with it in regard to contentious nuclear issues. In other words, we can affect the domestic balance of power in Russia over time in an arms control and nonproliferation context mainly not just by isolating and sanctioning it—a process that often results in strengthening precisely those coalitions that we do not wish to see in power—but also by actually negotiating viable nonproliferation accords. Once the security justifications for going nuclear and the associated material or intangible payoffs to interested elites from going nuclear diminish, these ruling coalitions either must find a new basis for exercising power, reach out to other groups with different agendas, or gradually lose relative power at home. This occurred in Soviet-American relations and could certainly happen again if this approach is adopted. And it would have the advantage of helping to realize the goals stated by Brzezinski above of intergrating Russia more securely into a Euro-Atlantic world.[255]

Russia too needs arms control and nonproliferation because it cannot meet missile threats in any other way or at least it cannot imagine meeting them in any other way than by deterrence, i.e., building more missiles. Thus Russian demands for leaving or universalizing the INF treaty are openly linked to the development by states like China, Pakistan, and Iran of IRBMs that can target Russia or its partners.[256] While the sale of military technologies to these states is a major Russian policy (except for Pakistan), and Russia considers them to be its friends, the fact that its friends and partners

257

constitute the truly greatest risk to Russia indicates that its policies have, in fact, hit a brick wall and that it has substituted animus toward the United States for clear thinking. In short, it has a threat peception that cannot be solved by means of Russian policy.

The only way out of this dead end for Moscow is bilateral arms control with the United States which benefits it because it opens up new possibilities for a détente with the United States that can ultimately help reduce global nuclear tensions through agreements with it on nonproliferation. Specifically, this means genuinely negotiating a new START agreement with Russia even while upholding the INF treaty. It also means giving Moscow the choice of committing to true defense integration or at least cooperation with NATO on theater missile defenses if it does not want American defenses in Poland and the Czech Republic even though they cannot threaten Russian targets or interests. Russia should be given to understand that failure to move this issue forward means being saddled with this unpalatable alternative and that its efforts to transfer nuclear technology, know-how, and conventional weapons to Iran materially increases the likelihood that such defenses will be built. This means confronting both Tehran and Moscow with the prospect of real costs if Iranian enrichment and weaponization programs continue. But it also means offering a basis for negotiations in which both sides' threat assessments and perceptions, as well as their force development concepts, can be discussed on an equal basis. As part of its revisionist demands, Moscow has claimed to want "total equality, including equality in the analysis of threats, in finding solutions, and making decisions."[257] But it obviously refuses to accept the validity of American assessments or to be willing to subject its own defense policy to any form of external monitoring or even cooperation, unlike NATO members.

The arms control agenda suggested here duly offers a basis for direct dialogue with Moscow and for redressing the consequences of inherent asymmetries of force in today's world. It does not give Russia a veto over American policy or vice versa, but it acknowledges Moscow's prestige as a nuclear player and forces it to start dealing with real as opposed to phantom threats. It also offers Russia the opportunity to move from defense relationships based on the presupposition of enemies and deterrence, which is inherently destabilizing as regards international nuclear agendas, even if deterrence may or may not have failed. It offers a chance to move to smaller nuclear arsenals, thus realizing the NPT's provisions and a world more dominated by defenses and nonproliferation where regional security actors have their security concerns dealt with more honestly than has previously been the case. This is by no means Nirvana or the promised land. But arguably the agenda outlined here represents steps forward to dialogue and accord rather than what we now see, i.e., regression towards discord, arms races, and multiplying sources of regional tensions. If Moscow rejects this alternative, it should then have the onus placed upon it to devise a more satisfactory alternative. And it will have to bear the consequences of its policies. Neither Washington nor Moscow may succeed in resolving nonproliferation or arms control issues soon, but to abstain from trying out of a misplaced and unjustified desire for self-aggrandizement or to use force to end threats and then fail at the task hardly represents a better alternative to what is proposed here.

ENDNOTES - CHAPTER 6

1. Nazila Fathi, "Iran Escalates Military Rhetoric," *www.nytimes.com*, August 5, 2008; Bruce Riedel, "Pakistan's Pathways to Proliferation," presented to the NPS-DTRA Conference on Proliferation Pathways, Belfast, ME, July 17-18, 2008; Dennis Gormley, *Missile Contagion: The Threat To International Security*, Westport, CT: Praeger Security International, 2008. Gormley was published as this volume was going to press and builds on Gormley's and other researchers' findings some of which are cited below.

2. National Intelligence Estimate (NIE), *Iran: Nuclear Intentions and Capabilities*, Washington, DC: National Intelligence Council, 2007, available at *www.dni.org* (Henceforth NIE).

3. *Ibid.*

4. J. Michael McConnell, *Annual Threat Assessment of the Director of National Intelligence for the Senate Select Committee on Intelligence*, February 5, 2008, pp. 11-12.

5. "Test of Iranian Space Launch Vehicle Causes Another Crack in Russian-Iranian Relations," *WMD Insights*, March 2008, *www.wmdinsights.com/I23/I23_ME1_TestofIranian.htm*.

6. Duncan Lennox, "WMD and Missile Proliferation," *RUSI Journal*, April 2006, p. 57.

7. "Russia Sees No Need for Iran To Continue With Uranium Enrichment," *RIA Novosti*, December 26, 2007.

8. McConnell, pp. 11-12; NIE.

9. McConnell, pp. 11-12.

10. NIE.

11. Mark Heinrich, "Iran Testing Advanced Centrifuges," *Reuters*, February 7, 2008.

12. "Interview With Shannon Kile, Iran: 'Skepticism in Order' on Claims Of Nuclear Progress," *Radio Free Europe Radio Liberty Features*, April 9, 2008.

13. McConnell, p. 12.

14. Conversation with Dr. Ariel Cohen of the Heritage Foundation, Washington, DC, December 5, 2007; Gerald Steinberg, "Decoding the U.S. National Intelligence Estimate on Iran's Nuclear Weapons Program," *Jerusalem Issue Brief*, December 5, 2007.

15. McConnell, p. 11.

16. "US Defense Secretary Sees Iran as Threat to US and Mideast," *AFP*, December 8, 2007; Hoosain Aryan, "Iranian Military Flaunts New Capabilities as Tensions Arise," *Radio Free Europe Radio Liberty Newsline*, October 24, 2007.

17. NIE.

18. John Bolton, "The Flaws in the Iran Report," *Washington Post*, December 6, 2007, p. A29.

19. NIE.

20. *Ibid*.

21. NIE.

22. Bolton, p. A29.

23. Steinberg.

24. *Northeast Asian Peace and Security Network (NAPSNET)*, December 6, 2007; *NAPSNET*, December 7, 2007; "Seoul: No Progress on Nuclear Disclosure by North Korea," *Deutsche Press Agentur*, December 6, 2007.

25. Jin Dae-woong, "N. Korea Persisting with Missiles," Seoul, Korea, *The Korea Herald Internet Version*, in English, February 29, 2008, Foreign Broadcast Information Service (hereafter *FBIS*) *SOV*,

February 29, 2008; "N.Korea Still Developing Nuclear Capable ICBM: U.S. Official," Kyodo, Japan, April 1, 2008; "N.Korea's Yongbyon Nuclear Facilities almost Scrapped-China," *RIA Novosti*, December 25, 2007.

26. "ROK Daily: US Defense Secretary: North Korea Exports Missiles to Iran," Seoul, Korea, *Dong-a-Ilbo Internet Version*, in English, November 3, 2007, *FBIS SOV*, November 3, 2007.

27. Choe Sang-Hun, "North Korea Says it Has Said Enough," *New York Times*, January 5, 2008, *www.nytimes.com*; "North Korea Says It Will Boost Its 'War Deterrent'," *Los Angeles Times Wire Services*, January 4, 2008.

28. Helene Cooper, "U.S. Sees Stalling by North Korea on Nuclear Pact," *New York Times*, January 19, 2008.

29. See the article in the Russian Journal (English language version) *Military Thought*, No. 2, 2007, from speeches given at a conference at the Academy of Military Sciences in Moscow, January 20, 2007; M.A. Gareev, "Russia's New Military Doctrine: Structure and Substance, pp. 1-14; Y. N. Baluyevsky, "Theoretical and Methodological Foundations of the Military Doctrine of the Russian Federation (Plans for a Report), pp. 15-22; A.S. Rukshin, "Doctrinal Views on Employment and Organizational Development of the Armed Forces of Russia," pp. 23-30. Gareev is President of the Academy; Baluyevsky is Chief of Staff; and Rukshin his Deputy.

30. "Putin Interviewed by Journalists from G8 Countries — text," *www.kremlin.ru*, June 4, 2007, retrieved from Nexis-Lexis; Moscow, *Agentstvo Voyennykh Novostey, Internet Version*, in English, May 16, 2007, *Open Source Committee, FBIS Central Eurasia, May 16, 2007*; Moscow, Ministry of Foreign Affairs *Internet Version, Press Conference of Foreign Minister Sergei Lavrov with Secretary of State Condoleezza Rice*, May 16, 2007, *www.mid.ru*.

31. Stephen Blank, *Towards a New Russia Policy*, Carlisle, PA: Strategic Studies Institute, U.S. Army War College, 2008.

32. *Ibid.*; Gareev, pp. 1-14; Baluyevsky, pp. 15-22; Rukshin, pp. 23-30.

33. "Putin Interviewed by Journalists from G8 Countries— text."

34. Yaroslav Cheslavovich Romanchuk, "When Silence Is a Weakness," Moscow, *Nezavisimaya Gazeta*, in Russian, August 31, 2007, *Open Source Committee, FBIS Central Eurasia*, September 11, 2007.

35. "Interview with Foreign Minister Sergei Lavrov," *Rossiyskaya Gazeta,* February 21-28, 2007, *www.mid.ru*; Dmitri Solovyov, "Russia Says It Must Have Nuclear Parity With U.S.," *Reuters*, December 7, 2007.

36. *Report of the Defense Science Board Task Force on Nuclear Capabilities: Report Summary*, Washington, DC: Office of the Under Secretary of Defense for Acquisition, Technology, and Logistics, December, 2006, pp. 11-12.

37. *Ibid.*, pp. 12-13.

38. *Ibid.*

39. "US Report Warns of Russian Nuclear Threat," *Jane's Intelligence Digest*, January 26, 2007, *jid.janes.com*.

40. Quoted in Paul Abelsky, "Agreeing to Disagree," *Russia Profile*, No. 29, 2007, p. 52.

41. "Moscow Unconcerned by Delays in N. Korea De- nuclearization," *RIA Novosti*, December 27, 2007.

42. Broadcast of Joint News Conference of Foreign Minister Sergey Lavrov and Armenian Foreign Minister Vardan Oskanyan, Moscow, *Vesti TV*, in Russian, December 5, 2007, *FBIS SOV*, December 5, 2007.

43. Stephen Blank, "The Foundations of Russian Policy in the Persian Gulf," Dubai, United Arab Emirates: Gulf Research Center, forthcoming.

44. Moscow, *Agentstvo Voyennykh Novostey Internet Version*, in English, December 5, 2007, *FBIS SOV*, December 5, 2007; Moscow, *Interfax*, in English, December 4, 2007, *FBIS SOV*, December 4, 2007; Moscow, *ITAR-TASS*, in English, October 30, 2007, *FBIS SOV*, October 30, 2007; Inga Kumskova, "What Will Moscow 'Present' Tehran With?," Moscow, *Moskovskiy Komsomolets*, in Russian, November 1, 2007, *FBIS SOV*, November 1, 2007.

45. Pavel K. Baev, "Moscow Raises Stakes in Iran Game," *Eurasia Daily Monitor*, January 8, 2008; "Iran: Russia Will Supply New Air Defense System," *Agence France-Presse*, December 26, 2007; "Russia Denies Selling Iran an S-300 Air Defense System," *Agence France-Presse*, December 27, 2007.

46. "Iran Lauds Russia, China For 'Opening Nuclear Splits'," *zeenews.com*, October 29, 2007, *www.zeenes.com/znnew/articles.asp?aid=332226&sid=wor*.

47. Anatol Lieven, "The Mutual Responsibility and Irresponsibility of the West and Russia," *International Affairs*, Vol. LIII, No. 5, 2007, pp. 24-27.

48. Leon Aron, "Putin's Cold War," *Wall Street Journal*, December 26, 2007, p. 11.

49. Moscow, *Agentstvo Voyennykh Novostey Internet Version*, in English, November 7, 2007, *FBIS SOV* November 7, 2007; "Events in Pakistan May Become Prologue to Nuclear War," Moscow, *www.forum.ru*, in Russian, November 6, 2007, FBIS *SOV*, November 6, 2007.

50. Gordon M. Hahn, *Russia's Islamic Threat*, New Haven, CT, and London, UK: Yale University press, 2007, pp. 228-229.

51. *Ibid.*, p. 229.

52. *Ibid.*, pp. 229-230.

53. "Russia Stops 120 Nuclear Smuggling Attempts in 2007," *NTI: Global Security Network*, January 3, 2008, *www.nti.org*.

54. Lawrence Scott Sheets and William J. Broad, "Smuggler's Plot Highlights Fear Over Uranium," *New York Times*, January 25, 2007, *www.nytimes.com*.

55. *A Secure Europe in a Better World: European Security Strategy*, Paris, France: European Institute for Security Studies, 2003, pp. 7-8.

56. Elaine Sciolino, "Iranian Pushes Nuclear Talks Back to Square 1," *New York Times*, December 2, 2007; Elaine Sciolino, "On Nuclear Seesaw, the Balance Seems to Shift to Iran," *New York Times*, November 30, 2007; "France's Chirac Backtracks After Downplaying Threat of Iran Nuke," *USA Today*, February 1, 2007.

57. Open Source Center, *OSC Analysius:* "Opposition Media on Burma's Alleged Nuclear Cooperation With Russia, N. Korea," *OSC Analaysis*, in English, *FBIS SOV*, December 8, 2007; Seoul, Korea, The Korea Herald Internet Version, in English, January 28, 2007, *Open Source Center FBIS SOV*, January 28, 2007; Moscow, *ITAR-TASS* in English, January 26, 2007, *FBIS SOV*, January 26, 2007; Uzi Mahnaimi, Sarah Baxter, and Michael Sheridan, "Israelis 'Blew Apart Syrian Nuclear Cache'," *Times Online*, September 16, 2007.

58. Peter Finn and Robin Wright, "'No Real Data' on Iranian Nuclear Ambitions, Putin Asserts," *Washington Post Foreign Service* Thursday, October 11, 2007, p. A12.

59. Moscow, *Interfax*, in English, October 10, 2007, *FBIS SOV*, October 10, 2007.

60. Robert O. Freedman, *Russia, Iran, and the Nuclear Question: the Putin Record*, Carlisle, PA: Strategic Studies Institute, U.S. Army War College, 2006.

61. Cited in Etel Solingen, *Nuclear Logics: Contrasting Paths in East Asia & the Middle East*, Princeton, NJ: Princeton University Press, 2007, p. 264.

62. *Ibid.*

63. Gilbert Rozman, *Security Challenges to the United States in Northeast Asia: Looking Beyond the Transformation of the Six-Party Talks,* in Gilbert Rozman and Chu Shulong, *East Asian Security: Two Views,* Carlisle, PA: Strategic Studies Institute, U.S. Army War College, 2007, p. 45; Dmitri Trenin, "Russia and Global Security Norms," *The Washington Quarterly,* Vol. XXVII, No. 2, Spring 2004, pp. 63-77.

64. "Progress Continues in U.S.-Russian Nuclear Threat Cooperative Threat Reduction Efforts," *WMD Insights,* December 2007-January 2008, *www.wmdinsights.com;* Richard Weitz, *Revitalizing US-Russian Security Cooperation,* Adelphi Papers, No. 377, Oxford, UK: Oxford University Press and the International Institute for Strategic Studies, 2005; Richard Weitz, *Russian-American Security Cooperation After St. Petersburg: Challenges and Opportunities,* Carlisle, PA: Strategic Studies Institute, U.S. Army War College, 2006.

65. Weitz, *Russian-American Security Cooperation After St. Petersburg.*

66. Weitz, *Revitalizing US-Russian Security Cooperation,* p. 14.

67. As stated by Daniel Flaherty of the State Department at a panel of the annual convention of the American Association for the Advancement of Slavic Studies, New Orleans, LA, November 16, 2007.

68. Cairo, *Al-Akhbar* in Arabic, February 27, 2007, *FBIS SOV,* February 27, 2007; James A. Russell, *Regional Threats and Security Strategy: The Troubling Case of Today's Middle East,* Carlisle, PA: Strategic Studies Institute, U.S. Army War College, 2007, pp. 17-21; Robert O. Freedman, "The Russian Resurgence in the Middle East," *China and Eurasia Forum Quarterly,* Vol. V, No. 3, 2007, pp. 19-23.

69. Karl Vick, "'Energy', Iran Spur Turkey's Revival of Nuclear Plans," *Washington Post Foreign Service,* March 7, 2006, p. A14; Burak Ege Bekdil, "Nukes, Regional Instabilities Threaten Turkey: Defense Chief," *Defensenews.com,* March 20, 2006, *www.defensenews.com.*

70. Duygu Bazoglu Sezer, "Turkish Security Challenges in the 1990s," in Stephen J. Blank, ed., *Mediterranean Security Into the Coming Millennium*, Carlisle, PA: Strategic Studies Institute, U.S. Army War College, 1999, pp. 272-274; *Idem*, "Turkey's New Security Environment, Nuclear Weapons and Proliferation," *Comparative Strategy*, Vol. XIV, No. 2, 1995, pp. 149-172; see also Ilter Turan, "Mediterranean Security in the Light of Turkish Concerns," *Perspectives*, Vol. III, No. 2, June-August, 1998, pp. 16-31.

71. *FBIS SOV*, January 26, 2007.

72. "Iran, Russia Sign 'Zohreh' Satellite Deal," Tehran (IRNA) January 31, 2005; Olga Bozhyeva, "Interview with Russian Space Forces Commander, Colonel General Vladimir Popovkin," Moscow, *Moskovskiy Komsomolets*, in Russian, October 4, 2007, *FBIS SOV*, October 4, 2007.

73. Dennis M. Gormley, "Missile Proliferation Challenges: Assessment and Prospects for Multilateral Solutions," Paper Presented at a Seminar Sponsored by the European Union's Institute for Security Studies, "The Hague Code of Conduct Against Ballistic Missile Proliferation," Vienna, Austria, May 30, 2007.

74. Duncan Lennox, "WMD and Missile Proliferation," *RUSI Journal*, April, 2006, p. 57.

75. *Ibid.*, p. 58.

76. Michael Evans, "Spy Photos Reveal 'Secret Launch Site' for Iran's Long-Range Missiles," *London Times*, April 11, 2008.

77. Scott Jones, "Focus on Cruise Threat," *Defense News*, April 11, 2005, p. 21.

78. *Ibid.*

79. Gormley.

80. *Ibid.*

81. *Ibid.*

82. *Ibid.*

83. G. V. C. Naidu, "Ballistic Missile Defense: Perspectives on India-Japan Collaboration," *Strategic Analysis*, Vol. XXXI, No. 1, January-February 2007, pp. 55-77.

84. Stephen Blank, "Strategic Rivalry in the Asia-Pacific Theater: A New Nuclear Arms Race?" *Korean Journal of Defense Analysis*, forthcoming.

85. Gordon Correra, *Shopping for Bombs: Nuclear Proliferation, Global Insecurity and the Rise of the A. Q. Khan Network*, Oxford, UK: Oxford University Press, 2006.

86. *Ibid.*

87. Rahul Bedi, "India Confirms Nuclear Boat Plans," *Jane's Defence Weekly*, December 12, 2007, *www4.janews.com/subscribejdw*; C. Raja Mohan and Klaus Voll, "An Alliance of Rivals," *Transatlantic Intenrationale Politik*, Winter 2007, p. 59.

88. Adrian Levy and Catherine Scott-Clark, *Deception: Pakistan, the United States and the Secret Trade in Nuclear Weapons*, New York: Walker & Company, 2007, pp. 447-448; "Khan's Nuclear Network Still Trying in 2004 to Buy Nuclear Technology: Swiss Report," *Associated Press*, May 26, 2005.

89. Gormley.

90. Rahul Bedi, "Who Is In Control of Pakistan's Nuclear Arsenal?" *London Daily Telegraph*, December 29, 2007.

91. Kurt M. Campbell and Robert J. Einhorn, "Avoiding the Tipping Point: Concluding Observations," Kurt M. Campbell, Robert J. Einhorn, and Mitchell B. Reiss, eds., *The Nuclear Tipping Point: Why States Reconsider Their Nuclear Choices*, Vartan Gregorian, Foreword, Washington, DC: Brookings Institution Press, 2004, pp. 321-325.

92. Harsh V. Pant, "A Great Time for a Nuclear Pakistan," *www.isn.ethz.ch*, November 22, 2007; Shaun Gregory, *The Security of Nuclear Weapons in Pakistan*, Pakistan Security Research Unit (PSRU) Briefing No. 22, November 18, 2007.

93. *Ibid.*

94. Peter Wonacott, "Inside Pakistan's Drive to Guard It's a-Bombs," *Wall Street Journal*, November 29, 2007.

95. Pant; Gregory.

96. "Questions Persist on Reported Russian Lease of Nuclear Sub to India," *WMD Insights*, December 2007-January 2008, *www.wmd.insights.com*; Stephen Blank, "Proliferation and Counterproliferation in Russian Strategy," and Remarks on Russia, *Proceedings from the Conference on Countering the Missile Threat: International Military Strategies*, February 22, 1999, Washington, DC: Jewish Institute for National Security Affairs, 1999, pp. 127-149 and 41-45, respectively; and *Korean Journal of Defense Analysis*, Vol. XII, No. 1, Winter-Spring 2000, pp. 149-191; Mohan Malik, "The Proliferation Axis: Beijing-Islamabad-Pyongyang," Korean Journal of Defense Analysis, Vol. XV, No. 1, Spring 2003, pp. 57-100.

97. "Did China's Autocracy Exploit India's Democracy to Stall the U.S.-India Nuclear Draft?" *WMD Insight,* Open Source Committee, November, 2007, *www.wmdinsights.com/120/120_EAI_Did China's Autocracy.htm.*

98. Henry Sokolski ed., *Gauging U.S.-Indian Strategic Cooperation*, Carlisle, PA: Strategic Studies Institute, U.S. Army War College, 2007, provides a comprehensive series of discussions on both sides of the issues raised by these agreements.

99. Shaun Walker, "Fueling India's Growth, " Russia Profile, I, No. 4, May, 206, p. 13-14; P. S. Suryanarayana, "Australia Assures Cooperation in Civil Nuclear Energy Sector," *The Hindu*, August 1, 2007, cited in *nuclearno.com/text.asp?12059*; "China May Seek N-Cooperation With India," *Expressindia.com*, September 5, 2007.

100. Swapna Kona, "Building an Edifice, Security Partnerships," *New Delhi Institute of Peace and Conflict Studies* website, in English, April 10, 2006, *FBIS NES*, April 10, 2006; V. R. Raghavan, "India's Quest for Nuclear Legitimacy," *Asia Pacific Review*, Vol. XIII, No. 1, 2006, p. 66.

101. Swapna Kona, "Russian Nuclear Fuel for Tarapur," New Delhi, *Institute of Peace and Conflict Studies*, Internet Version, in English, March 23, 2006, *FBIS NES*, March 23, 2006.

102. *Ibid.*; "China May Seek N-Cooperation With India"; Mohan and Voll, p. 59.

103. Solingen strongly argues that the decisive factor is the mode of political survival of regimes in proliferating states.

104. Harsh V. Pant, "The US-India Deal: The Beginning of a Beautiful Friendship?" *Cambridge Review of International Affairs*, Vol. XX, No. 3, September, 2007, p. 468.

105. *Ibid.*, p. 470.

106. A. Vinod Kumar, "Counterproliferation: India's New Imperatives and Options," *Strategic Analysis*, Vol. XXXI, No. 1, January-February 2007, p. 34.

107. Mohan and Voll, p. 59.

108. "N.Korea Dreams of Int'l Kudos as a Nuclear Power," Digital *Chosun* (English Edition), March 29, 2007, *english.chosun. com*.

109. Zbigniew Brzezinski, *Second Chance: Three Presidents and the Crisis of American Superpower*, New York: Basic Books, 2007, p. 172.

110. Mark Mazzetti and Neil A. Lewis, "U.S. Says India Broke Law to Get Weapons Technology," *International Herald Tribune*, April 3, 2007, *www.iht.com*.

111. Flaherty.

112. Freedman, "The Russian Resurgence in the Middle East," pp. 19-23, *FBIS SOV*, February 27, 2007; Russell, pp. 15-22.

113. "No Final Decision to Quit INF treaty - FM Lavrov," *RIA Novosti*, February 16, 2007; "Russia Made a Mistake By Scrapping Its Mid-Range Missiles-Ivanov," Moscow, *Interfax*, in English, February 7, 2007, *FBIS SOV*, February 7, 2007.

114. Moscow, *ITAR-TASS* in English, February 26, 2007, *FBIS SOV*, February 26, 2007.

115. *Ibid.*

116. *Ibid.*

117. Tehran, *Fars News Agency Internet Version*, in Persian, November 27, 2007, *FBIS SOV*, November 27, 2007.

118. "Iran Sees Progress in Nuclear Power," Atlanta *Journal-Constitution*, November 25, 2007.

119. "Russia Says IAEA Report on Iran Shows Progress But Much Still to Do," ITAR-*TASS*, in English, November 19, 2007.

120. *Ibid.*; Moscow, ITAR-TASS in English, September 12, 2007, *FBIS SOV*, September 12, 2007.

121. Tehran, *Jomhuri-ye Eslami Internet Version*, in Persian, September 11, 2007, *FBIS SOV* September 11, 2007.

122. Campbell and Einhorn, "Avoiding the Tipping Point," pp. 323-324.

123. U.S.Department of Defense, *Nuclear Posture Review*, (Henceforth NPR), *www.defenselink.mil/news/Jan2002/d20020109npr.pdf*; Kerry M. Kartcher, "U.S. Nuclear Weapons and Nonproliferation: Dispelling the Myths," Presentation to the Carnegie Moscow Center, February 2, 2007, available at *www.carnegie.ru/en/pubs/media/101192007.02.02.Presentation.ppt*.

124. Kartcher.

125. Stephen Blank, "Undeterred: The Return of Nuclear War," *Georgetown Journal of International Affairs*, Vol. I, No. 2, Summer/Fall 2000, pp. 55-63; China's test of an anti-satellite weapon (ASAT) in January 2007 is only the latest manifestation of these trends to weaponize space.

126. David Yost, "France's New Nuclear Doctrine," *International Affairs*, Vol. LXXXII, No. 4, pp. 701-721, 2006; NPR; Stephen Blank, "Nuclear Strategy and Nuclear Proliferation in Russian Strategy," *Report of the Commission To Assess The Ballistic Missile Threat To The United States*, Appendix III, Unclassified Working Papers, Pursuant to Public Law 201, 1998, pp. 57-77; Norman Bowen, "France, Europe, and the Mediterranean in a Sarkozy Presidency," *Mediterranean Quarterly*, Vol. XVIII, No. 4, Fall 2007, p. 5.

127. George Perkovich, "Bush's Nuclear Revolution," *Foreign Affairs*, Vol. LXXXII, No. 2, 2003, p. 2.

128. Louis Rene Beres, "Israel's Uncertain Strategic Future," *Parameters*, Vol. XXXVII, No. 1, Spring 2007, pp. 37-54; "Rules Set for Using PAC-3 Missile Defense: Intercept Could Be OK'd Before Enemy Launch," *The Yomiuri Shimbun*, March 26, 2007, *www.yomiuri.co.jp*.

129. "India Likely to Export Nuclear Technology," *NDTV Profit*, February 26, 2007, *www.ndtvprofit.com*.

130. Colin S. Gray, *The Second Nuclear Age*, Boulder, CO: Lynne Rienner Publishers, 1999.

131. Christopher Jones, "The Axis of Nonproliferation," *Problems of Post-Communism*, Vol. LIII, No. 21, March-April 2006, pp. 3-16.

132. *Ibid.*

133. Conversations With former U.S. officials, March 2007.

134. "US Defense Chief Sees Problems in Russian Withdrawal from INF," *ITAR-TASS*, February 16, 2007; Conversations with former Defense Department officials, March 2007.

135. *Radio Free Europe Radio Liberty Newswire*, February 26, 2007.

136. Ellen Laipson, "Syria: Can the Myth Be Maintained?" in Campbell, Einhorn, and Reiss, eds., p. 94.

137. "Moscow, No Basis for Interaction With U.S. Missile Defense in East," *www.tmcnet.com, from Interfax News Agency via Thomson Dialog News Edge, Europe,* April 6, 2007.

138. Rozman.

139. Charles L. Pritchard, *Failed Diplomacy: The Tragic Story of How North Korea Got the Bomb,* Washington, DC: Brookings Institution Press, 2007; Stephen Blank, "The End of the Six-Party Talks?" *Strategic Insights,* January 2007, *www.nps.navy.mil.*

140. Stephen Blank, "Strategic Rivalry in the Asia-Pacific Theater: a New Nuclear Arms Race?"

141. Naidu, pp. 64-68.

142. Tokyo, *Nihon wa Sudeni Kitaichosen Kakumisairu200KI no Shateika ni Aru,* in Japanese, March 6, 2008, pp. 218-232, *FBIS SOV,* March 24, 2008.

143. *Ibid., FBIS SOV,* March 25, 2008.

144. Herb Keinon, "Russia Set on Mideast Parley 'Whether Israel Likes It or Not'. Gov't Sources Describe Lavrov's Visit as 'Nasty'," *Jerusalem Post,* March 26, 2007, p. 1.

145. Hideya Kurata, "A Conceptual Analysis of the Six-Party Talks: Building Peace Through Security Assurances," *Asian Security,* Vol. III, No. 1, 2007, p. 16.

146. John Simpson, *The Nuclear Landscape in 2004: Past Present and Future,* The Weapons of Mass Destruction Commission, Paper No. 3, 2004, p. 16, *www.wmdcommission.org.*

147. *www.kremlin.ru*, October 14, 2007; *RIA Novosti*, February 16, 2007; *FBIS SOV*, February 7, 2007; *FBIS SOV*, February 26, 2007.

148. Neil King, "China-Iran Trade Surge Vexes U.S." *Wall Street Journal*, July 27, 2007, *www.wsj.com*.

149. "The ISCIP Analyst," Vol. XIII, No. 9, March 8, 2007, Institute for the Study of Conflict, Ideology, and Policy, Boston University, *www.bu.edu/iscip*; "Press Conference with Political Analyst Alexei Arbatov and Vice President of the Academy of Geopolitical Problems Leonid Ivashov on Russian Foreign Policy," *RIA Novosti*, February 6, 2007, *www.fednews.ru*; Alexei Arbatov, "An Unnecessary and Dangerous Step," *Nezavisimoye Voyennoye Obozreniye*, No. 7, March, 2007, *www.america-russia.net/eng/security/143683092*.

150. Kurt Kisler, "Star Wars, New Implications: Shooting Down of Satellite Shows Extent to which Washington Is Pursuing Military Exploitation of Space," Munich, Germany, *Suddeutsche Zeitung*, in German, February 22, 2008, *FBIS SOV*, February 22, 2008.

151. Richard Weitz, "Arm Wrestling," *The National Interest*, March-April, 2008, No. 94, pp. 72-74.

152. Stephen J. Cimbala, "Nuclear First Use: Facing the Inevitable or Playing with Fire?" Unpublished Paper, pp. 16-17.

153. Christopher Jones, "The Axis of Non-Proliferation," *Problems of Post-Communism*, Vol. LXXX, No. 2, March-April, 2006, pp. 3-16.

154. *Ibid.*

155. Brzezinski, *Second Chance*, p. 96.

156. Jones, pp. 7-8.

157. On Russo-American cooperation, see Richard Weitz, "Revitalizing US-Russian Security Cooperation," *Adelphi Paper*, No. 377, Oxford, UK: Oxford University Press, 2005; and Richard

274

Weitz, *Russian-American Security Cooperation After St. Petersburg: Challenges and Opportunities*, Carlisle, PA: Strategic Studies Institute, U.S. Army War College, 2007.

158. Carol Kessler, "Post-Cold War Effects on the Non-Proliferation Regime," *Problems of Post-Communism*, Vol. LIII, No. 2, March-April 2006, p. 37.

159. Quoted from Clifford Kupchan, "Real Demokratik," *The National Interest*, Fall 2004, cited in *ibid*.

160. "China Urges Iran to Cooperate With IAEA, Create Conditions for Talks," *Xinhua*, November 3, 2007.

161. "China Said to Provide UN Iran Nuke Info," *Associated Press*, April 3, 2008.

162. Brzezinski, *Second Chance*, p. 172.

163. *Ibid.*, pp. 172-173.

164. *Ibid.*, pp. 170-171; Minxin Pei, *Assertive Pragmatism: China's Economic Rise and its Impact on Chinese Foreign Policy*, Proliferation Papers, Institut Francais des Relations Internationales (IFRI), 2006, p. 17, *www.ifri.org*; David Kerr, "The Sino-Russian Partnership and U.S. Policy Toward North Korea: From Hegemony to Concert in Northeast Asia," *International Studies Quarterly*, Vol. XXXXIX, No. 3, September 2005, pp. 411-437; Constantine C. Menges, *China: The Gathering Threat*, Nashville, TN: Nelson Current Publishers, 2005.

165. Rozman, p. 45.

166. "Did China's Autocracy Exploit India's Democracy to Stall the U.S.-India Nuclear Draft?"

167. *Ibid.*

168. Kumar, p. 34.

169. "Iran Issues Missile Threat to U.S., Israel," *Middle East Newsline*, December 27, 2000; Ivo Daalder, "What Vision for the Nuclear future?" *Washington Quarterly*, Vol. XVIII, No. 2, Spring

1995, pp. 131-132; Lawrence Freedman, "Great Powers, Vital Interests and Nuclear Weapons," *Survival,* Vol. XXXVI, No. 4, Winter 1994-1995, pp. 46-47.

170. David Blair, "How To Defeat the United States: The Operational Effects of the Proliferation of Weapons of Mass Destruction," Henry Sokolski, ed., *Fighting Proliferation New Concepts for the Nineties,* Maxwell AFB, Montgomery, AL: Air University Press, 1996, pp. 75-88.

171. David S. McDonough, "Nuclear Superiority: The 'New Triad' and the Evolution of Nuclear Strategy," *Adelphi Paper,* No. 383, 2006; Keir A. Lieber and Daryl G. Press, "The Rise of U.S. Nuclear Primacy," *Foreign Affairs,* Vol. LXXXV, No. 2, March-April 2006, pp. 42-54; Keir A. Lieber and Daryl G. Press, "The End of MAD?: The Nuclear Dimensions of U.S. Primacy," *International Security,* Vol. XX, No. 4, Spring 2006, pp. 7-44; George Bunn and Christopher F. Chyba, eds., *U.S. Nuclear Policy: Confronting Today's Threats,* Foreword, William J. Perry, Washington, DC: Brookings Institution Press, 2006.

172. Keith Payne, "The Continuing Role for U.S. Strategic Forces," *Comparative Strategy,* Vol. XXVI, No. 4, July-September 2007, p. 271.

173. "Japan Intercepts Missile in Milestone Test," *Reuters,* December 17, 2007; Tokyo, *Kyodo World Service,* in English, December 14, 2007, *FBIS SOV,* December 14, 2007.

174. Mure Dickie and Jonathan Soble, "Missile Test Fails to Raise China's Ire," *Financial Times,* December 19, 2007, *www. ft.com;* "China Unmoved by Japan Missile Interception," *Reuters,* December 18, 2007.

175. Moscow, *Interfax,* in English, October 17, 2007, *FBIS SOV,* October 17, 2007.

176. *Ibid;* Tokyo, *Kyodo World Service,* in English, October 13, 2007, *FBIS SOV,* October 13, 2007.

177. Esook Yoon and Dong Hyung Lee, "A View From Asia, Vladimir Putin's Korean Opportunity: Russian Interests in the

North Korean Nuclear Crises," *Comparative Strategy*, Vol. XXIV, No. 3, 2005, p. 194.

178. Charles Pritchard, *Failed Diplomacy: The Tragic Story of How North Korea Got the Bomb*, Washington, DC: Brookings Institution Press, 2007; Stephen Blank, "The End of the Six-Party Talks?"

179. Alexander Lukin, "Russia's China Card: Eyes on Washington," Byung-Kook Kim and Anthony Jones, eds., *Power and Security in Northeast Asia: Shifting Strategies*, Boulder, CO: Lynne Rienner Publishers, 2007, p. 187.

180. Remarks of Ambassador Gleb A. Ivashentsov, Second Department for Asia Director, Russian Foreign Ministry, *Iran's Security Challenges and the Region*, Liechtenstein Colloquium Report, Vol. I, Liechtenstein, Germany, and Princeton, NJ, 2005, p. 39.

181. Yitzhak Shichor, "Evil From the North: The DPRK Axis and Its Strategic Dimensions," *Korean Journal of Defense Analysis*, Vol. XIX, No. 4, Winter 2007, pp. 81-82.

182. *Ibid.*, p. 91.

183. Cairo, *Al-Akhbar* in Arabic, February 27, 2007, *FBIS SOV*, February 27, 2007.

184. Riyadh, Saudi Arabia, "Putin Opens Saudi-Russian Economic Forum," *SPA*, Internet Version, February 12, 2007, *FBIS SOV*, February 12, 2007; Moscow, *Interfax*, in English, February 12, 2007, *FBIS SOV*, February 12, 2007; Moscow, *Vesti TV*, in Russian, February 12, 2007, *FBIS SOV*, February 12, 2007.

185. Alexei Vassilev, *Russian Foreign Policy in the Middle East: From Messianism to Pragmatism*, Reading, PA: Ithaca Press, p. 360.

186. This report is to be found in *Joint Publication Research Service Arms Control (JPRS TAC) 95-009*, April 6, 1995.

187. *Ibid.*, p. 7.

188. *Ibid.*; Tehran, Iran, *Voice of the Islamic Republic of Iran First Programme Network*, in Persian, August 22, 1994, *Open Source Committee, FBIS Near East Service*, (Henceforth *FBIS NES*), August 22, 1994, p. 52.

189. "The Non-Proliferation Treaty Must Be Prolonged," *Moscow News*, April 21-27, 1995, p. 13.

190. Stephen J. Blank, "Russia and Iran in a New Middle East," *Mediterranean Quarterly*, Vol. III, No. 4, Fall 1992, pp. 108-128.

191. See the remarks of Putin's special presidential representative on terrorism, Anatoly Safonov, in Mark Smith, *A Russian Chronology April-June 2006*, Camberley, Surrey, UK: Conflict Studies Research Centre, 2006, p. 31.

192. Moscow, *Mirovaya Ekonomika i Mezhdunarodnye Otnosheniya* (World Economy and International Relations), No. 1, January 1995, *FBIS-SOV*-95-056-S, March 23, 1995, pp. 11-16.

193. Tehran, Iran, *IRNA* in English, March 8, 1995, *FBIS NES*, 95-045, March 8, 1995, p. 51.

194. Tehran, Iran, *Abrar* in Persian, March 7, 1995, *FBIS-NES*-95-052, March 17, 1995, pp. 71-72.

195. *RIA Novosti*, June 21, 2007.

196. Zbigniew Brzezinski, "Living With Russia," *The National Interest*, No. 61, Fall 2000, p. 5.

197. Sergei Karaganov, "Maximizing Russia's Engagement With the West," *Internationale Politik, Transatlantic Edition*, 2002, No. 4, pp. 39-43.

198. Pan Zhengiang, *China's Non-Proliferation Policy and Practices*, Konrad Adenauer Stiftung, Online Info-Dienst Aufgabe, No. 1, 2004, January 15, 2004.

199. Moscow, *Interfax*, In English, October 22, 2007, *FBIS SOV*, October 22, 2007.

200. "IAEA in Full Control of Iran's Nuclear Program - Foreign Ministry," *RIA Novosti*, December 15, 2007; "Russia Says Fuel for Iran NPP Insufficient for Weapon Use," *RIA Novosti*, December 12, 2007.

201. Weitz, *Revitalizing US-Russian Security Cooperation*, pp. 17-59; Weitz, *Russian-American Security Cooperation After St. Petersburg*, pp. 19-36; Ferguson *et al.*, *The Four Faces of Nuclear Terrorism*, Monterey, CA: 2004.

202. NIE.

203. Joseph Cirincione and Carl Robicheaux, "Into the Breach: The Drive for a New Global Nuclear Strategy," Jeffrey Laurenti and Carl Robicheaux, eds., *Breaking the Nuclear Impasse: New Prospects for Security Against Weapons Threats*, New York: The Century Foundation Press, 2007, p. 13.

204. Thomas Friedman, "A Choice for the Rogues," *New York Times*, August 2, 2006, *www.nytimes.com*.

205. Conversations with U.S. officials, June 2005; Kerr, pp. 411-437.

206. *Ibid.* More recently see the Russo-Chinese reporting on Chinese President Hu Jintao's visit to Moscow on March 26-27, 2007, which repeatedly stressed the identity of viewpoints of the two states on Korea and Asian–Pacific issues.

207. *Ibid.*; Alexander Zhebin, "The Bush Doctrine, Russia, and Korea," in Mel Gurtov and Peter Van Ness, eds., *Confronting the Bush Doctrine: Critical Views From Asia*, Abingdon, UK, and New York: Routledge, 2005, p. 149.

208. Robert Jervis, "U.S. Grand Strategy: Mission Impossible," *Naval War College Review*, Summer 1998, pp. 22-36; Richard K. Betts, "Power, Prospects, and Priorities: Choices for Strategic Change," *Naval War College Review*, Winter 1997, pp. 9-22; John C. Gannon, "Intelligence Challenges Through 2015," *odci.gov/cia/publicaffairs/speeches/gannon_speech_05022000.html*.

209. Christopher Jones, "The Axis of Nonproliferation," *Problems of Post-Communism*, Vol. LIII, No. 21, March-April, 2006, pp. 3-16.

210. Etel Solingen, *Regional Orders at Century's Dawn: Global and Domestic Influences on Grand Strategy*, Princeton, NJ: Princeton University Press, 1998.

211. *Ibid.*; Etel Solingen, *Nuclear Logics*.

212. *Ibid.*, p. 5.

213. *Ibid.*, p. 12.

214. *Ibid.*, p. 42.

215. Stephen Blank, "Engaging North Korea: Issues and Challenges," *Korean International Unification Journal*, 2008.

216. Solingen, *Nuclear Logics*, p. 297; Jay Solomon, "U.S. Courts North Korea's Army," *Wall Street Journal*, December 29, 2007, p. 3.

217. "Gates Says U.S. Wants Diplomacy to Solve Iran Disputes," *Reuters*, April 5, 2008.

218. Sten Rynning, "Peripheral or Powerful? The European Union's Strategy to Combat the Proliferation of Nuclear Weapons," *European Security*, Vol. XVI, No. 3-4, September-December, 2007, p. 270.

219. *Ibid.*

220. *Ibid*; Jones, pp. 3-16.

221. Rynning, p. 271.

222. *Ibid.*, p. 275.

223. McDonough, *Nuclear Superiority*; Lieber and Press, "The Rise of U.S. Nuclear Primacy," pp. 42-54; Lieber and Press, "The End of MAD?" pp. 7-44; Bunn and Chyba, eds.

224. Rynning, p. 275; Justin Bernier, "The Death of Disarmament in Russia?" *Parameters*, Vol. XXXIV, No. 2, Summer 2004, pp. 84-103.

225. Stephen J. Cimbala, "Missile Defense and Mother Russia: Scarecrow or Showstopper?" *European Security*, Vol. XVI, No. 3-4, September-December, 2007, p. 294.

226. "Interview with Foreign Minister Sergei Lavrov," *Rossiyskaya Gazeta,* February 21-28, 2007, *www.mid.ru.*

227. NPR, *www.globalsecurity.org/wmd/library/policy/dod/ npr.htm*; Kerry M. Kartcher, "U.S. Nuclear Weapons and Nonproliferation: Dispelling the Myths," Presentation to the Carnegie Moscow Center, February 2, 2007, available at *www. carnegie.ru/en/pubs/media/101192007.02.02.Presentation.ppt.*

228. McDonough, *Nuclear Superiority*; Lieber and Press, "The Rise of U.S. Nuclear Primacy," pp. 42-54; Lieber and Press, "The End of MAD?" pp. 7-44; George Bunn and F. Chyba.

229. *Ibid.*, pp. 303-304.

230. George F. Kennan, "The Sources of Soviet Conduct," *Foreign Affairs*, July 1947.

231. Blank, "The End of the Six-Party Talks?"

232. Robert S. Litwak, *Regime Change: U.S. Strategy Through the Prism of 9/11*, Washington, DC, and Baltimore, MD: Woodrow Wilson Center Press and Johns Hopkins University Press, 2007, p. 10.

233. *Ibid.*

234. Derek D. Smith, *Deterring America: Rogue States and the Proliferation of Weapons of Mass Destruction*, Cambridge, UK: Cambridge University Press, 2006; Keith B. Payne, *Deterrence in the Second Nuclear Age*, Lexington: The University Press of Kentucky, 1996; Keith B. Payne, *The Fallacies of Cold War Deterrence and a New Direction*, Lexington: The University Press of Kentucky, 2001.

235. McDonough; Lieber and Press; Bunn and Chyba.

236. Kartcher and the sources cited therein.

237. Dov Lynch, "Same View, Different Realities: EU and US Policy Toward Russia," Marcin Zaborowski, ed., *Friends Again?: EU-US Relations After the Crisis*, Paris, France: European Union Institute for Security Studies, 2006, p. 166.

238. E. G. Sergei Karaganov, "Dangerous Relapses," *Russia in Global Affairs*, Vol. IV, No. 2, April-June 2006, pp. 82-85.

239. "Closed-Type Democracy," *www.gazeta.ru*, October 6, 2005, cited in *Johnson's Russia List*, October 6, 2005, available at *www.cdi.org*; Natalya Gevorkyan, "The Bottom Line," Moscow, *Kommersant*, in Russian, October 17, 2005, *FBIS SOV*, October 17, 2005.

240. Moscow, *ITAR-TASS*, in English, November 21, 2004, *FBIS SOV*, November 21, 2004.

241. Heinrich Vogel, "Prospects for Coordination of Western Policies," Stiftung Wissenschaft und Politik: Berlin and the Carnegie Endowment for International Peace, Hannes Adomeit and Anders Aslund, eds., *Russia Versus the United States and Europe – or "Strategic Triangle,"* Berlin, Germany, 2005, p. 92.

242. Ron Susskind, *The One-Percent Solution: Deep Inside America's Pursuit of Its Enemies Since 9/11*, New York: Simon & Schuster, 2006, pp. 224-228, 307-308; Peter Baker, "Russian Relations Under Scrutiny," *Washington Post*, February 26, 2006, p. 1; John Vinocur, "Putin's Brazen Moves Force Bush to Recalibrate," *International Herald Tribune*, February 27, 2006, p. 2, retrieved from Lexis-Nexis; "Russia: Friend or Foe of the USA?" *pravda.ru*, February 27, 2006, from *Johnson's Russia List*, February 27, 2006, available at *www.cdi.org*. On Korea, see C. Kenneth Quinones, "Dualism in the Bush Administration's North Korea Policy," *Asian Perspective*, Vol. XXVII, No. 1, 2003, pp. 197-224; David Ignatius, "A CEO's Weaknesses," *Washington Post Weekly*, September 12-18, 2005, p. 27; Karin Lee and Adam Miles, "North Korea on Capitol Hill," *Asian Perspective*, Vol. XXVIII, No. 4, 2004,

pp. 185-207; Robert M. Hathaway and Jordan Tama, "The U.S. Congress and North Korea During the Clinton years," *Asian Survey*, Vol. XLIV, No. 5, September-October, 2004, pp. 711-733; David E. Sanger, "Aftereffects: Nuclear Standoff, Administration Divided Over North Korea," *New York Times*, April 21, 2003, p. 15; David Rennie, "Rumsfeld Calls for Regime Change in North Korea," *Daily Telegraph*, April 22, 2003; Gordon Fairclough, "Talks Display U.S. Rift on Pyongyang," *Wall Street Journal*, June 28, 2004, p. 9; Bill Gertz, "USA Considers Reactor Deal With North Korea," *Washington Times*, May 19, 2004, cited by Aidan Foster-Carter, "Pyongyang Watch: Six-Party Glacier: Did the US Melt?" *Asia Times Online*, June 28, 2004, *www.atimes.com*; and the author can attest to those policy divisions on Central Asia from his conversations with U.S. officials from the Department of State, Defense, and the National Security Council over the period May-2005 to the present. See also "The Pentagon's Mission Creep," *Jane's Foreign Report*, June 1, 2006, *www.4janes.com/subscribefrp/ doc_view.jsp?K2DocKey=/content1/janesdat/mags*.

243. Robert D. Blackwill, "The Three R's: Rivalry, Russia, and 'Ran'," *Asia Times Online*, January 10, 2008.

244. *Ibid.*

245. *Ibid.*

246. "No Final Decision to Quit INF treaty - FM Lavrov"; "Russia Made a Mistake By Scrapping Its Mid-Range Missiles-Ivanov"; *FBIS SOV*, February 26, 2007.

247. Federal News Service, Official Kremlin International News Broadcast, "Without a Strong Army Russia Has No Future," Interview With Defense Minister Sergei Ivanov, February 22, 2002, retrieved from Lexis-Nexis.

248. Dmitri Trenin, "Russia and Global Security Norms," *Washington Quarterly*, Vol. XXVII, No. 2, p. 65.

249. *RIA Novosti*, June 21, 2007.

250. Stephen Blank, ""Russia Unfazed by North Korean Nuclear Test," *Eurasia Daily Monitor*, October 13, 2006; Stephen

Blank, "Russia Turns the Other Cheek on North Korean Missile Launch," *Eurasia Daily Monitor*, July 7, 2006.

251. Trenin, "Russia and Global Security Norms," pp. 65-70; Moscow, *Interfax*, December 1, 2005, *FBIS SOV*, December 1, 2005.

252. Gilbert Rozman, "Security Challenges to the United States in Northeast Asia: Looking Beyond the Transformation of the Six-Party Talks," Paper Presented to the XVIII Annual Strategy Conference, Strategic Studies Institute, U.S. Army War College, Carlisle, PA, March 28-29, 2007.

253. Blackwill.

254. Rynning, pp. 270-275; Bernier, pp. 85-104; Blank, "Nuclear Strategy and Nuclear Proliferation in Russian Strategy," pp. 57-77; Dmitri Trenin, *Russia's Threat Perception and Strategic Posture*, Carlisle, PA: Strategic Studies Institute, U.S. Army War College, 2007.

255. Brzezinski, "Living With Russia," p. 5.

256. Blank, *Towards a New Russia Policy*.

257. Moscow, *Vesti TV*, in Russian, March 17, 2007, *FBIS SOV*, March 17, 2007; "Address by Russian Foreign Minister at Moscow University," Moscow, *Ministry of Foreign Affairs Website (www.mil. ru)*, February 21, 2007.

CHAPTER 7

RUSSIAN AND AMERICAN STRATEGIC RIVALRY
IN UKRAINE AND GEORGIA

James Sherr

INTRODUCTION

Although the victory of Dmitri Medvedev in Russia's presidential elections might change the parameters of Russo-American rivalry for the better, it is unlikely to do so soon. The foundations of today's difficult relationship were put in place in the mid-1990s. Subsequent developments have reinforced these foundations and, in the eyes of Russia's leadership, confirmed their essential validity.

In April 1994 during the North Atlantic Treaty Organization (NATO)-backed offensive in Bosnia-Herzegovina, President Boris Yeltsin declared to the senior echelons of Russia's Foreign Intelligence Service that "ideological confrontation is being replaced by a struggle for spheres of influence in geopolitics" and added that "forces abroad" wanted to keep Russia in a state of "controllable paralysis."[1] These statements, along with several others marking the "end of the era of romanticism between Russia and the West"[2] brought to the surface several premises that are much in evidence today: a geopolitically driven (and, by implication, zero sum) view of Russian security interests and the threats that others pose to them; the view that successful interventions in conflict zones outside the former Soviet Union might enhance the propensity of the United States and NATO to intervene inside it;[3] And belief that instability on Russia's periphery and in the Russian Federation itself serves U.S. and NATO interests. As the decade advanced, Russia's requirement for long-term security cooperation also emerged: recognition of the former Union of Soviet Socialist Republics (USSR) as a zone of Russian "special interests."[4] The brief post-September 11, 2001 (9/11) partnership collapsed when it became clear to the Kremlin that the United States would not accept this implicit quid pro quo for Russia's support in the "global war on terror" (GWOT).

Two waves of NATO enlargement, the forward deployment of U.S. military infrastructure in two new NATO member states (and the deployment of missile defense components in two others), intensified dialogue with Ukraine and Georgia, the 1999 Kosovo conflict, and the 2008 recognition of Kosovo's independence have not diminished the force of these views which, since the "colored revolutions" of 2003-04 have migrated into the mainstream of Russia's political establishment. Moreover, during President Vladimir Putin's period in office, two pillars have been added to these foundations: a strong geo-economic impulse to policy and, with the rise in global energy prices and restoration of the "administrative vertical" in Russia itself, politically usable economic power. This has added a second requirement for long-term strategic cooperation: recognition of Russia's right to "control the entire value chain" in the supply and distribution of its energy resources. By comparison with previous periods — not only Russia in the 1990s, but the Soviet Union in the mid-1980s — Russia today is both unusually resentful and self-confident. This combination of indignation, vindication, and capability will make it uncommonly difficult for the United States to be perceived as it wishes to be perceived or to secure cooperation on terms that it regards as reasonable.

DIMENSIONS OF INTERACTION AND RIVALRY

The commonalities in Russia's approach to Ukraine and Georgia are defined by identity, sentiment, interdependence, and geopolitics. But they are weighted differently. When it comes to identity, Ukraine stands in a class of its own. Whereas many Russians might be persuaded to regard their country's long historical moment in the Caucasus in imperial terms, they simply are not capable of regarding Ukraine in this light: "St. Petersburg is the brain, Moscow the heart, and Kyiv the mother of Russia." Many who embrace this axiom regard Ukrainians and Russians as a "single people" while, without any hint of contradiction, also assert (*pace* President Putin at Bucharest, Romania) that "one third" of the inhabitants of Ukraine are ethnically Russian.[5] Those who view Russia and Ukraine as integral to one another would therefore invert Zbigniew Brzezinski's celebrated maxim about the relationship between Russia, Ukraine, and empire: *With* Ukraine, Russia is a European state; *without* it, a state doomed to become a Eurasian empire. Georgians can be spared these sentiments. Yet Russia's long Caucasian moment is also a factor in its own identity, because it has added a rich dimension to Russia's own culture and is a large part of what gives the term *rossiyskiy* (i.e., Russian) real meaning.[6] Moreover, the sectoral and elite linkages that have been established, the sovietized working culture of state administration, and (in the post-Soviet period) clannish, opaque modes of business have— again in both countries, but in different proportions— created a web of transnational connections with similar institutions in Russia and a mountain of obstacles to integration with the Euro-Atlantic community.

All of these factors have given point to the distinction between *nezavisimost'* (juridical independence) and *samostoyatel'nost* (capacity — the "ability to stand"). They also provided the foundation for the view, widespread among Russian democrats in the 1990s, that "there is a logic that will bring the former republics back our way." The fact that this "logic" belittled (or entirely overlooked) highly divergent views of the "common" Soviet and Great Russian (i.e., ethnic Russian) inheritance need not be pursued here. Neither need we elaborate upon the failure of Western liberals to anticipate that when the military and ideological demarcation lines of the Cold War disappeared, new demarcation lines based on political, administrative, and business culture would take their place.

But four factors bear underscoring. First, dependency and interdependence are not simply weaknesses to be exploited by Russia. They can become weaknesses of Russia. What happens in the South Caucasus, including Georgia"s separatist regions, has a bearing upon what happens in the North Caucasus which, despite "normalization" in Chechnya and the increasingly strong "vertical" of power, also lacks *samostoyatel'nost*. A realization of the expectations of Ukraine's *Maidan* (Kyiv's central square and the site of the 2004 demonstrations that led to the collapse of a fraudulently elected government there) would have challenged the art of the possible in Russia and across Eurasia.

Second, the gap between the Euro-Atlantic aspirations of states and the post-Soviet reality of their economies, force structures, institutions, and regional divisions have drawn both the West and Russia into their internal arrangements. In the 1990s, Russian interests were a structural component of the internal politics of both countries. In Moscow's eyes, Russian diasporas not only provided an additional structural link, but a justifiable basis for intervening in the internal affairs of neighbours. By the time of the colored revolutions, the web of Western institutional involvement had expanded to the point where it had become integral to internal arrangements as well.

Third, this interpenetration not only lends itself to antagonism; it has occasionally been defined in antagonistic terms at an official level. According to the draft military doctrine of May 1992, Russia will "vigorously oppose . . . the politico-military presence of third countries in the states adjoining Russia" and will ensure "the provision of . . . human and minority rights, particularly of Russians *and the Russian-speaking* population." Although the official military doctrines of November 1993 and April 2000 have been decidedly more nuanced, the position set out in the 1992 draft has been reiterated frequently and emotively during moments of tension, most recently in President Putin's Bucharest summit comments regarding Ukraine's possible admission to NATO.[7] These perceptions are deeply problematic for neighboring states, because they imply, first, that it is illegitimate for them to seek such a "politico-military presence"; second that ethnic Russians and Russian speakers (in Ukraine about 50 percent of the population) welcome the Russian Federation's "protection" and have no reason (or obligation) to be loyal to the states in which they live. While this might fairly sum up the views of many Russians who, through no wish of their own, have found themselves since 1991 living "abroad," it demonstrably does not reflect the views of others, the extent of their assimilation into neighboring countries or their attitudes to Russian policy. Fourth, the mode of interaction between the West and Russia has been decidedly different. Both NATO and the European Union (EU) seek strong partners, and each dreads closer integration with those who will drain collective resources or bring internal security problems into their own organizations. Strengthening *samostoyatel'nost* – the capacity of civil society and public institutions – has therefore become the core of their activity, and it often takes a highly intrusive form. If Ukraine or Georgia join Membership Action Plans (MAP) for NATO, it will become more intrusive still. In contrast, even a part of Russophile elite of these countries, has concluded that Russia seeks to undermine the *samostoyatel'nost* of their countries and secure partnership on the basis of dependency and weakness. Russia's role in Abkhazia and South Ossetia, along with its blockades on goods and transport, has not only imparted a particular intensity to this perception in Georgia, but has persuaded much of the country that direct pressure is its preferred *modus operandi*. Even Ukraine's Party of Regions is at pains to demonstrate that, while opposed to NATO membership, it is not anti-NATO and a withdrawal of Western commitment and influence would damage the security of the country. Yet while there is much truth in these perceptions, they are also simplistic. An equally strong part of Russia's *modus operandi* is to conclude strong, mutually beneficial arrangements with local elites that (in Dmitri Trenin's words) "have swiftly acquired wealth and dominance but feel insufficiently self-confident":

> Resting on strengthening economic links, Moscow will definitely be able to secure political loyalty from the CIS [Commonwealth for Independent States] countries. . . . The principal instrument for realising the "CIS project" will be the achievement of understandings with the

governing elites of the CIS. This will demand long-term and painstaking work to create and promote in neighbouring countries groups of influence orientated towards Moscow and a gradual weakening and neutralization of pro-Western circles.[8]

Even in the absence of any overarching geopolitical animus or antagonism between the West and Russia, this overlap between external and internal relationships and "civilizational" and "humanitarian" factors would have raised stakes on both sides and added to the pressures placed on the countries concerned. As it turned out, by the mid-1990s, the "Russia first" policy of the West disappeared, and the "era of romanticism between Russia and the West" came to an end.

THE PUTIN SYSTEM

In contrast to Gorbachev and Yeltsin — leaders who sought to create the international conditions necessary, in Shevardnadze's words, "to bring about change *inside* the country" — Putin reverted to an older pattern established by Stalin: restoring the "vertical of power" as a way of returning Russia to its rightful position on the world stage. Under Yeltsin, Russia functioned less as a state than as an arena upon which very powerful interests competed for power and wealth, often at Russia's expense. In contrast, Putin was determined that centers of power — the security services, the armed forces, the defense-industrial complex, the energy sector — should become instruments of national power rather than laws unto themselves.

From the start, there was a concerted attempt to ensure that foreign policy "conform[ed] with the general capabilities and resources of this country."[9] Where Russian capabilities and resources were weak (as initially they were in comparison with the West), the leadership sought new openings and common ground; where they were strong (as in Ukraine and Georgia), policy became, in the words of its Kremlin adherents, "cold," "harsh," and "much tougher." In Ukraine, the shift was felt as early as December 1999, when Russia cut the supply of oil to Ukraine for the fifth time. Those given responsibility for resolving the dispute swiftly perceived that the rules had changed, that Russia was no longer a mere problem, but a power. In early 2000, Deputy Prime Minister Mikhail Kasyanov linked the dispute to geopolitical issues as well as economic ones. Despite Ukraine's efforts, no progress was made until April 2000, when Putin stated his terms, and President Kuchma took the first steps to meet them. These terms included a readjustment in the respective weight of the eastern and western "vectors" of Ukraine's policy (dramatized in September 2000 by the dismissal of Foreign Minister Borys Tarasyuk and several other "unconstructive" officials) and agreement on a substantially new framework governing energy, payments, and the privatization of Ukrainian enterprises (codified in the Moscow and Dnepropetrovsk accords of December 2000 and February 2001 respectively). That crisis and its aftermath proved at least as damaging as the gas crisis of 2005-06. But because the damage was confined to Ukraine (and Moldova), few inside the EU grasped what a potent instrument energy would become.

Yet, as noted above, economic dependency would never have produced these results in the absence of less tangible dependencies rooted in the culture of power itself. Before 2003 this culture of power blocked the Euro-Atlantic course of Ukraine and Georgia just as firmly as Russia did, and the fact was well understood in the Kremlin. Moreover, in the wake of the events of 9/11, Putin assumed that the West, which now needed Russia in the "war on terror," would acquiesce in its preferred format for global cooperation. It took the Rose and the Orange revolutions to demonstrate conclusively that it would not acquiesce.

The emergence of antagonism reflects a divergence of thinking between the West and Russia that is still inadequately understood. With difficulty but conviction, not only the EU but NATO has replaced a Cold War view of European security with a post-Cold War view, emphasising "common security" and an extensive post-modern agenda of "common" challenges: state weakness, institutional incapacity, interdependence, integration and devolution, multiculturalism, illegal migration, and transnational organized crime. NATO's overriding emphasis in Ukraine and Georgia has been placed on defense and security sector reform—and along decidedly post-Cold War lines. Through the European Security and Defence Policy, a growing number of bridging institutions and the tangible influence of largely overlapping memberships, the menu of security cooperation between the EU and NATO in aspirant countries is widening. NATO's emphasis on hard power is now reserved for theaters of conflict far afield of Europe and Russia.

Russia's path of evolution has been decidedly different. By the time Yevgeniy Primakov replaced Andrey Kozyrev as Foreign Minister, a Cold War view of security had been replaced by a pre-Cold War view, emphasising balances of power, great power prerogatives, "zones of influence," and geopolitics. Whereas Western Europe's frame of reference (to the dismay of many in the United States and the incomprehension of Russia) is increasingly post-modern, Russia's emphasis on nation, state, and "the strict promotion of national interest" is emphatically modern.

NATO enlargement, too, has been seen in a totally different light by the respective parties. That former Warsaw Pact countries viewed NATO membership as protection against a renascent Russia is indisputable. But their primary, elemental, and transcendental motive was to escape the legacy of the "grey zone" and anchor their own institutions to the arrangements, interests, and "*schéma* of values" into which, by 1994, Russian "centrists" said they had no wish to "dissolve." Among the NATO 16, not one viewed enlargement as a means of containing Russia; all viewed Russia's objections as grounds for caution. For most NATO member states, but particularly for Germany, the first motive was to prevent the fragmentation of security and the "renationalization" of defense in brittle and immature ex-Warsaw Pact democracies. The second, but equally strong motive, was fear of U.S. withdrawal from Europe's security arrangements and the return of the "German problem," if not in fact, then in national psyches. Third, as enlargement got under way—and as Partnership for Peace became an adjunct rather than an alternative to it—NATO paradoxically became less geopolitical in its thinking rather than more. The process has merely strengthened the conviction that NATO will stand or fall as a community based on common affinities, values, interests, and capacity (the one starkly realist note in the equation). Moreover, with far less justification, the very emphasis on process— joint forums established, joint exercises conducted, the volume of meetings and exchanges—has, until recently, persuaded many NATO officials and national representatives that NATO-Russia cooperation was going well.

But to Russia's military establishment, the notion that NATO is anything other than a classically military alliance is risible. The notion that NATO is not what it used to be – an anti-Russian alliance – is, in Russian eyes, made equally risible by NATO enlargement. NATO's determination to maintain an "open door" to further enlargement without excluding Georgia or Ukraine has clinched the argument across virtually the whole political spectrum. Discussions about the stabilizing effects of NATO membership, the benefits to internal security, destruction of surplus weapons and toxic materials, force reductions and professionalization, the demilitarization of police and border services, democratic control of the security sector, and the right of independent states to choose their own models and partners fall on deaf ears. Since the mid-1990s, the premise of Russian military planning and policy has been that any activity undertaken by NATO near Russian territory is a threat to Russia. Within recent months, the sentiment seems to have grown rather than diminished that "any activity in the world [is] an intrigue against us."[10]

THE CRUCIBLE OF ENERGY

The first paragraph of the official *Energy Strategy of Russia to 2020* states that Russia's "powerful energy sector" is "an instrument for the conduct of internal and external policy" and that "the role of the country in world energy markets to a large extent determines its geopolitical influence."[11] Were Russian energy simply a geopolitical instrument, the problems faced by Russia's neighbours would be simpler than they are.

They are difficult for three additional reasons. First, while Russia's reserves of gas are, in principle, sufficient to supply all conceivable consumers for decades, in practice the greater portion of new reserves are undeveloped. Already there are abundant indications that supplies will not emerge in a timely way to meet rising demand at acceptable cost. Second, this is alarming news for Russia's rapidly growing economy and the Russian consumer, who has come to regard the provision of affordable energy as a primary function of the state. Third, *Gazprom's* model — "the regulation from a single center of regimes of extraction, transport, underground storage and sales" — has brought stability at the expense of market responsiveness and, thus, poses one of the greatest obstacles to meeting this rising demand.[12] Yet, fourth, this state dominated model has become an important prop for the authority of a Kremlin congenitally distrustful of decentralization, beset by demographic crisis and increasingly conscious of China's power. Thus, it will be modified with extreme reluctance and against multiple points of resistance. In sum, economic necessity, geopolitical ambition, and "subjective" clan interest combine to produce a cocktail more unhealthy than the sum of its parts.

The conclusions dictated by this picture are clear, but uncommonly difficult to accept or act upon. First, in Ukraine, Belarus, Moldova, and other chronically dependent states, Russia's economic imperatives and political goals will combine to ensure that the squeeze continues, and that spasms between stability and crisis grow shorter and sharper. Deals will be concluded with political forces who the Kremlin seeks to strengthen, yet economic pressures on the Russian economy will put them at risk. Second, countries like Ukraine which have resources of their own will not escape from this cycle until they become masters of their own energy sectors and confront their ills: opacity, venality, and barriers to honest, urgently needed investment. Despite the benefits derived from the Baku-Ceyhan and Baku-Ezerum pipelines, Georgia's problems are not dissimilar. Third, in order to confront these ills, they will need to confront some of the most powerful figures and forces in their own countries.

THE FUTURE PATTERN OF GEOPOLITICAL RIVALRY

The future is likely to be shaped by three variables: mood, leadership change in Russia, and the perceptions of neighbors.

Mood.

Putin came to power at a time of increased threat to Russia's geopolitical interests. He leaves power at a time when this threat is balanced by opportunity. The impact of the colored revolutions has been two-fold. First, they have strengthened the authoritarian impulse in Russia. Since 2004, the Putin project has acquired a more militantly self-righteous edge than it had in the past. Second, the colored revolutions have transformed disillusionment towards the West into antagonism. To circles schooled to believe *samostoyatel'noy Ukrainiy nikogda ne budet*, (a self-standing Ukraine will never occur), the Orange Revolution was a Western "special operation" from beginning to end. After the post-9/11 partnership and years of cultivating the EU, this was seen as nothing short of betrayal. When we wrote in September 2004 that "the worst scenario for Ukraine is not that Yushchenko loses the election [but that] he wins and then fails," it was out of apprehension that a sense of betrayal becomes dangerous when combined with a sense of vindication. As NATO considers the merits of MAP for Ukraine and Georgia, it should do so in the knowledge that, whatever the decision, it will enhance this sense of vindication.

The impact of the Iraq war and its failures is also two-fold. It has reinforced the view, firmly implanted by NATO's intervention in the 1999 Kosovo conflict, that the United States observes no limits in the conduct of its policy and has led to the conclusion that Russia need respect no limits where its own national interests are at stake and where it possesses the means to advance them. These means now exist. "Russia has earned a right to be self interested," and others can take it or leave it.

Leadership Change in Russia.

Unless appearances deceive entirely, Russia is headed for a weak presidency and a constitutional mess. Medvedev does not inherit a strong vertical of power, but a system that has been unravelling for the past 18 months. It is easy to forget that, by concentrating power and wealth in the Kremlin, Putin also concentrated rivalry there. A president as respected, skillful, and harsh as Putin might keep these rivalries in bounds, but his replacement by any one of these rivals had implications for the others. Hence, the determination of so many to keep Putin in power combined with their determination to ensure themselves against the looming reality of his departure. The October 2007 article by Viktor Cherkesov, Head of the Federal Counter-Narcotics Service, testifies to the lurid nature of these manoeuvres, which have rent sanguinary divisions in what once had been a relatively unified power base, the *siloviki*.[13] It would be outlandishly complacent to assume that a pliant successor and a constitutional sleight of hand will heal these divisions or even patch them.

How will internal rivalries play into this mood and disposition of forces? Three questions need to be considered. First, when the "question of power" is once again uppermost at home and Russia is once again "respected" abroad, who, if anyone, will be thinking about foreign policy in a careful and systematic way? Of course, it is not only in Russia that we find people who believe that if you are strong enough, you do not need to think. But that is not ground for comfort. There are already signs that methodology — reinforcing weakness wherever it can be found, emasculating potential partners through bribery and *kompromat*; *provokatsia* (compromising materials and provocations) and the setting of traps; mendacity, brutality, and threats — has taken the place of strategy: the tailoring of means to ends and an assessment of the longer-term effects of the successes that one's unpleasantness achieves today. In its own neighborhood, Russia has always had the ability to make life more difficult than it already is and antagonize those who never felt antagonistic. But it has not always profited. If *mezhdousobitsa* (mutual destruction) strengthens these tendencies, the risks to Russia's neighbors are obvious. But to pose the second question asked by Russians themselves: Are these tendencies not also self-destructive, and are they not launching Russia "once again on the path to isolation"?[14] If so, those determined to find opportunities for "engagement" might find themselves walking in circles.[15] The third question is no less ominous: are neighboring countries at risk of becoming theaters of internal Russian rivalry? Should they and countries further afield expect new tough and demonstrative actions (e.g., in Estonia, Ukraine, Georgia, or even the UK) to mobilize nationalist sentiment in Russia, distract attention from a swelling agenda of internal problems, compromise insufficiently tough rivals, or engineer the "extraordinary circumstances" needed to strengthen the coercive components of the political system? Surely we are at the point where these questions must be asked, but that does not mean they will be.

The Perceptions of Neighbors.

On Ukraine and Georgia, the point is not lost: Russians have recovered pride in their own traditions and values, but values that, increasingly, are defined in opposition not only to those of the West, but those of Europe and the liberal democratic order that has become synonymous with Europe in practice. During the same period, Ukraine has experienced a rite of passage from virtual democracy to immature democracy. Confusing and maddening as Ukraine's democracy is to its citizens and international partners, there is no authoritarian alternative to it on offer, and none with any foreseeable legitimacy. There is no Russian alternative either. Even if it is still the case that "no one is waiting for Ukraine in the West," threats to adopt another model of integration ring hollow. Those who oppose integration with NATO dare not oppose the "European course." Those who warn that Ukraine will not be "turned against" Russia dare not allow the Russian vector to become the determinant vector of their policy. With its own distinct patterns of upheaval and risk, Georgia has undertaken a similar rite of passage. The Georgian sense of national identity is indestructible. To the pro-Russian part of Ukraine's elite, Russian conduct frequently brings to mind the question *"protiv kogo viy druzhite?"* (Against whom are you waging friendship?). In Georgia, Russia's conduct has eviscerated this elite and made a pro-Russian stance untenable.

Western Policy.

In the United States, as much as in the EU, political establishments have grown accustomed to the luxury of debating how large a priority Russia should be. The beginning of wisdom is to accept that Russia will make itself a priority whether we wish it to be or not. The question is whether this wisdom will produce a further search for accommodation or a drawing of lines.

THE BUCHAREST SUMMIT: A DRAWING OF LINES?

The outcome of the NATO summit at Bucharest not only surprised most observers, it surprised most of the participants. The decision to postpone MAP for Georgia and Ukraine was, for most insiders, expected and mandated not by Russia's opposition but by the setbacks and reverses that occurred in both countries over the past year. Yet the balance of the text of Paragraph 23 of the Summit Declaration was not expected, and, paradoxically, it was the force of Russia's opposition and the public deference apparently paid to it that, in the end, persuaded 26 member states to endorse it.

NATO has always taken Russia into account when considering the modalities of enlargement, the timing of it, and the likely consequences of it. But it has been averse to granting Russia a veto over this process or a formal role to play in it. The nuance, understandable to professionals, is easily mangled by the mendacious, by the fearful and, of course, by the press. For this reason, allies have tended to exercise discipline when discussing the Russia factor in public. The breakdown of these disciplines before the Bucharest summit aroused apprehension in some quarters and, in others, a small amount of fury. Russian statements have also aroused apprehension and fury. It was not the leader of *Nashi* who threatened to target nuclear missiles on Ukraine, but the President of the country. It was not Gennadiy Zyuganov who called the collapse of the Soviet Union the greatest calamity of the 20th century, but the same President. It was not Vladimir Zhirinovskiy who said that "policy on Ukraine is not foreign policy; I believe it is domestic policy." It was Russia's Permanent Representative to NATO, and he did not make this comment in 1992 but in January 2008.[16] Thus, not for the first time in its history, NATO found itself under moral pressure to demonstrate that Russian political pressure would not succeed. Yet there would have been less need to respond so strongly to Russian pressure if it were not necessary to defer MAP invitations for the countries most exposed to it.

This paradox accounts not only for the extraordinary wording of Paragraph 23 — "[w]e agreed today that these countries will become members of NATO" — but the extraordinary words used to justify it:

> If there was an open door . . . there is now a wide open door, and a couple of questions have been laid to rest: the question of whether or not NATO would ever consider Ukraine off limits or whether NATO would consider it appropriate to have a member in the Caucasus; that question has been answered with the language that . . . these countries will become members of NATO. And so

these questions are now off the table, and it is a matter of when, not whether.

> Secretary of State Condoleezza Rice
> April 3

Relations with Russia did not play a role in this. This is a decision by NATO with the applicants. Others do not have the right to take part in this discussion.

> German Prime Minister Angela Merkel
> April 4

It also accounts for the way in which cooperation with Russia has been expanded and limited. The NATO-Russia Council and the Sochi summit have produced an agenda of NATO-Russia and U.S.-Russia cooperation that is serious but less wide ranging than many would like: missile defense, nonproliferation, counterterrorism, energy security, transit of forces to Afghanistan, and so on. NATO is clearly losing interest in discussing the future of NATO with Russia, and Russia is clearly losing its ability to influence NATO's future. The Bucharest summit reaffirmed the truth that, like the EU, NATO stands or falls as a community based on common affinities, values, and interests. If Russia does not share them, it will not be allowed to claim the prerogatives and benefits of those who do. Neither can it expect recognition of "zones of interests" that contradict the interests of countries residing in them. Russia has made its choice, and at Bucharest NATO told Russia to live with it. It remains to be seen whether NATO and Russia can live with that conclusion.

ENDNOTES - CHAPTER 7

1. At a closed address on April 27, 1994, excerpted (and partially paraphrased) by ITAR-TASS.

2. Vyacheslav Kostikov, *Trud*, February 22, 1994. Kostikov had only just retired as Yeltsin's press secretary. He also stated that "Russian interests will no longer dissolve in the interests of European diplomacy," adding for good measure that "Russia increasingly sees itself as a Great Power, and it has started saying this loudly."

3. Hence the verdict of *Krasnaya Zvezda* during the 1999 Kosovo conflict (March 27, 1999): "Today they are bombing Yugoslavia, but are aiming at Russia." The article goes on to say, "tomorrow they will bomb Russia because of Chechnya, Ukraine because of Crimea, Moldova because of Trans-Dnestria, and Georgia because of Abkhazia and South Ossetia." Along similar lines, Lieutenant General Leonid Ivashov, Head of the MOD's International Cooperation Directorate, told NTV America, "[i]f the world community swallows this large-scale aggression, this barbarity, then it is today difficult to say who will be next, but there will be a state that is going to be next in line without fail."

4. The theme emerged in conciliatory format as early as September 1992 in the first MFA report on the so-called "near abroad." Deputy Foreign Minister Fedor Shelov-Kovedyayev, *"Strategiya i taktika vneshney politiki Rossii v novom zarubezh'ye"* ("Strategy and Tactics of Russian Foreign Policy in the New Abroad"), September 1992. In a somewhat harder vein, the Foreign Ministry's December 1992 "Concepts" document stipulated the interest of "the leading democratic states" in the "provision of stability" on the former Soviet "geopolitical space" and warned that this would depend "on our ability to uphold with conviction, and in extreme cases with the use of means of force, the principles of international law, including human rights, and to achieve firm good neighborliness." In February 1993, Yeltsin called upon the UN to "grant Russia special powers as guarantor of peace and stability." By late 2000, Andrey Fedorov, former First Deputy Foreign Minister stated, "[t]oday we are speaking more or less openly now about our zones of interests. In one way or another we are confirming that the post-Soviet territory is such a zone. . . .

In Yeltsin's time we were trying to wrap this in a nice paper. Now we are saying it more directly: This is our territory, our sphere of interest."

5. According to the last Soviet census (1989) only 22 percent (11.4 million out of a population that was then 50 million) characterised themselves as ethnically Russian, and almost half of those who did resided in the Crimean Autonomous Republic, which was not transferred to Ukraine until 1954. At the time, many regarded this figure as inflated, given the perceived advantages of Russian nationality. How this figure has jumped to "one-third" will mystify many.

6. Whereas the term *russkiy* is strictly ethnic or national, *rossiyskiy* refers to membership of the wider Russian cultural or civilizational space. The former is a matter of origin (*proiskhozhdenie*), the latter of belonging or orientation (*prinadlezhnost'*). In the UK, many would interpret the distinction between "English" and "British" in a similar light—but this is a risky Pandora's box to open!

7. "[Ukraine] is a complex state formation. And if you introduce the issue of NATO, you can bring it to the point where its statehood can be called into question. We have no right of veto, there won't be one, and we don't claim one. But . . . so we all understand, we also have our own interests. Look, 17 million Russians live in Ukraine. Who can say we have no interests? In southern Ukraine, there are only Russians. Crimea was acquired by Ukraine simply thanks to a decision of the CPSU [Communist Party of the Soviet Union] Politburo. There wasn't even any state procedure for transferring this territory. We are not trying to stir anything up, but we ask our partners to reflect on the weight of their actions."

8. "'*Proyekt SNG' – noviy prioritet rossiyskoy vneshney politiki?*" ("'The CIS Project'—The New Priority of Russian Foreign Policy?"), February 2004.

9. Sergei Ivanov (then Secretary of the Russian Federation Security Council) outlining the Russian Federation's new "Concepts of Foreign Policy," approved by the President on June 28, 2000.

10. As Mark Urnov stated last month in a radio discussion with Dmitriy Ryzhkov, "Our calamity . . . lies in the fact that we interpret any activity in the world as an intrigue against us." *Ekho Moskviy, V kruge Sveta* (*"Sveta's Circle"*), February 12, 2008, *echo. msk.ru/programs/sorokina/58662/index.phtml.*

11. *Energeticheskaya strategiya rossii na period do 2020* (*Energy Strategy of Russia to 2020*), No. 1234-g, Government of the Russian Federation, August 28, 2003.

12. *Rasshirovka viystupleniya Predsedatelya Pravleniya OAO (Gazprom) Alekseya Millera na vstreche s poslami stran Evropeyskogo Soiuza v rezidentsii posla Avstrii,* Text of Alexei Miller's address to EU ambassadors, April 18, 2006, Moscow, p. 1.

13. Viktor Cherkesov, *"Nel'zya dopustit', chtobiy voiniy prevratilis' v torgovtsev"'* (*"We Cannot Allow Warriors to Become Traders"*), *Kommersant,* October 9, 2007.

14. *Ekho Moskviy.*

15. Maxim Litvinov's comment to Averell Harriman at the end of 1945 is once again pertinent. Asked "What can my government possibly do to allay suspicions of our intentions?" Litvinov instantly replied, "Nothing!"

16. Interview on *Ekho Moskviy,* January 3, 2008.

CHAPTER 8

OBSTACLES TO U.S.-RUSSIAN COOPERATION IN THE CAUCASUS AND UKRAINE

Andrei P. Tsygankov

INTRODUCTION

The potential for U.S.-Russian cooperation in the Caucasus and Ukraine exists and may be exploited in Georgia, Azerbaijan, and Ukraine in areas such as political stabilization, their relationships with the North Atlantic Treaty Organization (NATO), counterterrorism, demilitarization, and energy security. However, obstacles to such cooperation are formidable. Future cooperation between the United States and Russia will require considerable time and effort by both sides and may materialize only if we fully understand these obstacles and draw correct conclusions for policy. This chapter first reviews the existing potential for cooperation, then addresses difficulties of developing it on the Russian and American sides. I argue that within the next 2 to 3 years, important domestic considerations will prevent Russia and the United States from engaging in a systematic and mutually beneficial relationship.

The most important of these considerations concern the two nations' political elites and is mainly of a psychological nature. Russia is only recovering from the state collapse of the 1990s, and the fragility of this recovery is felt in the weakness of the country's governing institutions, as well as in its perception of the outside world, particularly the United States. While the weakness of governing institutions makes it difficult for the state to isolate various lobbies and form a coherent policy, an inadequate perception of U.S. intentions at times undermines the Kremlin's will to reach out to its principally important partner. In the United States, the problem is different albeit also psychological. Its institutions are stronger and more mature, yet the policymaking process, too, has been wide open to influences of lobbies—mostly of a Russophobic nature—largely because of weak presidential leadership. In the absence of a strong commitment to relationships with Russia coming from the White House, any bilateral cooperation becomes a hostage to special interests. In addition, the United States suffers from what Michael Gorbachev called the "complex of a winner"[1]—a psychological inability to adjust to new international realities and incorporate others, including Russia, into the process of governing the world.

After reviewing the potential for, and obstacles to U.S.-Russia cooperation, the chapter provides a tentative conclusion on the current state of their relationships and reflects on their future.

POTENTIAL FOR COOPERATION

The United States and Russia could cooperate in at least five distinct areas of security relations in the Caucasus and Ukraine. One such area is political stability and territorial integrity. Azerbaijan and Georgia have developed acute issues of secessionism. Having passed the stage of active military confrontation, they have made little progress in bringing secessionist territories under control and continue to live in the shadow of war. Ukraine's problem is that of a deeply divided political elite, and it continues to experience serious risks to territorial integrity. In time Crimea has a potential of becoming a secessionist headache for Kiev. The historically pronounced regional divisions[2] — with the East favoring stronger ties with Russia and the West eager to minimize those ties — have been threatening the unity of the ruling elite.[3]

Assuming sufficient trust and political will on both sides, the United States and Russia could assist the three nations in strengthening their territorial integrity. For example, some joint security guarantees could be offered to Georgia in exchange for its signing a nonaggression pact against its secessionist territories. The United States and Russia could also offer some forms of assistance to the states in the region for alleviating poverty and building functioning law enforcement institutions. If anything, Russia's large market and currently booming economy should continue to be of significance in addressing instability in the region.[4] It is time to realize that the challenge of the 21st century is that of building viable state institutions, rather than promoting Western-style democratization. Without important social and security preconditions in place, attempts to promote democracy may in fact breed instability,[5] thereby exacerbating the nations' problems.

The second issue concerns expansion of the North Atlantic Treaty Organization (NATO). Georgian and Ukrainian leaderships have expressed a desire to join the Alliance, while Russia continues to view the process as threatening its security interests. Following the April 2008 summit of NATO in Bucharest, Russia reiterated that it would do everything in its power to prevent expansion of the Alliance and extension of its membership to Georgia and Ukraine. According to Foreign Minister Sergei Lavrov, Moscow will do all it can to prevent such membership in order "to avoid an inevitable serious exacerbation of our relations with both the Alliance and our neighbors."[6] President Vladimir Putin stated, "We view the appearance of a powerful military bloc on our borders, a bloc whose members are subject in part to Article 5 of the Washington Treaty, as a direct threat to the security of our country. The claim that this process is not directed against Russia will not suffice. National security is not based on promises."[7] In the aftermath of the summit, to signal its dissatisfaction to Georgia, the Kremlin extended an additional assistance to the secessionist South Ossetia and Abkhazia.[8] Moscow also expedited negotiations with Moldova over incorporation of Transnistria, provided that Moldova stays a neutral state and does not join NATO.[9] Moscow may be feeling that not all is lost in Georgia, and the no-NATO membership in exchange for territorial integrity deal may still be possible.

One possible way to address Russia's NATO concerns may be in separating the issue of membership from that of military presence. For instance, in response to Russia's concerns, President Victor Yushchenko has recently suggested that he has no plans of stationing any military troops on Ukrainian territory,[10] effectively committing his nation to the status of a neutral state. If NATO is indeed a political organization and not merely a military alliance as many in the West claim, then such a solution should not seem unfeasible. Enforcement of Article 5 in such cases should be the subject of a separate negotiation. Other joint security arrangements, with or without NATO participation, must also be considered.

The third issue is counterterrorism in the Caucasus. Related to the already articulated concern about

Georgia's instability, which the Rose Revolution has not adequately addressed, Russia remains concerned that Georgian territory may continue to be used by international terrorists as a transit point on their way to the North Caucasus. In the past, Pankisi Gorge and several other areas near the Georgian border with Chechnya were known to have terrorist camps. The United States, Russia, and Georgia have cooperated successfully in clearing Pankisi of terrorist camps. With Chechnya largely secured, there remains an important issue of stabilizing the larger Northern Caucasus which is plagued by the weakness of political institutions, regional instability, and ethnic separatism. A growing number of terrorist attacks and jihadist networks in Dagestan, Ingushetiya, Northern Ossetia, and Karachayevo-Cherkessiya[11] leave the Kremlin few options but to increase its military presence there and improve security measures in the short run. In principle, there is potential for Russia and the United States to cooperate in addressing the issue through joint military exercises, antiterrorist centers, or establishment of limited counterterrorist contingents to prevent possible border crossings from Turkey and Iran.

The forth issue is demilitarization of the Caucasus. With the United States and Russia arming their "clients" in the region — Azerbaijan and Georgia in the case of the United States; Armenia, Abkhasia, and South Ossetia in the case of Russia — the region has become heavily militarized. One implication of this is a constant fear of war among the region's residents. Armenia, for example, has no territorial integrity problem, but its citizens live under a constant threat of war with Azerbaijan. The latter has sharply increased its military budget, and on many occasions threatened to use force to persuade Armenia to give up its political support for Nagorno-Karabakh.[12] Azerbaijan's economy is now seven times larger than that of Armenia, and Azerbaijan's military budget is over $1 billion.[13] Some strategy of demilitarization is in order. Such strategy must include U.S.-Russia guarantees of security for the states in the Caucasus and measures aiming to develop energy cooperation in the region.

To speak of the latter, one must acknowledge that the United States and Russia are increasingly at odds over how to exploit energy reserves and transportation routes in the Caspian Sea. For the United States, with its constant concerns over energy supplies, the region has been of importance since the end of the Soviet breakup. Russia's economic interests include the need to protect energy pipelines, particularly the one that stretches through Dagestan to Novorossiysk. Energy continues to be the largest part of Russia's exports, and its share of foreign trade with European nations is around 50 percent. Without reliable protection of energy transportation, Russia's energy-export dependent economy is in an extremely risky position. The energy issue directly affects the overall security situation in the Caucasus partly because the U.S. concept of oil supplies is linked to militarization and geopolitics. Ever since the crisis in the 1970s when the Organization of Petroleum Exporting Countries (OPEC) imposed an oil embargo and raised the prices, American policymakers have pursued hegemonic policies to control energy supplies. With Russia's sharply declining ability to dominate in the region, Washington moved to develop a unilateral advantage in exploiting the Caspian Sea reserves and fostered special ties with Azerbaijan, the richest state in the Caucasus. With involvement of major Western oil companies, Washington built the Baku to Ceyhan

(BTC) pipeline to bypass Russia in carrying oil to the territory of the Mediterranean coast. Extremely expensive and 1,090 miles (1,750km) long, the pipeline was completed in 2005 and is able to carry 1 million barrels per day.[14] This approach continues to breed militarization in the region and is hardly conducive to development of an energy partnership with Russia.

A more productive way of exploiting energy opportunities in the Caspian region might include searching for joint U.S.-Russian exploitation of oil and gas pipelines going through territories of third parties, as well as attempts to institutionalize relationships.[15] For example, the BTC could be exploited jointly. In the past Russian companies were invited to participate in the BTC pipeline, and the experience should be resumed and built upon. Another positive example is the Caspian Pipeline Consortium (CPC) that was established with memberships of Chevron-Texaco, Arco, Mobil, Shell, and the governments of Russia and Kazakhstan to carry oil from Kazakhstan's Tenghiz oil field (the world's sixth largest) to the Russian Black Sea port of Novorossisk. If the objective is to develop an energy partnership, then developing Russia-bypassing routes, such as the Trans-Caspian or Nabucco pipelines, may only further exacerbate the mistrust from Russia, while pushing Kazakhstan and Turkeminstan to seek partners elsewhere (e.g., China). Opportunities for cooperating with Russia are both political and economic. Politically, energy partnership will contribute to development of U.S.-Russian cooperation in solving other vital issues, such as terrorism, weapons proliferation and narcotics trafficking. Among other things, diversification of energy supplies away from the Middle Eastern countries will help to bring down oil prices and undermine funding for prominent terrorist organizations. For Russia, partnership with the United States promises new technologies, greater integration into the world economy, and strengthening of political ties between the two countries.

OBSTACLES

The Russian Side.

On Russia's side, obstacles to developing broad cooperation with the United States are two-fold: Internally, the key obstacle is a continuous crisis of state legitimacy. Rather than viewing the Kremlin's policies as indicative of imperialism,[16] a productive way to understand Russia is to view it as a nation that has relinquished the Soviet state model and is now struggling to establish new political and economic foundations of its statehood. The post-Soviet Russia is a new state because it acts under new international conditions that no longer accept traditional patterns of imperial domination. Throughout the 1990s, the country almost became a failed state[17] in response to its original shock therapy choice of reforms at home and poorly conceived policies abroad. Having abstained from attempts to restore its empire and having created the necessary macroeconomic environment, Russia has revived its economy and a good measure of political viability under the leadership of Vladimir Putin. The country's leadership has pragmatically integrated the previously excluded security elites in the ruling class and concentrated on building a "normal great power"[18]—not by means of imperial grandeur, but through reformed macroeconomic conditions, favorable world energy prices, and a stable political environment for economic growth and rising living standards.[19] Although some have suggested that security elites became prominent and indeed dominant in influencing political circles and policymaking process,[20] in reality the state did not become a hostage to those influences. Putin's designation of the liberally-minded Dmitri Medvedev is an important testament to this fact.

Still, Russia's political class remains divided, and domestic influences continue to be important— excessively so—in forming foreign policy. The state has not been consolidated enough to isolate pressures from these influences. Although Putin has been very popular with the general public, the elites have pulled him in different directions. For instance, with regard to the Caucasus and Ukraine, some have long advocated stimulating and recognizing separatism in "politically disloyal" Georgia, Moldova, and Azerbajian, and demanding a greater independence for Crimea in Ukraine, while others have insisted on preservation of the status quo.[21] The Kremlin has yet to work out an ideological formula among elites and to develop a policy capacity for purging the most odiously corrupt and hawkish representatives of the political class. The emergence of a formally dualistic power structure with Dmitri Medvedev as President and Putin as Prime Minister may become an important step in the direction of forming an ideological consensus within the elite circles. By ruthlessly eliminating narrow political extremes, such as Mikhail Kasyanov and Dmitri Rogozin, the Kremlin has forged a liberal-conservative consensus that will guide Russia's modernization for the next 5 years or more. While sharing fundamental principles of reforming the economy and political system, Medvedev and Putin are otherwise ideologically distinct. The former may emerge as a prototypical Russian liberal with a greater emphasis on developing civil society and rule of law, whereas Putin may be viewed as a modern conservative with his concerns for preserving stability, governance, and independence.

Externally, the key obstacle to development of Russia's cooperation with the United States has to do with the Kremlin's deeply-held suspicion toward U.S. intentions and policies in the Caucasus and Ukraine as undermining Russian security interests. That suspicion has its roots in the American support for the colored revolutions that many in the Kremlin view as directed at Russia as well. President Putin insisted on Russia's right to "decide for itself the pace, terms, and conditions of moving towards democracy," and he warned against attempts to destabilize the political system by "any unlawful methods of struggle."[22] Putin's concern for noninterference in Russia's domestic developments from outside only became stronger over time, and in his addresses to the Federation Council in May 2006 and April 2007, he put an even greater emphasis on the values of sovereignty and strong national defense.[23] The Kremlin's ideologists and theorists sympathetic to the official agenda have developed concepts of "sovereign democracy" and "sovereign economy,"[24] insisting on the need for Russia to protect its path of development and natural resources. The Kremlin has also trained its own youth organizations, restricted activities of Western nongovernmental organizations (NGOs) and radical opposition inside the country, and warned the United States against interference with Russia's domestic developments. Russia's elections, too, demonstrated the ample fear of outside interference and willingness by politicians to resort to an anti-Western rhetoric.[25]

In addition, Russia feels humiliated by what it sees as lack of appreciation of its foreign policy interests. More importantly, a strong conviction developed in Moscow that the United States was indeed preparing to isolate Russia economically, politically, and morally. Even mainstream politicians and analysts were now concluding that there was little in America's political class that suggested a constructive attitude toward Russia in the future. For example, Director of the Institute of the U.S.A. and Canada Sergei Rogov spoke of the formation of a very negative consensus about Russia that united left-wing liberals and right-wing conservatives in the United States. In his assessment, the Cold War thinking that Russia must be contained and isolated has returned, and "it is a very dangerous situation."[26] President Putin's criticism of the U.S.-led "unipolarity" beginning with his speech at the Munich Conference, as well as his threats to withdraw from already signed international treaties such as the Intermediate-Range Nuclear Forces Treaty, was meant to convey Russia's frustration with its inability to develop more equitable relations with the United States. Rather than sending the message of a threat, the Kremlin was desperate to be heard that it was Russia, not America, that had to swallow the war in the Balkans, two rounds of NATO expansion, the U.S. withdrawal from the antiballistic missile (ABM) treaty, military presence in Central Asia, the invasion of Iraq, and, now, plans to deploy elements of nuclear missile defense in Eastern Europe.

That post-revolutionary Georgia and Ukraine had expressed their desire to join NATO only added to Russia's sense of being vulnerable and politically isolated by the West. As Western officials demonstrated their support for Georgia,[27] the Kremlin felt it had only one option left—a toughest possible response short of using force—and it sought to send a strong warning for both Tbilisi and officials of the West. After the "spy scandal" in late 2006, the Kremlin imposed tough sanctions against Georgia which were met with almost universal condemnation in the West, but also served to validate Russia's already formed suspicions vis-à-vis Western, particularly American, intentions in the Caucasus. Although Western nations helped to defuse the crisis with the arrest of Russia's officers, and sought to discourage Tbilisi from using force against its separatist territories, the Kremlin did not see such efforts as sufficient in recognizing Russia's vital role in the region. In June 2006, Russia's Foreign Minister said that Ukraine or Georgia joining NATO could lead to a colossal shift in global geopolitics.[28] The Kremlin was determined to stop the Alliance expansion, and the spat with Georgia seems to be a crucial test of will for Moscow. The so-called "frozen conflicts" are merely leverage in the Kremlin's hands, and they will remain frozen until NATO bears out plans to continue its march to the East. The Russia-Georgia crisis therefore has became an indicator of a bigger Russia-West crisis. Some Russian analysts argue that if membership in NATO is most important to Georgia, then Tbilisi is likely to obtain it at the cost of its territorial integrity.[29] South Ossetia and Abkhasia continue to oppose Georgia's membership in the Western Alliance and to press for integration with Russia. Such integration came one step closer after U.S. recognition of Kosovo's independence, although the Kremlin is still not prepared to legally recognize Georgia's separatist territories.

In Georgia, Russia's policy and its new attitude of frustration only further reinforced the already strong sense that the Kremlin had no respect for Georgia's independence. Just as Russia was frustrated with lack of recognition by the United States and NATO, Georgia demonstrated anger at what it saw as Russia's lack of respect for its choice of foreign policy orientation. President Mikheil Saakashvili and other officials were defiant, and condemned Russia's "imperialism" and unwillingness to honor Georgia's independence. The discourse of anger and frustration clearly comes through in many policy statements, such as the following from President Saakashvili (2007):

> In my opinion, Russia is unable to reconcile itself with Georgia's independence. It wants to revert to the Soviet rule, although this is impossible. Georgia is no longer a country that it was some 4 or 5 years ago, when we did not have either an army or police and corruption was rife in this country. Georgia is now able to protect its territorial integrity and sovereignty.

Capitalizing on special relationships with the United States and determined to benefit from the Russia-West growing confrontation, Tbilisi seemed determined to humiliate Russia further. Rather than discussing military neutrality after Russia's withdrawal, a discussion in Tbilisi was under way that a future Georgia may not have objections against possible future deployment of weapons of mass destruction (WMD) on their territory by NATO. The issue comes full circle when Russia insists that Georgia's foreign policy choices are not independent, but instead are formed by the United States, Tbilisi's most important ally in the Caucasus.

The U.S. Side.

The U.S. psychological problem is that of a superiority complex that is evident in a broad range of its policies and attitudes, from the "we won the Cold War" mood, to expanding NATO, blocking development of Russia's energy infrastructure, and pushing the Kremlin to adopt Western-style democratization. Each of these policies betrays a fundamental misunderstanding of international and former Soviet realities. Russia is not a defeated power and has greatly contributed to the end of the Cold War. It has its own security and economic interests in the Caucasus and outside, that are principally undermined by the process of NATO expansion and unilateral exercise of energy policies. Finally, Russia's current imperatives are those of a state-building nature, broadly supported by the public. Further democratization may come, but no earlier than a strong middle class emerges and a sense of security from external threats sets in. That the United States has generally abstained from offensive language without changing its unilateral approach is patronizing, and Russians justifiably see such behavior as offensive. As far as they are concerned, they are not going to gain an additional confidence from hearing that NATO expansion does not threaten their interests — even if it is repeated hundreds of times — because it is actions that matter, not words. And those actions include breaking the promise of not expanding the Alliance that was given to Mikhail Gorbachev, denying Russia's requests to be considered as a potential member, and failing to consult the Kremlin on the Balkans and other issues critical to Russia's security

In addition to this general attitude of superiority shared by the American political class, there are three distinct Russophobic groups within the U.S. establishment that have pushed for a tougher Russia policy at least since the late-1990s. One important group includes military hawks or advocates of American hegemony, who fought the Cold War not to contain the Soviet enemy, but to destroy it by all means available. A number of military hawks, in fact, advocated a nuclear strike against the Soviet Union during the 1970s. An important part of this group also formed the core of the Committee of Present Danger and "Team B" that had produced a highly inflated assessment of the Soviet threat.[30]

The second group may be called liberal hawks and has important roots after World War II and an agenda of protecting freedom and human rights in the world. Over time, however, the initial agenda of such agencies as Freedom House and Human Right Watch had been hijacked by the Cold War warriors and successfully transformed into a tool for fighting the Soviets. During the 1990s era of Bill Clinton's presidency, the group got stronger. That the Soviet threat had been eliminated has strengthened the sense of superiority of America's liberal values and the determination to promote those values across the world. In 1990 Francis Fukuyama first formulated his triumphalist "end of history" thesis, arguing a global ascendancy of the Western-style market democracy.[31] Marc Plattner declared the emergence of a "world with one dominant principle of legitimacy, democracy."[32] When the Soviet system had indeed disintegrated, the leading establishment journal, *Foreign Affairs*, pronounced that "the Soviet system collapsed because of what it was, or more exactly, because of what it was not. The West 'won' because of what the democracies were—because they were free, prosperous, and successful, [and] because they did justice, or convincingly tried to do so."[33] The group had gotten comfortable with the Russia of the 1990s and had assumed that the weakened and submissive state it had become would become a normal (and convenient) state of affairs.

Finally, there is a group consisting of Eastern European nationalists, or those who fled from the Soviet system and the Warsaw Pact and now dreamed of destroying the Soviet Union as the ultimate way to gain independence for their people. After the Cold War, this group worked in concert with ruling elites of Eastern and Central European nations to oppose Russia's state consolidation as well as to promote NATO expansion. They also supported deployment of the American missile defense system in Poland and the Czech Republic, and energy pipelines circumventing Russia, seeing these as important guarantees against restoration of the neo-Soviet empire. East European nationalists have been typically pessimistic about prospects of Russia becoming a democracy, and they tend to side with military hawks in promoting the American hegemonic agenda in the world. For instance, a former Estonian ambassador to Russia referred to it as a "growing monster that the world has not yet seen before." He claimed that after the 2008 presidential elections, Russia would turn into "the most dangerous terrorist regime in the world and an exporter of terrorism next to which Hamas and al-Qaeda would pale."[34]

What brought these diverse groups together was the belief in the supremacy of American power and ideas, and a hatred toward the Soviet system that, at the time, was justifiably perceived as the most important obstacle to the establishment of a U.S.-centered international system. Most members of the anti-Russian lobby never believed in a peaceful transformation of the Soviet system, and, after that transformation finally took place, they never trusted the intentions of the new Russia and its leaders. The Cold War struggle instilled in them hatred not just for the Soviet empire, but for any political system that the Russians might create so long as such a system presented a challenge to America's world leadership and hegemony. Although post-Soviet Russia in the 1990s represented a sorry state of affairs — an impoverished population, an economy in shambles, and leaders desperate for Western advice and assistance — the Russophobic elites worried about Russia's revival. Fear of such a revival of the "old Russia" became the unifying subject of their concern, as well as a successful strategy for rallying supporters, mobilizing the media, and promoting an anti-Russian policy agenda.

These groups have diverse but compatible objectives of isolating Russia from Euro-Atlantic institutions and reducing its interests to those of West-controlled domestic transformation. With regard to the Caucasus and Ukraine, they have insisted on absorbing these regions into the Western area of interest and values. The colored revolutions to them were predominantly about increasing the West's influence at the expense of Russia. For example, the leading advocate of U.S. unipolarity, Charles Krauthammer, insisted during the 2004 U.S.-Russia conflict over election outcomes in Ukraine that "this is about Russia first, democracy only second. This Ukrainian episode is a brief, almost nostalgic throwback to the Cold War. . . . The West wants to finish the job begun with the fall of the Berlin Wall and continue Europe's march to the east."[35] Similar objectives have been set vis-à-vis the Caucasus in terms of including its states into

NATO and the West-led system of energy security—
at the expense of Russia's interests and influence.
These groups have been generously publicized in the
American media to the point that balanced analysts such
as Charles Kupchan of Georgetown University wrote
that "an anachronistic Russophobia is triumphing over
a more sober assessment of Russia's intentions and
capabilities."

Due to several conditions, these groups' influence
on policymaking has been notable. Among those
conditions are lack of commitment to a strong
relationship with Russia in the White House, a largely
uninformed public, and the absence of a Russian lobby
within the United States. Although Russophobia is not
in American national interests, the identified groups
have generally succeeded in feeding the media the
image of Russia as a country with a well-consolidated
and increasingly dangerous regime. A testament to it,
for example, are thousands of articles in the mainstream
American press implicating the Kremlin, and Putin
personally, in murdering opposition journalists and
defected spies,[36] relative to only a handful of pieces in
less prominent outlets questioning such interpretation
and insisting on lack of evidence.[37] The lobby has also
created a relatively cohesive group, in which elites with
diverse core interests often converge on the subject of
Russophobia by participating in joint events and signing
joint public letters that push the policy line of taking
a tough stand against Russia.[38] Organizations such as
Project for a New American Century, Committee for
Peace in the Caucasus, Freedom House, and the Center
for Security Policy advocate different aspects of U.S.
hegemony, yet Russia is invariably presented by them
as a leading threat. Finally, the lobby has succeeded in
having leading members of the American political class

advocate the Russia-threat approach. Some influential members of Congress and policymakers in the White House have been sympathetic to the lobby's agenda and prone to use of Russophobic rhetoric.[39]

CONCLUSION

Overall, progress in U.S.-Russian relations in the region remains sporadic and crisis-driven, not systematic or strategically thought out. The two nations cooperated in cleaning terrorists out of the Pankisi Gorge when the situation became especially difficult and when, along with Georgia, the sides agreed on the urgency of acting to prevent the threat. They have also found ways to cooperate in restraining Georgia's especially militaristic and ethno-nationalist policies. For instance, in late 2007, tacitly supported by Moscow, Washington presented Saakashvili with an ultimatum of removing from office the most odiously hawkish Minister of Defense Irakli Okruashvili. The United States and Russia also continued to share important counterterrorist intelligence information. However, the bigger picture of the two nations' cooperation is less than impressive, mainly because Washington continues with its unilateral policies in the region. While restraining Saakashvili's most extreme plans, it continues with policies of bringing Georgia into NATO without addressing Russia's concerns. Washington also continues to push Ukraine in the direction of gaining NATO membership. It continues to arm narrowly-based militaristic regimes in Azerbaijan and Georgia. And it continues to seek control of Caspian Sea reserves while trying to isolate Russia from energy infrastructure in the region.

Although it matters greatly who comes to the White House in November 2008—John McCain, Hillary Clinton, or Barrack Obama—the larger issue is still the American political class, and a psychological adjustment that needs to be made by both Washington and Moscow. The above-described superiority-inferiority complex cannot be conducive to a robust bilateral cooperation. The U.S. healing of its imperial complex is going to take time, maybe a long time, if the country's leadership continues to disregard new international realities and insists on remaining the governing center of the world. Winston Churchill once famously commented that American politicians "always do the right thing in the end—they just like to exhaust all the alternatives first." If this indeed is the case, then meaningful cooperation with Russia is going to be delayed. Also, Russia needs to get comfortable with its newly acquired wealth and influence and act as a more responsible world power. It is only natural that after years of decline and humiliation the Kremlin would emerge as more assertive in defending its interests. When there is greater room for Russia in the world—in terms of its regional influence, economic integration in Europe and Asia, and meaningful participation in international security institutions—there will be new opportunities to engage the Kremlin. Although in the short run chances of the U.S.-Russia partnership are slim, in a longer run the leaders of the two countries may learn—to quote George Kennan—to defend their interests as real statesmen must; that is without "assuming that these can furthered only at the expense of others."

ENDNOTES - CHAPTER 8

1. Mikhail Gorbachev, "History Is Not Preordained: A New Cold War Can Be Averted," *The Guardian*, January 18, 2007.

2. For analyses of Ukraine as a regionally divided nation, see Mikhail Molchanov, *Political Culture and National Identity in Russian-Ukranian Relations*, Austin: Texas University Press, 2002; Andrew Wilson, *Ukrainian Nationalism in the 1990s: A Minority Faith*, Cambridge, UK: Cambridge University Press, 1998; Andrew Wilson, *The Ukrainians: Unexpected Nation*, New Haven, CT: Yale University Press, 2000.

3. As of this writing, the Ukrainian parliament cannot convene for 2 month due to a split between the Orange coalition and the Party of Regions.

4. For a broader argument about the role of Russia's economic attractiveness and soft power, see Fiona Hill, *Energy Empire: Oil, Gas, and Russia's Revival*, Washington, DC: Brookings, 2004; Andrei P. Tsygankov, "If Not by Tanks, then by Banks? The Role of Soft Power in Putin's Foreign Policy," *Europe-Asia Studies*, Vol. 58, No. 7, November 2006.

5. See Edward D. Mansfield and Jack Snyder, *Electing to Fight: Why Emerging Democracies Go to War*, Cambridge, MA: The MIT Press, 2000.

6. "Russia again Vows to Block NATO Enlargement," *RFE/RL Newsline*, April 9, 2008.

7. Vladimir Putin, "Press Statement and Answers to Journalists' Questions Following a Meeting of the Russia-NATO Council," Bucharest, Romania, *Kremlin.ru*, April 4, 2008.

8. C. J. Chivers, "Russia Expands Support for Breakaway Regions in Georgia," *New York Times*, April 17, 2008.

9. "Moldovan President, Transdniester Leader Hold Landmark Talks," *RFE/RL Newsline*, April 14, 2008.

10. Victor Yuschenko, "Ukraine's Membership in NATO Will Pose No New Threats to Russia," *Vremya Novostei*, No. 29, February 22, 2008.

11. Gordon Hahn, *Russia's Islamic Threat*, New Haven, CT: Yale University Press, 2007.

12. Richard Giragosian, "Military Buildup in South Cacausus Adds to Tensions," *Radio Free Europe/Radio Liberty*, October 16, 2006, available online at *www.rferl.org/newsline/5-not.asp*.

13. Sohbet Mamedov, "Baku vooruzhayetsya," *Nezavisimaya gazeta*, June 25, 2007.

14. Ariel Cohen, "U.S. Interest and Central Asia Energy Security," *The Heritage Tribune*, November 26, 2006, *www.heritage.org/Research/RussiaandEurasia/bg1984.cfm*.

15. Analysts proposed, for example, that Russia and Western nations build an energy consortium and that Russia be brought into the International Energy Agency. See Ira Straus, "Why a U.S.-Russia Alliance Makes Sense," *The Russia Journal*, April 26, 2002, *http://www.russiajournal.com/node/6182*.

16. For such view, see Zbigniew Brzezinski, *The Grand Chessboard*, New York: Basic Books, 1998; Charles Clover, "Dreams of the Eurasian Heartland," *Foreign Affairs* Vol. 78, No. 2, 1999.

17. For characterizations of Russia in the 1990s as a weak or failing state, see Stephen Holmes, "What Russia Teaches Us Now: How Weak States Threaten Freedom," *The American Prospect*, No. 33, July-August, 1997; Peter J. Stavrakis, "The East Goes South: International Aid and the Production of Convergence in Africa and Eurasia," in Mark R. Beissinger and Crawford Young, eds., *Beyond State Crisis? Postcolonial Africa and Post-Soviet Eurasia in Comparative Perspective*, Washington, DC: Woodrow Wilson Center Press, 2002; Jens Meierhenrich, "Forming States after Failure," in Robert L. Rotberg, ed., *When States Fail: Causes and Consequences*, Princeton, NJ: Princeton University Press, 2004; Vladimir Popov, "The State in the New Russia (1992-2004): From Collapse to Gradual Revival?" PONARS Policy Memo 324, *www.csis.org/ruseura/ponars*; John P. Willerton, Mikhail Beznosov, and

Martin Carrier, "Addressing the Challenges of Russia's 'Failing State'," *Demokratizatsiya*, Vol. 13, No. 2, 2005.

18. Andrei P. Tsygankov, "Vladimir Putin's Vision of Russia as a Normal Great Power," *Post-Soviet Affairs*, Vol. 21, No. 2, April-June 2005.

19. The ratings developed by Russian analysts differ from those of Western agencies, such as Freedom House and Fund for Peace, considerably. For details, see these organizations' websites at *www.freedomhouse.org* and *www.fundforpeace.org*. One example is its publication of "Geopolitical Atlas of Contemporary World," A. Yu. Melville *et al.*, "Opyt klassifikatsiyi stran," *Polis*, No. 5, 2006. While recognizing the constraining role of various threats on Russia's development, Russian analysts assign for their country relatively high ratings of "stateness" and "international influence." Unlike Freedom House, they also classify Russia as a democracy, albeit an imperfect one, which may invite scholars to reevaluate the meaning of the concept in Russia's situation.

20. Both Russian and Western analysts have speculated that the security class has become omnipresent in policymaking. See, for example, O. Kryshtanovskaya and S. White, "Putin's Militocracy," *Post-Soviet Affairs*, Vol. 19, No. 4, 2003; Daniel Treisman, "Putin's Silovarchs," *Orbis*, Winter 2007. For alternative perspectives on the objectives and the role of the security class, see Sharon Werning Rivera and David W. Rivera, "The Russian Elite under Putin: Militocratic or Bourgeois?" *Post-Soviet Affairs*, Vol. 22, No. 2, 2006; and Bettina Renz, "Putin's Militocracy? An Alternative Interpretation of *Siloviki* in Russian Politics," *Europe-Asia Studies*, Vol. 58, No. 6, September 2006.

21. Moscow Mayor Yuri Luzhkov and a number of State Duma deputies, in particular, have been active in advancing these kinds of objectives.

22. Vladimir Putin, "Poslaniye Federal'nomu Sobraniyu Rossiyskoy Federatsiyi," March 2005, *www.kremlin.ru*.

23. Vladimir Putin, "Poslaniye Federal'nomu Sobraniyu Rossiyskoy Federatsiyi," May 10, 2006, April 26, 2007, *www.kremlin.ru*.

24. Vitali Tretyakov, "Suverennaya demokratiya. O politicheskoi filosofiyi Vladimira Putina," *Rossiyskaya Gazeta*, April 28, 2005; Vladislav Surkov, "Suverenitet—eto politicheski sinonim konkurentnosposobnosti," *Moscow News*, March 3, 2006; Aleksandr Tsipko, "Obratno puti net," *Literaturnaya Gazeta*, No. 19, May 2006. Not all in the Kremlin share the notion of sovereign democracy. For an alternative perspective from the current President Dmitri Medvedev, see his "Dlya protsvetaniya vsekh nado uchityvat' interesy kazhdogo," *Ekspert*, No. 28, 522, July 24, 2006, *expert.ru*.

25. Neil Buckley, "Clan with a Plan: All the Contradictions of Vladimir Putin's Russia," *Financial Times*, November 29, 2007; Robert Coalson, "For Russia's Most Powerful Man, Fear Still A Factor," *RFE/RL*, November 30, 2007.

26. "Leading Russian Americanist Fears U.S. and EU Will Rally on 'Anti-Russian' Basis," *RFE/RL Newsline*, February 23, 2005.

27. Many Western officials insisted on immediate cessation of the sanctions, and special representative of the NATO Secretary-General Robert Simmons extended his support for Tbilisi during his demonstrative trip to Georgia in the midst of the crisis.

28. *RIA Novosti*, 2006.

29. Anatoly Tsyganok, "On the Consequences of Georgia's NATO Entry," *Fondsk.ru*, January 2, 2008, *www.fondsk.ru/article.php?id=1148*.

30. "Team B" was commissioned to provide an alternative to the CIA intelligence reports on the Soviet Union. It faulted the CIA for relying on "hard" data rather than "contemplat[ing] Soviet strategic objectives," thereby setting up the United States for defeat by the Soviets. It also credited the Soviet Union with developing some new types of weapons, and it underestimated the Soviet economic weaknesses. Among those involved in organizing "Team B" and directly participating were William Van Cleave, Daniel Graham, Foy Kohler, Paul Nitze, Richard Perle, Richard Pipes, Seymour Weiss, and Paul Wolfowitz.

For details, see Anne Hessing Cahn, *Killing Détente: The Right Attacks the CIA*, University Park: Pennsylvania State University Press, 1998; Paul C. Warnke, "The B Team," *Bulletin of the Atomic Scientists*, January/February 1999; *Team B Strategic Objectives Panel*, International Relations Center, Silver City, NM, *rightweb. irc-online.org/profile/2822*, accessed on September 27, 2007.

31. Francis Fukuyama, "The End of History?" *The National Interest*, Vol. 16, Summer 1989.

32. Marc Plattner, "The Democratic Moment," in Larry Diamond and Marc Plattner, eds., *The Global Resurgence of Democracy*, Baltimore, MD: Johns Hopkins University Press, 1992. Plattner later became co-editor of the *Journal of Democracy*. Also see Marc C. Plattner, "Democracy Outwits the Pessimists," *Wall Street Journal*, October 12, 1988.

33. William Pfaff, "Redefining World Power," *Foreign Affairs*, Vol. 70, No. 1, 1999, p. 48. This vision was finally legitimized at the highest policy level when President George H. W. Bush announced the cold war "victory" of the United States in his 1992 State of the Union message.

34. As cited in Yelena Shesternina and Maksim Yusin, "Goryachi estonski paren' soskuchilsya po 'kholodnoi voine'," *Izvestia*, January 31, 2007.

35. Charles Krauthammer, "Why Only in Ukraine?" *Washington Post*, December 3, 2004.

36. It would be impossible to cite all of them, but some examples include "Russia's Murder Mystery," *Washington Post*, August 31, 2006; Anders Aslund, "Putin Gets Away with Murder: It's time to confront the Russian leader," *The Weekly Standard*, October 23, 2006; David Satter, "Russia: Rebuilding the Iron Curtain," Testimony to U.S. House of Representatives, Committee on Foreign Affairs, May 17, 2007; "Russian Poison," *Wall Street Journal*, May 23, 2007; "Charged With Murder," *Washington Post*, May 23, 2007; Jim Hoagland, "Dealing With Putin," *Washington Post*, May 27, 2007; "Geopolitical Diary: The Curious Politkovskaya Case," *Stratfor.com*, August 28, 2007; Fred Weir, "Suspicion of Kremlin's tack in Politkovskaya murder case," *Christian Science*

Monitor, August 29, 2007; Jim Hoagland, "With Russia, Pray for Cynicism," *Washington Post*, September 2, 2007; Michael Weiss, "The Cool Peace? Resolved: Russia Is Becoming Our Enemy Again," *The Weekly Standard*, November 7, 2007.

37. See, for example, Charles Ganske, "One Cold War Was Enough: Russia Needs Our Help, Not Our Condemnation," *World Politics Review*, November 19, 2007, *www.worldpoliticsreview.com*; Justin Raimondo, "Is Russia Democratic? Yes, But So What?" *Antiwar.com*, December 3, 2007, *www.antiwar.com*.

38. *An Open Letter to the Heads of State and Government Of the European Union and NATO*, September 28, 2004, *www.cdi.org/russia/johnson/8385-24.cfm*, accessed on October 4, 2007.

39. See, for example, the bipartisan Council of Foreign Relations report, *Russia's Wrong Direction*, as well as multiple statements by Senator John McCain (R-AZ) on Russia's new "imperialism."

ABOUT THE CONTRIBUTORS

ALEXEI ARBATOV has served as Head of the Center for International Security, Center of the Institute for International Economy and International Relationships of the Russian Academy of Sciences from 2002 to the present, and Vice chairman of the YABLOKO party from 2002 to the present. His previous assignments have been as an academician and professor of the Academy of Defence, Security and Policy by the President of Russia in 2003, Head of a department at the Institute for International Economy and International Relationships of the Russian Academy of Sciences and a consultant to the Russian Ministry for Foreign Affairs in 1997, Head of a department at the Institute for International Economy and International Relationships of the Russian Academy of Sciences from 1985 to 1994, Head of a section at the Institute for International Economy and International Relationships of the Russian Academy of Sciences from 1983 to 1985, and Research fellow at the Institute for International Economy and International Relationships of the Russian Academy of Sciences from 1976 to 1983. Dr. Arbatov was a member of the Russian Parliament (State Duma), the YABLOKO party, and Deputy Chairman of the Duma Defence Committee from 1994 to 2003; a member of the Research Council of the Russian Ministry of Foreign Affairs; Head of the School Board of the Foundation for Families of the 76th Airborne Division's Servicemen; a member of the Governing Board of the Stockholm International Peace Research Institute (SIPRI), the International advisory board of the Geneva Centre for the Democratic Control of Armed Forces (DCAF) Institute, and the Center on Nonproliferation of the Monterey Institute; a member of the Russian Council for Foreign and Defence policy; a

333

member of the Nuclear Threat Initiative; and a member of the International Commission for Nuclear Non-Proliferation and Disarmament. Dr. Arbatov holds an M.A. from the Moscow State Institute of International Relations, and a Doctorate of History from the Russian Academy of Sciences.

STEPHEN J. BLANK has served as the Strategic Studies Institute's expert on the Soviet bloc and the post-Soviet world since 1989. Prior to that he was Associate Professor of Soviet Studies at the Center for Aerospace Doctrine, Research, and Education, Maxwell Air Force Base, and taught at the University of Texas, San Antonio, and at the University of California, Riverside. Dr. Blank is the editor of *Imperial Decline: Russia's Changing Position in Asia*, coeditor of *Soviet Military and the Future*, and author of *The Sorcerer as Apprentice: Stalin's Commissariat of Nationalities, 1917-1924*. He has also written many articles and conference papers on Russian, Commonwealth of Independent States, and Eastern European security issues. Dr. Blank's current research deals with proliferation and the revolution in military affairs, and energy and security in Eurasia. His two most recent books are *Russo-Chinese Energy Relations: Politics in Command*, London, UK: Global Markets Briefing, 2006 and *Natural Allies?: Regional Security in Asia and Prospects for Indo-American Strategic Cooperation*, Carlisle Barracks, PA: Strategic Studies Institute, U.S. Army War College, 2005. He holds a B.A. in History from the University of Pennsylvania, and an M.A. and Ph.D. in History from the University of Chicago.

LYNTON F. BROOKS is an independent consultant on national security issues. He served from July 2002 to

January 2007 as Administrator of the U.S. Department of Energy's National Nuclear Security Administration, where he was responsible for the U.S. nuclear weapons program and for the Department of Energy's international nuclear nonproliferation programs. Ambassador Brooks has over 4 decades of experience in national security, including service as Assistant Director of the Arms Control and Disarmament Agency, Chief U.S. Negotiator for the Strategic Arms Reduction Treaty, Director of Defense Programs and Arms Control on the National Security Council staff, and a number of Navy and Defense Department assignments as a 30-year career naval officer. Ambassador Brooks holds degrees from Duke University, the University of Maryland, and the U.S. Naval War College.

JACOB W. KIPP is the Deputy Director of the U. S. Army's School of Advanced Military Studies (SAMS). Before coming to SAMS, he served as Director of the Foreign Military Studies Office (FMSO) of the U.S. Army Training and Doctrine Command at Ft. Leavenworth, Kansas, from 2003 to 2006. During the same period, he also served as Director of the Ft. Leavenworth Joint Reserve Intelligence Center, one of 27 such centers supporting the Intelligence Community. FMSO was the Army's leading center for mid and long-range open-source research on foreign militaries and emerging security issues and has been recognized for excellence by the Under Secretary of Defense for Intelligence, Intelink, the Director of National Intelligence, and Congress. During his tenure, FMSO provided the institutional foundation for the creation of the Human Terrain Teams (HTT), which were created to provide cultural insights into the operating areas of Army brigades in Iraq and Afghanistan. In 1971, Dr. Kipp joined the

History Department of Kansas State University, where he taught Russian, Soviet, East European, and Military History. In 1985, he was promoted to the rank of Full Professor. In 1986, he joined the newly founded Soviet Army Studies Office (SASO) at Ft. Leavenworth as a senior analyst. In 1990, SASO became FMSO. As senior analyst, Dr. Kipp led research efforts on Soviet military doctrine, perestroika, and military reform; ethno-nationalism in Eastern Europe and the former Soviet Union; and the revolution in military affairs. In 2003, Dr. Kipp became the director of FMSO. Over the next 3 years, he oversaw the growth of its budget, the expansion of its mission, the renovation of its building, and the initiation of major programs in Chinese, Latin American, and Middle Eastern studies. Dr. Kipp has published extensively, including nine books and over 40 articles in professional journals and 40 chapters in books. He has also been actively involved in editorial work as associate editor of *Military Affairs*, *Aerospace Historian*, and the *Journal of Slavic Military Studies*, and as editor of *European Security*. He also serves on the editorial board of the modern War Studies Series of the University Press of Kansas. He is a recognized expert on Russian and Soviet naval history. His most recent book publication was the English translation of M. Gareev and V. Slipechenko's *Future War*, which he edited, and to which he provided an introduction. Dr. Kipp holds a B.S. in Secondary Education from Shippensburg State College and a Ph.D. in Russian History from the Pennsylvania State University.

ALEXANDER A. PIKAYEV is Director of the Department for Disarmament and Conflict Resolution at the Moscow based Institute of World Economy and International Relations (IMEMO). His previous assignments were as a professional staff member at the Duma Defense Committee from 1994-1997, and he directed a weapons of mass destruction nonproliferation program at the Carnegie Moscow Center from 1997 to 2003. Dr. Pikayev lectured to audiences at the United Nations, the Russian Duma, the U.S. Congress, the German Bundestag, and the Europarliament. He is a member of the International Institute for Strategic Studies. Dr. Pikayev authored more than a hundred of books, chapters and articles on weapons of mass destruction, disarmament, and nonproliferation; Iraninan and North Korean nuclear issues; and Russia's foreign and security policy. He is one of the most frequently cited by media Russian experts in the field.

JAMES SHERR is Head of the Russia and Eurasia Programme at the Royal Institute of International Affairs (Chatham House) in London. Between 1995 and May 2008, he was a Fellow of the Advanced Research and Assessment Group (formerly Conflict Studies Research Centre) of the Defence Academy and is now Senior Visiting Fellow of that institution. Since 1993, Mr. Sherr has also been a member of the Faculty of Social Studies of Oxford University. Over the past 10 years, he has been a consultant to NATO on Ukraine and regularly advises the British government and parliament as well as others inside NATO about Russia as well as security problems in the Black Sea region. In Ukraine, he collaborates closely with official bodies and NGOs and is a regular contributor to *Zerkalo Nedeli* and *Den'*. Mr. Sherr has spoken at the NATO-Russia Council and delivered papers at the first and second official NATO-Russia workshops in Moscow. In addition, he is a regular participant in Wilton

Park conferences on Russia, Ukraine and NATO, the Harvard Russia Security Programme, the Harvard Black Sea Security Programme and the workshops and seminars of the German Marshall Fund of the United States. Mr. Sherr's latest monograph for the Defence Academy, *Russia and the West: A Reassessment*, was published as a *Shrivenham Paper* in January 2008. He is a frequent contributor to *Nezavisimaya Gazeta*, and has published in the journal, *Russia in Global Affairs*, most recently in April 2008.

ANDREI P. TSYGANKOV is a Professor at the departments of Political Science and International Relations at San Francisco State University. He has taught Russian/post-Soviet, comparative, and international politics since August 2000. He served as Program Chair of International Studies Association (ISA) from 2006 to 2007. Dr. Tsygankov co-edited *New Directions in Russian International Studies* (2004), *Pathways after Empire* (2001), *Whose World Order?* (2004), *Russia's Foreign Policy* (2006), and *Russophobia* (forthcoming), as well as many journal articles. In Russia, his best known books are *Russian Science of International Relations* (2005, co-edited with Pavel Tsygankov, also published in Germany and China) and *Sociology of International Relations* (2006, co-authored with Pavel Tsygankov, also published in China). His editorial opinions have appeared in *Asia Times*, *Johnson Russia List*, *Moscow Times*, *Korea Herald*, *Los Angeles Times*, Radio Free Europe/Radio Liberty, and *Russia Profile*. Dr. Tsygankov is a Candidate of Sciences from Moscow State University and holds a Ph.D. from the University of Southern California.

www.ingramcontent.com/pod-product-compliance
Lightning Source LLC
Chambersburg PA
CBHW081357270326
41930CB00015B/3327